CW01024512

STUDENTS, PLACES AND IDENTITIES IN ENGLISH AND THE ARTS

In an age when national identities are a subject of popular debate, along with issues of place in relation to immigration, displacement and mobility, it is particularly important that educators are supported in their reflections on how best to respond to such pertinent issues in their daily practice. This book accessibly and sensitively explores the ways in which teachers can work with places and identities in English and related expressive arts to create a rich experience for students in schools and beyond.

A team of carefully selected contributors present practical ideas and critically examine diverse contexts and viewpoints. Exploring the significance of identity and place in education, the central notion is that language and arts are vital to enhancing understanding and empathy. The book provides an approach that offers teachers and other professionals ways to engage critically with these themes, as well as practical strategies for opening up debate and creative work in a broad range of curriculum areas.

This insightful book will be of interest to teachers, teacher educators, training teachers and researchers in education.

David Stevens is Senior Lecturer in the School of Education, University of Durham, UK.

Karen Lockney is Senior Lecturer in Working with Children and Families, University of Cumbria, UK.

NATE

The National Association for the Teaching of English (NATE), founded in 1963, is the professional body for all teachers of English from primary to Post-16. Through its regions, committees and conferences, the association draws on the work of classroom practitioners, advisers, consultants, teacher trainers, academics and researchers to promote dynamic and progressive approaches to the subject by means of debate, training and publications. NATE is a charity reliant on membership subscriptions. If you teach English in any capacity, please visit **www.nate.org.uk** and consider joining NATE, so the association can continue its work and give teachers of English and the subject a strong voice nationally.

This series of books co-published with NATE reflects the organisation's dedication to promoting standards of excellence in the teaching of English, from early years through to university level. Titles in this series promote innovative and original ideas that have practical classroom outcomes and support teachers' own professional development.

Books in the NATE series include both pupil and classroom resources and academic research aimed at English teachers, students on PGCE/ITT courses and NQTs.

For a full list of titles in this series, please visit: www.routledge.com/National-Association-for-the-Teaching-of-English-NATE/book-series/NATE

Titles in this series include:

Teaching Grammar Structure and Meaning
Marcello Giovanelli

Researching and Teaching Reading
Gabrielle Cliff Hodges

Introducing Teacher's Writing Groups
Jenifer Smith and Simon Wrigley

Creative Approaches to Teaching Grammar
Martin Illingworth and Nick Hall

Knowing about Language
Marcello Giovanelli and Dan Clayton

English and its Teachers
Simon Gibbons

International Perspectives on the Teaching of Literature in Schools
Andrew Goodwyn, Cal Durrant, Louann Reid and Lisa Scherff

Students, Places and Identities in English and the Arts
David Stevens and Karen Lockney

STUDENTS, PLACES AND IDENTITIES IN ENGLISH AND THE ARTS

Creative Spaces in Education

Edited by David Stevens and Karen Lockney

LONDON AND NEW YORK

First published 2018
by Routledge
2 Park Square, Milton Park, Abingdon, Oxon OX14 4RN

and by Routledge
711 Third Avenue, New York, NY 10017

Routledge is an imprint of the Taylor & Francis Group, an informa business

© 2018 selection and editorial matter, David Stevens and Karen Lockney; individual chapters, the contributors

The right of the editor to be identified as the author of the editorial material, and of the authors for their individual chapters, has been asserted in accordance with sections 77 and 78 of the Copyright, Designs and Patents Act 1988.

All rights reserved. No part of this book may be reprinted or reproduced or utilised in any form or by any electronic, mechanical, or other means, now known or hereafter invented, including photocopying and recording, or in any information storage or retrieval system, without permission in writing from the publishers.

Trademark notice: Product or corporate names may be trademarks or registered trademarks, and are used only for identification and explanation without intent to infringe.

British Library Cataloguing-in-Publication Data
A catalogue record for this book is available from the British Library

Library of Congress Cataloging-in-Publication Data
Names: Stevens, David, 1952– editor. | Lockney, Karen, editor.
Title: Students, places and identities in English and the arts : creative spaces in education / edited by David Stevens and Karen Lockney.
Description: Abingdon, Oxon; New York, NY: Routledge, 2018. | Includes bibliographical references and index.
Identifiers: LCCN 2017007658 | ISBN 9781138694545 (hardback : alk. paper) | ISBN 9781138694552 (pbk. : alk. paper) | ISBN 9781315528014 (ebook)
Subjects: LCSH: Language arts–Social aspects–Great Britain. | English language–Study and teaching–Social aspects–Great Britain. | Arts–Study and teaching–Social aspects–Great Britain. | Language and education. | Identity (Philosophical concept) | Place (Philosophy)
Classification: LCC LB1631.S837 2018 | DDC 428.0071–dc23
LC record available at https://lccn.loc.gov/2017007658

ISBN: 978-1-138-69454-5 (hbk)
ISBN: 978-1-138-69455-2 (pbk)
ISBN: 978-1-315-52801-4 (ebk)

Typeset in Bembo
by Out of House Publishing

CONTENTS

Notes on contributors   vii
Introduction   xi

1 From place to planet: the role of the language arts in reading
   environmental identities from the UK to New Zealand   1
   Sasha Matthewman

2 Connecting community through film in ITE English   14
   Joanna McIntyre and Susan Jones

3 Muslim youth identities through devotional songs and poetry
   in South Yorkshire communities   28
   Andrey Rosowsky

4 Creative spaces for developing independent writing with
   English teachers   42
   Lorna Smith

5 Durham city as an educational resource in initial teacher
   education for English: seeing the city with new eyes   55
   David Stevens

6 Shakespeare, Turgenev (and Kalashnikov) in Siberia   67
   Nicholas McGuinn and Amanda Naylor

7 Poetry, place and identity   82
   Karen Lockney

8 An exploration of immigrant-background children's identities
   and their ideas of place in relation to their global imaginaries
   and languages   94
   Oakleigh Welply

9 Negotiating 'third space' through popular children's
   literature: creating democratic spaces   112
   Sarah Pfenninger

10 'To see oursels as ithers see us': constructions of Scotland's
   place and identity within a changing Scottish curriculum
   and context   123
   Karen Lowing

11 'Thank the Lord for the internet!': identity, social media
   and space online   135
   Anna Llewellyn

12 A fable: *The Happy Teacher*   148
   Deirdre Diffley-Pierce

Index   *162*

CONTRIBUTORS

Deirdre Diffley-Pierce is a Lecturer of English Education at UCL, IOE. Following 25 years teaching English, she teaches PGCE English and the Masters of Teaching. Formative experience early on, working in different mediums such as icon-making with poplar, gesso and gold leaf, helped shape a lifelong, multimodal approach to English. Latterly, leading the relatively young 'Literacy, Language and Communication' core module for BA Education Studies at UCL, she draws, cru-cially, on interdisciplinary approaches to literacy. Deirdre's chapter embodies this approach, combining different literacies of image, iconography and text in an old form, the illustrated fable.

Susan Jones is Assistant Professor in English Education at the School of Education, University of Nottingham. Working with beginning teachers of English as well as in informal family and community-based contexts for learning, Susan's research focuses on how language, literacies and the arts relate to the agency and identities of individuals and communities. She has a strong interest in place-based research and pedagogy. Recent projects include a British Academy-funded study of the everyday literacies of families living on a Midlands council estate.

Anna Llewellyn has worked as an academic at Durham University for the past 12 years; prior to this she spent several years teaching in various secondary schools. Her role as Programme Director for the Education Studies undergraduate degree allows her to combine her passion for inspiring students with the academic pursuit of education. Academically, Anna is interested in how ways of being and knowing come to be accepted as the 'truth', rather than as cultural, social and political pro-ductions. She has a philosophical take on sociology and uses social theory to inform analysis. Anna also has a strong interest in equality, diversity and social justice.

Karen Lockney is a Senior Lecturer at the University of Cumbria where she teaches on the Working with Children and Families undergraduate programme. After ten years working as an English teacher and Head of English in Cumbria and East London, Karen worked in Initial Teacher Education across primary and secondary courses. Her PhD is in Creative Writing, specializing in poetry. She is a member of the national development team for the Poetry by Heart competition and also works occasionally as an editor specializing in creative non-fiction.

Karen Lowing is a Teaching Fellow at Durham University where she teaches on the PGCE English programme, is module convenor for Professional Issues and the MA Education Enquiry module, and is Pathway Lead for the MA QTS. Karen taught English in several schools across Scotland, and Scottish Studies at Strathclyde University, before moving to Newcastle University to run the PGCE English and Drama course. Karen was awarded full Chartered Teacher Status, and a Senior Fellowship of the Higher Education Academy. Karen's current research explores Scots language and Scottish identity in the Scottish classroom, with further interests in wider sociolinguistic themes, national identity and cultural studies.

Nicholas McGuinn has been involved in English and education for more than 40 years, either as a classroom teacher, examiner or course leader for undergraduate and PGCE secondary English programmes. He is currently an Honorary Fellow in the Department of Education at the University of York, where he is engaged in a number of global projects exploring literature and social justice. His most recent book, *Take Off into English Teaching*, will be published by Routledge in Autumn 2017. In 2013, he was honoured to be selected as one of the members of staff chosen to mark the university's fiftieth anniversary.

Joanna McIntyre is Associate Professor in English Education; Jo teaches on a range of ITE and Masters programmes. Jo is also course leader on the MA CALL (Creativities, Arts, Literacies and Learning). Previously, as a teacher of English, she developed a strong philosophy regarding the importance of English as a means of personal expression, developing cultural values, and critical enquiry. This has led to an interest in research that focuses on creativity. Jo is particularly interested in young people's creative practices in and out of school as well as research on the discourses surrounding schools and the teachers that work in them.

Sasha Matthewman is Senior Lecturer at the University of Auckland and Principal Investigator on a New Zealand research project that is exploring how school subjects shape a sense of our place in the world – 'our environment, our culture and our identity'. From 2005 to 2012, Sasha was the English course leader for initial teacher education at the University of Bristol where she worked with English and geography teachers to develop subject initiatives in sustainability. Sasha's book *Teaching Secondary English as if the Planet Matters*, published by Routledge in 2011, was first in the series *Teaching Secondary School Subjects as if the Planet Matters*.

Amanda Naylor is currently a Senior Lecturer in English in Education at the University of York. Her main research interests are the teaching of literature and poetry, teacher training and digital pedagogy. Amanda has experience of teaching and management in secondary, further and higher education settings. She has been an Advanced Skills Teacher in English, Head of English in two comprehensive schools, a Lecturer in FE and Subject Lead for the University of Hull PGCE English programme. Amanda is involved in research projects on mobile and digital learning, teaching poetry post-16 and into the reading experiences of undergraduate students.

Sarah Pfenninger is currently Assistant Professor of Literacy Education and Director of the Literacy Center at University of La Verne located in Southern California, USA. Previously, Sarah has taught in a range of schools in the USA, and in both American and British higher education sectors, including Manchester Metropolitan University. Her work focuses on the ways in which students engage with children's literature, with a particular emphasis on issues of social justice and diversity in American and British contexts. Sarah is also very interested in Montessori models of education, both as creative practitioner and critical theoretician.

Andrey Rosowsky is a Senior Lecturer in the School of Education at the University of Sheffield. His research explores literacy and language practices of faith-based supplementary schools. He has an interest in Qur'anic literacy and its relationship to notions of performance and how poetry and song in heritage languages and English are instrumental in reviving both religious and linguistic practices. He currently leads an Arts and Humanities Research Council international interdisciplinary research project on performance and religious practice entitled 'Heavenly Acts – Aspects of Performance through an Interdisciplinary Lens'. He is the author of *Heavenly Readings: Liturgical Literacy in a Multilingual Context* (Multilingual Matters, 2008).

Lorna Smith is a Senior Lecturer in Education at the University of Bristol and leads the PGCE English programme. Her current research focuses on the effect of the National Curriculum (2014) on creative writing in secondary English. She launched a Teachers as Writers group in 2013 which explores the impact of teachers' writing on their work with children in the classroom. She is also interested in technology-enhanced learning, particularly the contribution that ICT can make to an English classroom, and is a former Chair of the NATE ICT committee. Lorna began her career teaching in a South Gloucestershire school.

David Stevens is a Senior Lecturer and English tutor for the PGCE secondary course at Durham University, having previously taught English in four schools, in two as Head of English. David's research, writing and teaching interests centre on English pedagogy, working towards a synthesis of different views of English while focusing on its radical Romantic roots and the implications for the contemporary world: a broad vision of English as an arts subject in a critically intercultural context. Major influences include Blake, Coleridge and other Romantics, and libertarian thinkers such as William Morris, John Dewey and Paulo Freire.

Oakleigh Welply is a Lecturer in Intercultural and International Education at the School of Education, Durham University, UK. Prior to joining Durham in 2014 she was a Lecturer in Sociology of Education at the Faculty of Education, University of Cambridge. Her research adopts a cross-national perspective in order to investigate the experiences and identities of immigrant-background children in primary schools in France and England. She has a particular interest in developing cross-national research and methodologies to conduct research with diverse communities in European countries, to explore the relationship of education to issues of language, religion, immigration and citizenship.

INTRODUCTION

In compiling and editing the book, we intend to present and critically explore diverse contexts and viewpoints (the contributor list suggests the diversity) linked by a general concept: the significance of identity and place in education, a potentially pluralistic but often intensely fraught social context. In their different ways, the contributing writers seek simultaneously to problematize such notions and to use them positively to increase understanding of the complexities of the world through education. As may be readily seen in the range of chapter themes, the notion of education at stake here is a broad one, but the overarching idea is to do with the language arts as crucial to enhancing understanding and empathy. By the same token, each writer speaks with a distinctive voice: this we see as a real strength, echoing the range of possibilities inherent in the subject matter in both form and content. In the sense that Paulo Freire envisaged radical education, our proposed book seeks to present a dynamic combination – or, rather, synthesis – of word and world: 'a reading of the world and a reading of the word… both together, in dialectical solidarity' (Freire 2004: 90).

The current context for our proposed book, both nationally in the UK and internationally, strikes us as particularly fertile, if distinctly challenging. We seek to draw upon two related pedagogical traditions: the celebratory and Romantic on the one hand, and the critically discursive on the other. At a time when, in the field of initial teacher education and subsequent professional development, and often for broadly ideological reasons, the emphasis is frequently purely on the practical – the 'how?' in effect – we seek to restore and explore the relationship between practical and theoretical dimensions, praxis in effect, in ways that should resonate with the actual interests of student teachers, practising teachers and teacher educators. Both of us spend much of our time in the professional company of people in such roles, often in schools, and have abundant anecdotal and more formally researched evidence to support the quest for such a synthesis. The relationship between celebratory and critical stances may be further relevant in today's (and the likely future's) climate through a further highly topical context: the popular and academic emphasis on celebration of place through heightened ecological awareness, and, perhaps by way of critical contrast, the current stress on notions of identity, not least in the highly contentious and contested – not to say confused and confusing – notion of nationalistically conceived values. This book seeks to explore these areas, and the relationships between them, in distinctively educational sites.

Sasha Matthewman's opening chapter brings an immediate international perspective to the theme of the book, dealing as it does with the role of English and related arts-based secondary school subject areas in responding to and shaping identities relating to environment and place in New Zealand. Matthewman in this chapter draws upon her pedagogical experiences in both New Zealand and the UK, and specifically on her research and writing concerning ecocritical approaches to school curricula and practice. In so doing, she pays particular regard to the social and historical contexts of such exploration, and the distinct particularities of the New Zealand educational experience. In Chapter 2, Joanna McIntyre and Susan Jones offer a critical exploration of film-making projects involving English student teachers working alongside their own pupils. The success of these projects lies not only in the emphasis on important media-based skills in teacher education and the cementing of positive teacher–pupil creative relationships, but, at a deeper level, the concern for giving secondary English teaching roots in local communities through their often complex senses of identity and place. Through a critical and celebratory examination of the processes and products, as collaborative constructions of place and identity, the authors show both the significant complexity and the creative potential of community-based educational partnership. Andrey Rosowsky follows with a wide-ranging discussion of identities of Muslim youth in South Yorkshire. Rosowsky explores how such identities may develop through diversity of artistic and cultural influences. Notions of education are central here, especially in the context of local cultural intersections beyond the authorized versions of schooling on offer. In celebratory mode, often with a radically critical edge, traditional Islamic songs and verse mix with elements from prevalent contemporary youth cultures, frequently focusing on notions of unstable, creatively evolving identities and on ideas clustering around a sense of place – whether physically envisaged in the geographical environment, or in more metaphorical terms.

The focus in Chapter 4, written by Lorna Smith, is on beginning teachers as creative practitioners themselves of the language arts, partly for their own personal, aesthetic and professional development, and partly as modellers of creative practice for their own pupils. The research underpinning the chapter explores how such an enterprise may both critically sharpen and creatively epitomize the nature of language arts. The context of identity and place is consciously presented not simply as backdrop for many of the writing processes and products exemplified through the project, but as the very centre of the enterprise itself: teachers' identities, and the places so invariably intertwined with such identities. Such issues are also central to Chapter 5: the experiences of beginning teachers lie at the heart of this chapter, as David Stevens explores how identities of places may vary enormously through the eyes of people in different roles – including, crucially, teachers and their pupils. A group-based project undertaken early in the PGCE year is central to this exploration, encouraging student teachers to see aspects of places as potential teaching resources to foster a telling combination of critical and celebratory learning. In so doing, the chapter plays with notions of how a particular place may lend itself to diverse educational projects focusing on ideas of identity as both liberating and extending. Nicholas McGuinn and Amanda Naylor follow with an illuminating chapter based on research through which British and Siberian students considered together points of similarity and difference in their responses to classical texts from each other's literary traditions, through active exploration of how authors may be presented in and shaped by an educational context. In the case of Shakespeare, the context is far removed, both geographically and culturally, from that with whom his work is more usually associated. The chapter explores the means whereby notions of Shakespeare as quintessentially English in terms of language and identity are critically challenged with reference to the Russian experience of a similarly feted playwright, while alternative interpretations and dramatic constructions may be simultaneously celebrated.

Karen Lockney's chapter is based on empirical qualitative research into poetry writing by pupils in two schools, one primary and one secondary, on their own places and identities. Pupils undertook observational writing, creative photography and group discussions about their relationships to places lived in; these activities were followed by the shaping of such experiences into poems. The chapter raises pertinent questions around the nature of young people's complex identities in areas often side-lined as rural backwaters, and either denigrated or idealized as such. Because the focus is ultimately on poetry, further, there is a distinctly celebratory aspect to the activity, but the process towards poetic creation (and sometimes the product too) reveals fascinating critical thinking. In Chapter 8, Oakleigh Welply examines the role of global imaginaries for immigrant-background children's identity constructions in primary schools in France and England, showing how references to global representations allow children to renegotiate national frameworks through wider references to other languages and cultures. In a broadly educational context relating to language arts, Welply critically appraises the thoughts and feelings of a historically – and all too often currently – marginalized group. Identity and place have a special place in relation to those who have immigrated into other countries or areas, for whatever reasons, and here Welply seeks to explore complex notions and feelings in a spirit at once celebratory and critical. In the ensuing chapter, Sarah Pfenninger presents the literacy practices that emerged through research into an in-school, extra-curricular book club centred on a British popular book series, Jacqueline Wilson's Tracy Beaker books. Drawing upon Rosenblatt's ideas centred on reader response, and on third space hybridity theory, this work explores the role out-of-school literacies may play within the third space. Pfenninger considers the possibilities of re-conceptualizing popular fiction, to consider the ways in which young children negotiate spaces of critical literacy. Implicit, and often explicit, throughout the chapter is a radical sense of expanding boundaries of definition for place and identity in an educational setting.

Chapter 10, written by Karen Lowing, is something of a contrast: here, the focus is on contested notions of place and identity in a particularly volatile educational context, with reference to the marginalization of certain groups' identities through language, and the potential of that same language as a tool of liberation. Based on extensive recent research undertaken in recent years by Lowing into Scottish pupils' linguistic experiences, the chapter critically explores the relationship of Scots to other minority languages, to hegemonic English (at a time of vigorous Scottish nationalistic feeling and activity) and to a sense of place in both macrocosmic and microcosmic senses. Anna Llewellyn's chapter examines how these concepts and experiences may exist in the contexts of schooling, teachers and the cultures of young people, in a fluctuating, sometimes oppositional and often tentative way, along with the potential for pedagogical development in the broadest sense. The exploration focuses on the internet and social media as virtual places, and how these play with hegemonic space. This area is of particular importance in that Twitter and similar social media are relatively recent phenomena with still-emerging, and often contested, characteristics and conventions. Deirdre Diffley-Pierce's final chapter offers a vivid contrast to all the others, and also a fitting end-piece for the book as a whole: it takes the form of an illustrated fable in which issues of teacher identity and professional space are explored, harking back to an idealized age of innocence in the mind of the teacher protagonist with idealized notions of education set against mechanized, assessment-driven approaches. It raises questions about the creative spaces open to beginning teachers and about what it might mean to be a teacher. A creative sense of mystery for both students and teachers lies at the heart of the story, as does the idea that the creative spaces of classrooms are powerfully and inextricably linked to teachers' own senses of creativity and identity.

We hope that the book is a genuinely helpful survey of ways in which teachers can work with places and identities in English and related expressive arts to create a rich experience for pupils in schools. The lived experience of young people is indeed central here, mediated through adult educators, researchers and writers, and our hope is that such a project will appeal to teachers, teacher educators and all those interested in education as a positive force for understanding and promoting diversity. Many of the chapters present interesting practical suggestions as to how teachers may use localities and perceived identities in a positive, enabling spirit, and all contributors are concerned to contextualize such ventures within a broad pedagogical outlook. The guiding principle here is that suggested by Sasha Matthewman, one of the contributors here, in a previous book: 'ecocritics think and teach outside (or at least look out of the window)' (Matthewman 2011: 23). In an age when national identities are a subject of popular debate, along with issues of place in relation to immigration, displacement and mobility, we feel it is particularly important that schools and other educational sites are supported in their reflections on how best to respond to such pertinent issues in their daily practice.

In achieving these aims we seek to build, in a critical and celebratory spirit (that tricky but potentially vital combination), on excellent work done already in the field – especially by Gabrielle Cliff Hodges and Cambridge colleagues. In terms of theoretical underpinning for the entire book, more distantly, but crucially, we intend to make an explicit connection to the groundbreaking work undertaken by Raymond Williams in *The Country and the City*, initially published in 1973 but, more than 40 years on, showing remarkable prescience in suggesting both the nature of the problems of place and identity, as historically divisive and defensive, and potential ways forward:

> All the conventional priorities are again being questioned. ... The theoretical if not practical confidence of defenders of the existing system has gone. The position in ideas is again quite open, ironically at the very time when the practical pressures are almost overwhelming. ...
>
> This is the position, the sense of shape, for which I have worked. Yet it is still, even now, only beginning to form. It is what is being done and is to do, rather than anything that has been finally done. ...
>
> And to see the negative effects, with whatever urgency, can be to paralyse the will. The last recess of the division of labour is this recess within ourselves, where what we want and what we believe we can do seem impassably divided. We can overcome division only by refusing to be divided.
>
> *(Williams 2011: 305–6)*

It seems to us that such words, the concluding pages of the book, relate in an even more timely and pressing way to the world of 2017 than they did in 1973, and, furthermore, signal a positive direction to take.

David Stevens and Karen Lockney
January 2017

References

Freire, P. (2004) *Pedagogy of Hope*. London: Continuum.
Matthewman, S. (2011) *Teaching English as if the Planet Matters*. London: Routledge.
Williams, R (2011) *The Country and the City*. London: Spokesman.

1

FROM PLACE TO PLANET

The role of the language arts in reading environmental identities from the UK to New Zealand

Sasha Matthewman

From here to there

The environmental crisis is now a prominent theme in literature, media and non-fiction and more recently in theatre. This is the cultural arena where environmental identities are tried on and tested by writers, readers and audiences. Teachers of the language arts have a vital role in mediating environmental identities through their engagement in this discourse and debate. There are many possible avenues to follow (see Matthewman 2011) but the representation of place is a good starting point, not least in relation to its currency and value in educational discourse (see Comber 2015; Gruenewald and Smith 2008). In this chapter I will examine the ways that teachers in New Zealand secondary schools have worked to inform environmental identities through a focus on place and belonging. I began writing about the connections between English and environment as a teacher educator in the UK. My move to New Zealand has highlighted for me how a sense of place and identity is central to an interpretation of texts.

Cockney translation

When I read Andrew Motion's poem 'Sparrow' in 2004 and designed a lesson activity to use with Year 7 students in Bristol, UK, my focus was on the bird and its habitat while the sense of place was taken for granted (Motion 2004: 143). I followed Motion's account of his poem, which talks about place in general terms as 'country' or 'town' (Burnside and Riorden 2004: 246). However, when I used this poem as part of a professional development day with Auckland teachers in New Zealand in 2015, the interconnection between culture and ecology and the specificity of place was brought into sharper focus. In the next section I will outline the moves in the lesson sequence as it was framed in the UK and follow with an account of how this evolved in relation to the nature and culture of New Zealand.

The first move in the sequence was to withhold the title but to notice that each line is an act of naming, a noun phrase that follows the form of the Anglo-Saxon 'kenning' – something is being named; what is it? These range from the descriptive 'puddle bather' to the punning 'hedgerow flasher' to the lyrical 'heaven filler' (Motion 2004: 143). Conveniently there are 30 of these kennings that can be distributed around the average class and analysed individually and in pairs to draw out clues and connotations. Thoughts in relation to the kennings were collated on the board under headings such as: 'characteristics of the species', 'habitats' and 'human attitudes to the species'. This was usually a good point to reveal that the lines make up a whole poem, leading into a performance with students standing to read out their lines (in numbered order) with the teacher voicing the refrain 'no longer'. Students had probably already begun to make guesses at the species and this was encouraged in relation to the teaching point that 'this is a species that has adapted to live alongside humans in multiple environments – both urban and rural'. Before the answer of 'sparrow' was either guessed or finally revealed by the teacher, the possibility of a range of various birds and creatures such as spiders, rats, and pigeons had been considered. The significance of the refrain 'no longer' is brought into focus once the sparrow has been considered as a familiar bird held in some affection by the poet. Why no longer? What has happened to the sparrow? What have we lost? What is the purpose and value of this 'ecopoem', which appeared in the anthology *Wild Reckoning* (Burnside and Riorden 2004)? This anthology commemorated the fortieth anniversary of the publication *Silent Spring*, the seminal text of the environmental movement (Carson 1962). For older students, the sparrow poem segued well into a reading of the opening fable in *Silent Spring*, which describes a small town in America where nature has been steadily poisoned and where no birds sing. A creative alternative was to research their choice of an endangered species as a prelude to writing their own kenning poem. Teaching the poem to student teachers of English, I suggested that pupils could write an ecocritical introduction to the poem for an environmental publication based on their research into the disappearance of the sparrow.

But in New Zealand, sparrows are plentiful. When I arrived in Auckland I was pleased to see masses of them everywhere, jumping onto urban cafe tables, squabbling in the kanuka trees or flocking for bread in my 'backyard'. Clearly the refrain 'no longer' did not apply here. Also, when I came to teach the poem in New Zealand I realized more acutely that rather than capturing the 'sparrowness of sparrows wherever they are (or are not any more)', the sparrow in Motion's poem is viewed through the lens of Englishness and lives in English places (Burnside and Riorden 2004: 246). Expressions such as 'cocky bugger', 'hedgerow flasher', 'stubble scrounger' and even 'country clubber' need glossing, as these reflect the idioms of English speech, there are no hedgerows in New Zealand and the only stubble to be seen around Auckland is of the designer variety. Rather than being a problem, this difference is a point of interest, raising a new set of questions. How would the poem change if it was written about sparrows in New Zealand? What lines would need to be altered? What lines could be added? One teacher commented that sparrows in New Zealand count as pests because as scavengers they compete more success-fully for scraps than the native bird scavengers. This New Zealand environmental perspective could be set against environmental perspectives that suggest that other environmental focuses such as habitat loss are more important (Inger et al. 2015; Peach et al. 2008). Of course the elegiac tone of the poem does not make sense in New Zealand in relation to the abundance of sparrows but at one time, not so long ago, it would not have made sense in England. 'The best-documented change has occurred in London where numbers of breeding sparrows declined by 60% between 1994 and 2004' (Raven et al. 2005 in Peach et al. 2008: 1). This might be especially poignant as sparrows were part of a London identity and argot – the 'cockney sparrer' – an underfed city child. Moreover the decline of the sparrow has been linked to the 'great thinning' of the insect population in Britain (Summers-Smith 2003). Nature writer Michael McCarthy's book *The Moth Snowstorm: Nature and Joy* (2015) describes the rapid disappearance of British wildlife since the Second World War, which is closely linked to the intensification of farming and the use of pesticides, herbicides and fertilizers. McCarthy (2015) writes: 'The country I was born into, possessed something wonderful it absolutely possesses no longer: natural abundance… Blessed, unregarded abundance has been destroyed.' His most sober-ing example is the blizzard of insects that used to obscure the windscreen of the car on a summer's evening in England, a phenomenon that will only be remem-bered by people over the age of 50. This example makes the teaching point of how rapidly the ecology can change and natural *taonga* (treasures) can be lost, requiring awareness of threats and the importance of protection not just of species but of ecosystems. It is easy to transfer the activity to a bird in danger of extinction in New Zealand – unfortunately there are plenty of critical and endangered species to choose from, the most familiar ones being the kiwi (all five species), takahe, black robin and the kea.

Of course the significance of the lesson sequence is lost if all the cultural, envi-ronmental and ecological context is stripped away in the rush to guess, or to per-form, or to write. This is the basis for an ecological lesson sequence rather than a standalone lesson, and it would work well as part of a cross-curricular collaboration. Teaching this sequence ecocritically requires the teacher to impart and to man-age knowledge and research into environmental issues in relation to the text. But good English teachers have always researched and prepared the contexts of texts – knowing that a strong interpretation is informed by knowledge – rather than leav-ing students with only their own hunches, guesses and feelings. The difference is that the environment has only relatively recently emerged as a context for literary criticism, whereas race and gender have long been 'hot topics' (Glotfelty 1996: xvi). Motion's stated aim in writing the poem is environmental: 'to invite readers to consider the plight of all kinds of endangered species – the humble as well as the exotic' (Burnside and Riorden 2004: 246). In teaching 'Sparrow' in relation to a sense of place, teachers can inform the local environmental identities of students with a sense of pride and wonder. For instance, when asked about significant wild-life in New Zealand that could be equivalent to the sparrow, one student quipped derisively 'Well, we've got a flightless bird'. This could have been countered with 'Yes, and do you know why the kiwi is unique to New Zealand and has become the defining symbol of our culture?' Followed by 'How many other native species do we have?'[1]

Environmental identities

In New Zealand I have been leading a two-year research project *Tuhia ki te Ao: Write to the Natural World* (Matthewman 2016), which is focusing on the ways that teachers can engage ecocritically with texts so as to inform students' environmental identities.

Within the project we have used the term 'environmental identities' to refer to the shifting mix of knowledge, understanding, values and attitudes that people hold regarding their relationship to the natural world, their understanding of their physical place in the world and the relationship between their culture and nature. Environmental identities may be shaped by a wide variety of influences including the mass media and the everyday acts of living within a culture. We seek to emphasize in the project that environmental identities are not fixed; they develop and change over time, and are affected by physical and social location. Underpinning the project is the idea that school subjects are important sources of feelings, knowledge and values that can inform and draw on environmental identities. Clayton (2003: 45) emphasizes the 'sense of connection to some part of the non-human natural environment, based on history, emotional attachment, and/or similarity, that affects the ways in which we perceive and act toward the world'. From this we derive four aspects of environmental identity to consider in our planning: a sense of place and belonging; attitudes to animals and plants; involvement in group activities related to the environment; and a sense of the natural world as interconnected. Crompton and Kasser (2009: 7) argue that 'it is at this level of values and identity that environmental communication must aim since only a change of identity can make a real difference to people's behaviour'. This sits easily with the focus in English on 'personal growth,' albeit from a less familiar angle.

Another continuity arises from within the wider discipline of English in relation to the significant addition of ecocriticism to the canon of literary criticism.[2] Put simply, ecocriticism studies the relationship between the physical environment and cultural representations. Lawrence Buell, one of the most influential ecocritics, also draws a link between identity and environmental action. He examines a range of literary representations of environmental issues alongside reviews of prominent historical environmental case studies (such as Love Canal and the *Exxon Valdez*), which lead him to conclude that 'an awakened sense of physical location and of belonging to some sort of place-based community have a great deal to do with activating environmental concern' (Buell 2001: 56). Initial work in our project *Tuhia ki te Ao* has gravitated towards articulating place and belonging in relation to the themes that teachers have chosen to pursue in their work. In the context of New Zealand, the question of who belongs and who *most* or *really* belongs is both fraught and sensitive. Cultural protocol decrees that greetings must be given in a certain order, first to Māori (as the first people), then to the colonial islands in order of their historical connection. Formal meetings in our education department begin with a welcome in Māori with the speaker stating his or her place and ancestry (the '*pepeha*'). These expressions of a hierarchy of belonging mean that individuals from any culture (including Māori) are already inserted into a discursive history of post-colonial territorial disputes. Belonging in Aotearoa New Zealand involves negotiating your part in sedimented layers of history and protocol, which can feel exclusive and hierarchical whoever you are. Our research shows that students have affiliations and views of place and environment that are part of their cultural identity and that are embedded or *implicit* within cultural literacy practices. Conversely, alienation from the natural environment and the experience of displacement through migration or through changes to home environments can cause a profound sense of dissonance (Nixon 2011). To attempt to counter this alienation, the school curriculum – and the teaching and learning that take place in subjects – has the potential to inform, draw on and help *explicitly* develop students' environmental identities in positive ways.

Environmental identity is not just a matter of dimensions of environmental concern but involves cultural mediation and labelling. Students are exposed to available constructions of environmental identity in the media, literature and the culture of everyday life. In New Zealand these can be recognized as: Māori *kai-tiakitanga*; *pakeha* settler; New Zealand conservationist; New Zealand 100% Pure; and the global eco-being. These environmental identities may be provisionally sketched as follows:

Māori *kaitiakitanga*: This indigenous perspective holds that Māori have a literal ancestry and kinship to the natural world (Mataamua and Temara 2010). This is expressed through myths and stories of relationship and belonging to the land. Māori groups (*iwi* and *hapū*) have particular historical connections to land areas and they have the status of *kaitiakis* – guardians with an inherited obligation to protect the land. While the status of *kaitiaki* is often appropriated in mainstream environmental discourse, the meaning of this word is held to be sacred and appropriate only to Māori as people of the land (Mutu 2010). But as many Māori are now urban dwellers with broken links to the land, this may be an equally difficult identity to inhabit for most Māori as well as for *pakeha*. However, it offers an important and high-status alternative to a resource-based view of the environment.

***Pakeha* settler identity:** *Pakeha* (non-Māori or more commonly used in relation to New Zealanders of European descent) have long ties to farming reflecting the historical importance of New Zealand agriculture to Britain. This may be represented as a caring and productive relationship (Stephenson 2010). It is, of course, a contested environmental position as the waterways are increasingly polluted by dairy farming, and fertilizer and pesticide run off. As former All Black captain and 'national hero' Richie McCaw said in a recent advert for the milk company Fonterra – 'people say that farmers don't care much about the land' and then he listens, nodding to the farming couple who explain their efforts to protect, plant and regenerate. This identity of working your land is very strong in New Zealand and is present in many a suburban backyard cum smallholding. Homes are referred to routinely as 'properties' in general conversation and improvement of both land and property is part of a deep-seated belief in ownership, progress and development. 'Bring on the weekend' is the advertising slogan of DIY giant Mitre 10 reflecting and constructing a Kiwi obsession with weekend improvement projects.

New Zealand conservationist: This identity is dominant within education and aligned to the New Zealand Department of Conservation. It is focused on the protection of native species. New Zealand has a delicate ecosystem highly vulnerable to foreign fauna and flora. The solution is radically anti-alien with poison dropped to kill pests in remote forest areas, strict biosecurity and gated 'pure zones'. It is a dominant attitude to nature that views any non-native, even if innocuous, as suspect, or at least valueless. 'It's non-native' means it can be easily dismissed, culled or chopped down. Planting days and 'working bees' to clear weeds are common activities in rural and semi-rural primary schools but are less prevalent in secondary schools where the main focus is on high stakes assessment.

New Zealand = 100% Pure: This is the view of New Zealand that is most likely to be available to British readers through the famous 2016 Ministry of Tourism advertising campaign: 'The 100% Pure New Zealand brand has defined how our country and our exports are viewed across the globe.' It is an identity that embraces the recreational potential of New Zealand, natural spaces and accepts uncritically the notion of New Zealand as environmentally enlightened and blessed; as one social sciences teacher in the project commented, 'we still have a lot of nature compared to other countries'. The concept of *kaitiakitanga* is juxtaposed with the values of the market: 'The product we are selling is New Zealand itself – the people, the places, the food, the wine, the experiences.' The main problem with this identity is that it can lead to a complacent celebration of landscape and amenities without an awareness that the environment is a process and is under threat (see Matthewman 2014 for discussion).

The global eco-being: This is a more general environmental identity, which involves shopping second-hand, growing food, taking sustainable transport options, eating vegetarian or at least organic, and being involved in environmental campaigns. However, given that this is a global *middle-class* identity, air travel is likely to be a blind spot. Embracing this identity may earn you the dismissive epithet of 'greenie' or 'hippy', which is a common response in New Zealand to anything that threatens the 'common-sense' of maximizing the resource potential of the land.

The problem is that these identities may not seem especially attractive or available to urban and suburban children, many of whom are immigrants not fully enculturated into being 'New Zealanders'.[3] And evidently there are problematic and contradictory elements in all of these positions. These identities have all been raised in our project classroom observations largely as implicit 'givens' rather than as positions to be explored and critiqued. For example in social sciences the teacher listed essentialized comments about Māori made by students such as: 'land is sacred to them', 'they are very traditional and respect their land', 'the land is like family to them', which was contrasted with a destructive *pakeha* viewpoint: 'we don't think of the consequences'. These views were left uncontested, creating a problematic in-group versus out-group identity that can work against constructive behaviours (Crompton and Kasser 2009). The environment remains someone else's responsibility (Māori) or conversely someone else's fault (*pakeha*). A resonant example is the often-studied play *Waiora* in which the *pakeha* mill-owner Steve surveys the view and says to Hone, his Māori foreman:

> It's a beautiful place here, eh? You could do a lot with it. That land over there – you could pick it up for a song. Burn it off, plant pine and in 30 years' time you could mill it. Make a fortune... the Maoris I know they'd probably get up on that hill and watch the sunset.
>
> *(Kouka 1997: 81)*

It is challenging to move students on from stereotypes to consider that identities are not fixed and are always nuanced – and this would be possible and available in this play through a sensitive reading of the character of Hone. Working towards a more nuanced and critical understanding of the complexity of environmental identities is an important function and potential of close reading of text and place in relation to environmental context. However it requires strong teacher mediation in leading debate and discussion and offering alternative perspectives and readings. For instance, students were introduced to a recognizably 'New Age' definition of an ecopoem on YouTube, which led one student to respond that ecopoems are written by 'greenies' and another to offer that it sounded like 'the sort of thing that hippies would write'. The YouTube representation of ecopoetry could have been contrasted with a more political definition such as that available in the anthology *Earth Shattering* (Astley 2007). Working with a strong example, such as 'Sparrow' or *Waiora*, allows the teacher to prepare to discuss the differences between cultural perspectives on environmental issues. Learning to be ecocritical means being aware of the identities that are available and represented and debating the contradictions and problems in a global as well as a national context.

Environmental knowledge

One of the major challenges for teachers in the project has been judging how to introduce ecological knowledge to be integral to the activity and consistent with the subject discipline. Students may be unaware of what they need to know or how to research and this is reflected in the vignette that follows:

A feeling for somewhere...

It is July and a chilly winter's day (for Auckland). Students huddle outside a temporary classroom building but once inside, it is stiflingly hot and Newton comments that he has had to complain about the heating. The room is cramped and dark and the computers have a heavy look. Students sit down and the familiar complaints about slow log-in begin. Newton is busy settling the class and dealing with issues. It becomes clear that several of the computers are not working or have no internet access. The students with working computers know what they have to do and are scrolling and selecting images from the internet. There are maps, flags, pictures of beaches, waterfalls, *Marae*,[4] food, a couple of city scenes. Newton prompts, 'It's got to be about you. Remember we talked about culture – where you live… where your family is from.' Later he interjects, 'Remember that idea of sustainability – how is that perspective in your culture?' and again picking up on an individual question he reminds the class, 'What does sustainability mean? How will we keep the environment for future generations? Like how do we sustain a conversation – keep it going?'

Diane is working on her PowerPoint presentation. She has chosen iconic tourist scenes of the Coromandel: a picture of the famous railway and an image of the viewpoint tower. I am surprised when she says that she has never been on the train or to the viewpoint. 'It's just a picture of the environment.' She selects an image of a beach in Coromandel. To her, this represents the beach where her father and grandfather built their own bach,[5] although she can't remember where exactly in the Coromandel this is or give any place names. She says that she goes on holiday there every year and has good memories of it. Diane works in a fairly leisurely but focused way on compiling her three slides. She has discussion with her partner about what the task is about:

'It's culture!'

'No, it's environment!'

'It's a bit of both.'

They confirm this with Newton, who tries to draw out how her work connects to sustainability. He asks her about how she would feel about the beach if there were buildings there.

This vignette illustrates a common feature of our observations and discussion with students at the school about their favoured places, which are often located far from where they live. Diane clearly has a long history with her place in the Coromandel and a deep feeling for it as she describes how her father has taken up the task of working on and renovating the family bach, built by her grandfather. To her, the precise location does not seem to matter while the images are generic and symbolic, representing her imaginary sense of the Coromandel in relation to her small and special place within it. It is far from the urban and often edgy setting of South Auckland.

While this feeling for place is important in terms of environmental identity, our aspiration in the project is to begin to deepen this work through attention to the interconnections of place, text and context. In the second iteration of this work, the teacher plans for students to be introduced to the form of the '*pepeha*' and to write place-based haiku connecting text and image. The *pepeha* requires the ritual naming of geographical, cultural and ancestral connections relating to self. This is a prompt to finding out about the place that you connect with – your place to stand on the earth (*Tūrangawaewae*). There are many ways to do this but you would usually begin by naming your mountain, your river and your harbour before naming your tribal and family affiliations. It is a Māori form for an intro-duction but it can also be a resonant form for *pakeha* (non-Māori) and it may be adapted to suit personal circumstances. The structure creates an opportunity for learning the Māori language version (*Te Reo*) and could also be an opportunity for working in other languages. It was notable that when students prepared for this, only one out of the sample group of 12 could name a mountain and a river, while their knowledge of family and ancestry was much more developed. This reflects the strong focus on cultural identity in New Zealand but suggests that the eco-logical dimension of this identity has not been part of these students' experience as Gruenewald (2008: 144) states: 'Environmental education in schools is rare and rarely intersects with culturally responsive teaching.' He suggests that the failure to know about the unique places in our lives is to remain in 'a disturbing sort of igno-rance' (2008: 143). More poetically, Wendell Berry writes: 'Not knowing where you are, you can lose your soul or your soil, your life or your way home.' (Berry 1983: 103 in Buell 2001: 75).

The material impact of the school environment and culture is significant in rela-tion to developing and informing connections to the local place. The connection between positive experiences of nature, place and environmental identity is well documented (see Gruenewald 2003). However, James Cook School is set in a low socio-economic area, it is difficult and costly (without parental contributions) to arrange field trips – so none took place. Also, students typically don't have mobile phones or access to digital cameras to take original images and have to work on old computers that are not regularly maintained.

In contrast, during the same period of six-week observation at Honsonville Point School in a high-income catchment area, the target Year 9 class (13–14 years old) went on four field trips in the Auckland area and took part in two poetry workshops on different days led by writers. This disparity in opportunity between the two schools has been unexpectedly stark in the project while the demands in terms of tasks set have been remarkably similar. However, during the period of observation it has been the ability of the second school to afford experiences out-side the classroom that has been the major point of difference for students' learn-ing rather than the superior resources and technology. For example, the following vignette from the second school suggests the potential of the field trip as part of work on setting and location in drama.

Comparing locations from then to now

It is the day of the trip to Takapuna beach. Leigh has prepared a set of activi-ties for the students to complete as part of the field trip for drama. In activity one, students are asked to read the opening monologue from *The End of the*

Golden Weather (Mason 1962), highlighting descriptions of the landscape in the text, finding and photographing the locations and then noting how they have changed from the description in the play. Activity two involves looking for the places where a series of photos from the 1940s–1960s were taken, and again noting how the location has changed over time. Activity three asks students to investigate a newly built playground on the small reserve next to the beach (which used to be a regular performance space for the play) and reflect on who has been affected by this change in land use.

On the bus, students chat and text but some read the extract from the play. The script begins with a long monologue from a narrator, remembering this place from his childhood and reflecting on the changes that have been wrought there from European settlement to the setting in the 1930s. Students spill out onto the beach. They take pictures using their phones of viewpoints mentioned in the script. The teacher has put together a set of old photos of the same location. Students seem excited by the challenge of matching their photos to the ones from the past.

Back in the drama studio the next day, students discuss the ways that the place has changed over time, referring to the play, their own images and the old photos. The teacher directs their attention to the new Astroturf playground, which has replaced the grassy performance space used by the playwright. They are asked to consider in their groups how to produce this script to give a sense of the layers of environmental change and the ecological impact of people on the place. Some students plan to use their slide show as a backdrop, while others are prompted to consider an interrupting narrator who adds in comments about the present in relation to the play's portrayal of the past. One student group is attempting to create parallel scenes, one group is representing the environment as it is now, and another group as it is represented in the play. In directing their script they are asked to take an environmental angle on the performance.

This combination of the playscript with its explicit theme of environmental change in the opening monologue and the school's proximity to the setting location (also historically a performance site for the play) is a perfect opportunity to develop ecocritical literacy. Ecocritical literacy requires a critical understanding of how texts represent particular ecological interests. The shared model allows the teacher to draw attention to the ecological issues that the text raises in relation to the ecological issues presented at the location. A shared model of place for study has the advantage of building students' place awareness rather than leaving them stuck in a place that they already connect with (but may know little about). Learning how to read a place and knowing that places are in process and changing tends to relate to geography while English and the arts are focused on the work of representation and the feelings, values and emotions that make *space* become *place*. However, the process of place-making happens as much through this active mediation of 'texts, images and instruments' as through real experience (Massey and Thrift 2003: 292). In this unit we see the potential for both experience and mediation to work together as students explore the representation of the environment as a process reflecting on the multiple changes and shifts in the real and fictional location and their ecological significance. Given our observations of the value of the field trip when working with place, the project is planning to support a field trip for James Cook School in relation to their work on pepeha, haiku and image.

Conclusion: moving from place to planet

We have introduced teachers on the project to a three-part heuristic model drawn from geographers' conceptualizations of place: place as a bounded container; place as part of a web of relations; and place as a centre of flows (see Massey and Thrift 2003).

A sense of place as bounded can be discerned in the student's feeling for a bach situated 'somewhere' in the Coromandel. Knowing 'your' place better is a starting point but students also need an understanding of how places relate to each other; comparing the different ecologies and attitudes to place in relation to texts such as 'Sparrow' and other texts that represent nature, the land, the sea, animals and cities. Most texts provoke questions about our relationship to the natural world and have implications for sustainability of place. In the Takapuna example, place is represented as a centre of flows as the play describes the influx of settlers, and the ecological changes that have occurred in relation to cultural change. Arguably students need to develop both a sense of place (as in their place or their *Tūrangawaewae*) and a sense of planet as they look beyond the confines of their own place to see the environment as a complex and interconnected process (Heise 2008). At James Cook, the students who had explored their own place also learned about the plight of the pacific island of Kiribati in social sciences as part of the project. A majority of the students have family links to the Pacific and they wrote impassioned and carefully structured letters to Prime Minister John Key about the human impact of climate change on this place. This extends imaginations outwards from the dominant New Zealand environmental identities that are strongly centred on New Zealand as a bounded place, with a unique fauna and flora requiring protection from the threats of outside. But as a student once said to his environmentalist lecturer: 'It's hard to care about the environment when someone's foot is on your neck' (Gruenewald 2008: 145). Social disparities and opportunities have been marked in relation to the two schools and it is important to make explicit the links between social and environmental justice as in the case of Kiribati. Helping students to develop a robust and critical environmental identity requires an *eco*critical literacy approach within all subjects as a dimension of critical literacy. This means that texts are seen not only as serving particular *human* interests but also *ecological* purposes and interests. The hope is that *eco*critical literacy can support students to become powerful advocates for their places, communities, trees, animals, insects, birds and plants while also caring for wider communities and the fragile planet that supports us all in a web of living beings.

Notes

1 There are 70,000 native species of plants and animals and many of these, like the kiwi, are endemic (Brockie 2016).
2 Ecocriticism is now an established field with entries in the major introductions to literacy criticism and theory (see for example Barry 2002).
3 Over 3.25 million of the 4.5 million people in New Zealand live in a main urban area; www.stats.govt.nz/browse_for_stats/Maps_and_geography/Geographic-areas/urban-rural-profile-update.aspx.
4 A Māori meeting house.
5 Traditionally a wooden holiday home by the sea.

References

Astley, N. (ed.) (2007) *Earth Shattering: Ecopoems.* Tarset: Bloodaxe.
Barry, P. (2002) *Beginning Theory: An Introduction to Literary and Cultural Theory*, 2nd edn. Manchester: Manchester University Press.
Brockie, B. (2016) Native plants and animals – overview – Species unique to New Zealand. *Te Ara – the Encyclopedia of New Zealand.* Retrieved from www.TeAra.govt.nz/en/native-plants-and-animals-overview/page-1.
Buell, L. (2001) *Writing for an Endangered World: Literature, Culture, and Environment in the US and Beyond.* Cambridge, MA: Harvard University Press.
Burnside, J. and Riorden, M. (eds.) (2004) *Wild Reckoning: An Anthology Provoked by Rachel Carson's* Silent Spring. London: Calouste Gulbenkian Foundation.
Carson, R. (1962) *Silent Spring.* Boston, MA: Houghton Mifflin.
Clayton, S. (2003) Environmental identity: a conceptual and an operational definition. In S. Clayton and S. Opotow (eds.) *Identity and the Natural Environment*, 45–66. Massachusetts, MA: MIT Press.
Comber, B. (2015) *Literacies, Place, and Pedagogies of Possibility.* New York and London: Routledge.
Crompton, T. and Kasser, T. (2009) *Meeting Environmental Challenges: The Role of Human Identity.* Totnes: WWF-UK. Retrieved from http://assets.wwf.org.uk/downloads/meeting_environmental_challenges___the_role_of_human_identity.pdf?_ga=1.152114362.2075886703.1475022460.
Glotfelty, C. (1996) Introduction: literary studies in an age of environmental crisis. In C. Glotfelty and H. Fromm (eds.) *The Ecocriticism Reader: Landmarks in Literary Ecology*, xv–xxxvii. Athens, GA: University of Georgia Press.
Gruenewald, D. (2003) The best of both worlds: A critical pedagogy of place. *Educational Researcher* 32(4), 3–12.
Gruenewald, D. (2008) Place-based education: grounding culturally responsive teaching in geographical diversity. In D. Gruenewald and G. Smith (eds.) *Place-Based Education in the Global Age.* New York: Lawrence Erlbaum.
Gruenewald, D. and Smith, G. (2008) *Place-Based Education in the Global Age.* New York: Lawrence Erlbaum.
Heise, U.K. (2008) *Sense of Place and Sense of Planet: The Environmental Imagination of the Global.* Oxford: Oxford University Press.
Inger, R. Gregory, R., Duffy, J.P., Stott, I, Voříšek, P. and Gaston, K. (2015) Common European birds are declining rapidly while less abundant species' numbers are rising. *Ecology Letters* 18(1), 28–36.
Kouka, H. (1997) *Waiora.* Wellington: Huia Publishers.

Mason, B. (1962) *The End of the Golden Weather: A Voyage into a New Zealand Childhood.* Wellington: New Zealand University Press and Price Milburn.

Massey, D. and Thrift, N. (2003) The passion of place. In R. Johnston and M. Williams (eds.) *A Century of British Geography*, 275–99. Oxford: Oxford University Press for the British Academy.

Mataamua, R. and Temara, P.T.R. (2010) Ka mate kāinga tahi, ka ora kāinga rua. Tūhoe and the environment: the impact of the Tūhoe diaspora on the Tūhoe environment. In R. Selby, P. Moore and M. Mulholland (eds.) *Māori and the Environment: Kaitiaki*, 95–107. Wellington: Huia Publishers.

Matthewman, S. (2011) *Teaching Secondary English as if the Planet Matters.* Abingdon: Routledge.

Matthewman, S. (2014) Clearing the ground for a greener New Zealand English. *English Teaching: Practice and Critique* 13(1), 95–111.

Matthewman, S. (2016) *Tuhia ki te Ao: Write to the Natural World.* Wellington: Teaching Learning and Research Initiative. Retrieved from www.tlri.org.nz/tlri-research/research-progress/school-sector/tuhia-ki-te-ao-write-natural-world.

McCarthy, M. (2015) *The Moth Snowstorm: Nature and Joy.* London: John Murray.

Motion, A. (2004) Sparrow. In J. Burnside and M. Riorden (eds.) *Wild Reckoning: An Anthology Provoked by Rachel Carson's* Silent Spring, *143–4. London: Calouste Gulbenkian Foundation.*

Mutu, M. (2010) Ngāti kahu kaitiakitanga. In R. Selby, P. Moore and M. Mulholland (eds.) *Māori and the Environment: Kaitiaki*, 13–35. Wellington: Huia Publishers.

Nixon, R. (2011) *Slow Violence and the Environmentalism of the Poor.* Cambridge, MA: Harvard University Press.

Peach, W.J., Vincent, K.E., Fowler, J.A., Grice, P.V. (2008) Reproductive success of house sparrows along an urban gradient. *Animal Conservation* 11(6), 493–503.

Stephenson, G. (2010) Of rocks and recollections: our home in the South Waikato. In J. Stephenson, M. Abbott and J. Ruru (eds.) *Beyond the Scene: Landscape and Identity in Aotearoa New Zealand*, 39–53. Dunedin: Otago University Press.

Summers-Smith, J.D. (2003) The decline of the house sparrow: a review. *British Birds* 96, 439–46.

2

CONNECTING COMMUNITY THROUGH FILM IN ITE ENGLISH

Joanna McIntyre and Susan Jones

Introduction

As the landscape of English is shaped by global educational reform, character-ized by standardization and performativity, the subject is increasingly defined as a prescribed skillset, and the lived experiences of learners is sidelined by a narrow, assessment-driven curriculum. Within this landscape, beginning teachers of English face the challenge of developing critical, research-informed practice. This chapter outlines the work undertaken by beginning teachers of English who took part in a voluntary collaborative film-making project during their training year. The project involved them working alongside learners in their placement schools, and with cre-ative professionals, to produce short films exploring questions of community, place and identity.

The chapter begins with an exploration of the current place of English in the wider educational context, and in the experience of learners and teachers in English secondary schools. We then discuss three examples of films made by beginning teachers of English who opted to take part in the film project with young people in their placement schools. We examine both the process of the film project and the products made by those involved, and explore the potential for place in an English curriculum that engages creatively with community.

The place of English in the contemporary policy context

Although the subject of English has been the focus of debate for decades, recent years have seen the particularly acute impact of neoliberal policy on the experience of learners and teachers in English classrooms. Within a wider climate of intense performativity, the subject itself has been increasingly reduced to that which can be measured by standardized assessment. Comber (2016: xiv) outlines the 'fickle literacies' that can dominate the experience of learners in this context; these include 'rote learning, repeated test preparation, copying... and other challenge-free, thought-less activities, which will not build their capacity for academic learning and complex literacies'. Writing in the context of New Zealand, Locke (2008: 308) also describes the impact of competency-driven regimes which are 'distorting students' understandings of genre, marginalizing real-world textual practices... and drilling students in arid and formulaic responses to literary texts'.

This reduction of the subject has left little space for the experience of young people to be included in English classrooms. In England, non-dominant voices have been further marginalized by the most recent iterations of the National Curriculum Programmes of Study (Department for Education 2014). Speaking and listening have been abandoned as core elements of the English curriculum, which emphasizes canonical texts of 'British heritage' at the cost of media, film and drama. Alongside a policy context that has shaped this model of the subject, deficit discourses of youth continue to pervade the media to the point where young people are further disenfranchised as members of the community whose experiences and funds of knowledge (Gonzalez et al. 2005) do not count as valid resources for classroom learning (McIntyre 2016; Jones and Chapman 2017; Jones and McIntyre 2014; Vasudevan and Campano 2009).

The impact of this context on the experience of teachers has been well documented across jurisdictions subject to neoliberal education reform (e.g., Sandretto and Tilson 2015; Comber 2012; Ravitch 2010; Ball 2003). We have explored elsewhere the particular experience of teachers new to the profession in navigating this landscape (McIntyre and Jones 2014). The teachers in that study described how they perceived the experience of the learners in their subject:

> Ed: I think they now perceive English as a series of milestones rather than as something that is particularly coherent or, dare I say it, enjoyable.
>
> Will: [My Year 9s] have absolutely no idea of English outside the assessment focuses.

The place of English for learners in contemporary classrooms was, for these beginning teachers, often reduced to being fixed on the page of an examined text, or the whiteboard screen in a lesson preparing for assessment. The reduction of the places engaged with in the subject is illustrated by Heather's comment about a theatre trip she proposed for her class, which was seen by her colleagues and mentor as 'risky':

> They have never taken any kids to the theatre before. I think they see it as 'we are going to read this play because they are going to sit the exam on it', not that students need to see it as a wider thing.

For beginning teachers of English facing the tensions encountered when navigating the enactment of a narrow, mandated curriculum and a culture of performativity, their Initial Teacher Education (ITE) course provides a critical space in which to explore different possibilities. Turvey and Lloyd (2014: 77) offer an account of a beginning teacher's exploration of learning rooted in the social relationships of his English classroom, arguing that '"subject knowledge" in English should not be seen as a stable, pre-existing entity'. Allard and Doecke (2014) describe early career teachers' negotiation of their professional knowledge and values, the mandated curriculum, and the standards by which they themselves are measured in their practice; in doing so, the authors argue, these teachers are 'marshalling [their] knowledge *against* those standards' (2014: 42, emphasis in original) and pushing at the boundaries imposed by a standardized curriculum. Paradoxically, in so doing, they are demonstrating how drawing upon diverse experiences in the classroom is central to meeting the standards agenda by which teachers are themselves measured. This work is not without challenge for those entering the profession, however. Will, a beginning teacher in our previous study (McIntyre and Jones 2014), recognized that, in his placement school, 'it would be a very brave member of staff who would try to do things differently'. The film project we discuss in this chapter is one way in which beginning teachers are supported to explore the possibilities of doing just that.

Place in English: doing things differently

We approach the work we outline in this chapter with a perspective afforded by our experience as teachers of English now working as literacy researchers and teachers on a one-year university-based postgraduate secondary English ITE course. Our institution offers both a university-based PGCE as well as school-based routes. These programmes are informed by a conception of literacy in its broadest form and beginning teachers of English are invited to engage with paradigms of literacy that include print, digital, multimodal and material resources drawn upon in a range of contexts. Within the core programme for all beginning teachers of English, there is recognition of the pedagogical processes involved in working with media and film, and the affordances of these for engaging the creativity, voice and agency of young people (Bazalgette and Buckingham 2013; Parry 2014). While the assessment of individual skills can dominate in contemporary English classrooms, this model of literacy includes participatory, collaborative and intergenerational practice. There is a strong emphasis on the local and the transformative potential of place-based pedagogies (Comber 2016; Garcia and Morrell 2013; Jones and McIntyre 2014; Jones and Chapman, 2017). Literacy practices are therefore understood as inherently social actions: 'things which people do, either alone or with other people, but always in a social context – always in a place and at a time' (Barton and Hamilton 1998: 23).

The power of the film project to engage learners and teachers in a collaborative disruption of the mandated curriculum is rooted in its close focus on people in place. The concepts of place and space are far from simple, of course, and have been the focus of academic debate across disciplines for decades, including a specific focus on their relationship with literacy (Leander and Sheehy 2004). In our work with beginning teachers, as is made explicit in the film project, we understand place as a 'meaningful location' (Cresswell 2004: 5), which results from the 'interplay of people and the environment' (Cresswell 2004: 11). As such, we argue that the creative process of making these films, as well as the resultant films themselves, have the potential to be place-making (Jones et al. 2013). For Comber (2016: 101), 'the study of place affords complex opportunities for collective meaning making practices' that result in collaborative text production. This, she argues, 'can be a positive site for identity work, community building and the development of literate repertoires' (2016: 103). The agency that is suggested by such a position on meaning-making and text production is in direct opposition to the framing of the learner and the teacher in a mandated, performative culture. It challenges the new market discourse of education by reminding us that knowledge cannot be fixed. As Massey (2005: 38) warns, the essentializing of cultural meaning 'to try and hold the world still […] eliminates also any possibility of real change'.

Massey's (2005) conception of place as a 'spatio-temporal event' is helpful to our understanding of the films we explore here and their representation of young people and their communities. Such a way of understanding place is important in two key ways. The first is that, rather than being a fixed, emotionally and ideologically neutral geographical point, place is representative of broad constellations of what we might describe as specific, local and contemporary realities. Equally important to this understanding of place is a connection between realities in a given context and many others across space and time; these include a past from which these realities emerge, a present in which they are experienced and a future that they will impact. As well as representing the places and communities that are important to them, these young film-makers engage narratives which move across space and time. The resonance of the films is also enriched by the meanings brought to them by the audience at each viewing. In making films explicitly about place, therefore, participants in the film project are involved in a continued (re)creation of that place. The multidimensional meanings and complex interplay of mode and form that are generated through engaging with place are powerful outcomes for learning in English classrooms. They can inform understanding not only of young people's creative work but also of their role as critically literate members of their communities.

We move now to discuss the film project in more depth. Following some background about how the project has worked, we examine films produced in three different schools. Through a focus on the role of place, we analyse how each film challenges dominant and reductive models of subject English and what this means to young people and the communities in which they live and learn.

The film project

Beginning in 2010 and running annually with each of our cohorts, the film project was devised to offer beginning teachers of English a way of engaging with their learners in authentic, purposeful, real-world contexts (Lankshear and Knobel 2011). The project involves trainees from across the ITE English routes at the university working in a partnership with local creative practitioners. All English trainees attend a workshop facilitated by the creative practitioners, where they learn skills of practical film-making and project management. The range of experience within each cohort varies hugely in terms of practical skills and familiarity with film and media terminology and practice. The emphasis in this workshop is on the range of roles needed to create a film and, as a group, the participants are invited to take on responsibility as script writers, art department, sound and lighting as well as directing, camera work and appearing on screen. The focus on inclusivity, along with the accessibility of technical elements, makes the project easily transferable to trainees' own classrooms.

Beginning teachers can then opt to go on to develop a film-making project in their placement schools, identifying a group of pupils with which to work on planning and producing a short film of no longer than five minutes, using the media equipment available to them in their schools. More often than not, this equipment is relatively low-tech, low-cost and easy to use, such as FlipCams. One of the challenges faced by the young film-makers is learning how to creatively navigate the practical issues raised by the technology used, such as working with cameras with inbuilt microphones when filming shots at a distance from the actors, or the impact of the wind on sound quality when filming outdoors. The beginning teachers and their groups are free to choose the genre and content of their film, but a broad theme is given: 'This is my place.' Over the course of the project, which typically takes place in the spring and early summer terms, the beginning teachers who are leading film-making groups in their schools are invited back to campus for additional workshops led by a creative practitioner, with further input on filming, editing and project management. Many of those who take part enlist the support of other colleagues or older students at school, in particular those working in the media and ICT departments, or studying media post-16. This support can range from loaning or demonstrating equipment and software to support with the final edit of the film.

At the end of the project, all of the young film-makers are invited, along with their teachers, friends and families, to a celebratory screening at an arts venue in the city centre. At this event, each group, led by the beginning teacher with whom they worked, is asked to share their experiences of making their film and they are presented with a certificate and an engraved 'Oscar' trophy, which has made its way to the trophy cabinet in some schools.

The films

The three films we explore here were all made by groups of students in Key Stage 3 (aged 11–14).[1] One of the beginning teachers to have taken part in the project with a Year 7 group commented on why working with the younger pupils was important to her:

> Georgina: As is seemingly the case in schools entirely focused on achieving a C at GCSE, KS3 is marginalized. We decided we wanted to change this and realized by not focusing on Year 7 early on, as a school we often contributed to the 'switch-off' of students to English long before reaching KS4.

The examples we have chosen each focus on the school as the 'place' of the film, both in terms of its physical location and its topic. It is perhaps unsurprising that the school is such a key location given the restrictions on time and movement in a typical secondary school. Although there are some examples of films made during the course of the project that have used the school as a 'set' in a film such as a horror or a romantic comedy, in interpreting the broad title they are given, the majority of participating students chose their school as their explicit focus. In their representation of their school, the young film-makers present a view of it as 'the epitome of place in terms of it being a site of trajectories and negotiation' (Comber 2016: 23). Two of the films in particular show how the young film-makers deal quite explicitly with 'the situatedness of their school in its economic, social, cultural, historical, political and ecological environment' (Comber 2016: 23). The first of these is the film made by Lisa and her group at the Kingsville school.

'Our Place': the Kingsville School

Lisa made the decision to run the film-making project with her Year 7 class (aged 11–12) during one lesson a week over the course of the spring term. She was keen for all members of the class to have a role and as a group they explored the significance of each different person's contribution to a finished film. The film they made was aimed at primary school children about to leave Year 6 and start secondary school (aged 10–11). It is a film that therefore informs its audience about their new school. It also tells the story of the school's wider community, its history and a vision of its future.

The film opens with a title frame reading 'This was our place' and a shot of two performers addressing the audience directly from behind folders made to look like learned tomes on local history. They give some of the history of the school and its community. The school was built in 1964 to serve the children of its surrounding villages, once inhabited by the workers of local collieries and their families. As the film informs us, the closest colliery to the school was closed in 1994. Although 20 years on since this event, it is interesting to note that the pupils chose to open their film with this aspect of their local history. There is also reference to the legend of Robin Hood, described as 'just folklore, but still part of our story'. The next scene is a depiction of a primary school classroom, and one of the performers addresses the camera with a tale of how he felt he hadn't fitted in initially, before eventually finding his 'place'. The film then cuts to a depiction of transition, with a shot of pupils approaching the school entrance and an interview with one of the group about how she felt about coming to Year 7 for the first time. We hear about this pupil's fears of being 'swirled' ('where the older children flush your head down the toilet'), before she is reassured that this is merely an urban myth and that everyone is friendly. Life in secondary school is depicted through shots of pupils moving up stairs and along corridors, and an interaction with a teacher (more of which later). The final scenes are introduced with the caption 'This will be our place'. In a fictionalized encounter, a doctor bumps into a prime minister and both realize that they went to the school.

'This is Our Place': High Bridge

Like Lisa at the Kingsville School, Ella decided to work on the film project with her Year 7 group as part of a wider module she had devised to explore genre. The film made at High Bridge was aimed at promoting the school to an outside audience as a place to learn. The school is located on a large estate in one of the most deprived wards on the edge of an already deprived city. Although small as a geographic location, the area is served by two secondary schools, one of which is a new-build that attracts the greater share of intake and has led to a falling roll for High Bridge, which finds itself not only having to work to challenge the wider discourses of deficit that affect the community in which it is located, but also dealing with competition for pupils at a local level.

The film opens with a celebratory title frame – 'This is our place' – and takes the audience through a sequence of focuses throughout the school, framed around the experiences of students in the Year 7 group. One of the early comments heard on the film is made by one of the film-makers: 'Just because the building looks old doesn't mean it is a bad school.' The film states that pupils at the school are 'adventurous', as it moves into a spoof wildlife documentary, with boys walking down the corridor as if it were a jungle and a voiceover huskily describing the fact that they are looking for a 'wild creature'.

This wild creature is revealed, after much screaming and wobbly camera action, to be their English teacher, shown cheerfully greeting them at the door of their classroom. The film includes head-to-head interviews with the principal, deputy and assistant principals, a maths teacher, a PE teacher (who is described in a caption as 'a former pro-cricket player') and a member of the pastoral team. There are long and lingering shots of Cornflake, the school snake, who lives in one of the science labs, looked after by the science teacher, and is clearly a key presence in the

FIGURE 2.1 High Bridge film-makers 'looking for a wild creature'

film-makers' experience of their school. The film splices a range of voices describing the school and what it means to be part of its community with shots of the Year 9 girls (aged 13–14) dance group, students cooking, making pottery and learning in maths. There is a lot of pride evident in the film, from staff and pupils, and a strong message of being 'part of something that's bigger than yourself'.

It has been recognized that 'students' sense of belonging affects the extent to which they can embrace and negotiate the school as a learning space' (Comber 2016: 23). This sense of belonging to a community is the focus of the third film.

'This is My Place': Silver Hill

Unlike the groups led by Lisa and Ella, the group at Silver Hill, led by Kirsty, met after school to plan and produce their film. They were all in Year 9 and were nominated by their English teachers to take part. Silver Hill is located in a rural village that serves a broad community, including the surrounding ex-mining villages.

Kirsty explained that the students 'interpreted their "place" in school as meaning how many friends you had, whether you were bullied and how you felt when at school'. Of the three films we describe, this is the only one to feature a narrative storyline, although the plot features themes that are common across many of the films made as part of the project as a whole. It is also the only film without dialogue; the scenes are accompanied by a track by the musician Badly Drawn Boy. The film features a young male protagonist who arrives on the school bus one morning, and is seen in a series of scenes feeling isolated and being excluded from social interaction. We can assume that the boy is new to the school and trying to find his 'place'. The scenes depict different places around the school, including an English classroom and the dinner hall. In each, the boy struggles to find his 'place', ignored and excluded by his peers. The final scenes show him outside in the grounds of the school, where he joins a group of students sitting under a tree; the group get on well, passing away the rest of the afternoon as we cut back to the classroom clock showing the end of the school day. The final scene shows the new group of friends walking away from the school together.

FIGURE 2.2 The closing shot of 'This is My Place' made by pupils at Silver Hill

Discussion

The project aimed to develop a range of skills among beginning teachers of English, including subject and technical expertise, experience of leading extra-curricular projects and creative collaboration with students and other colleagues, in and out of school. One participant explained the potential for classroom learning that she saw as emerging from the project; this includes examining film shots alongside sentence types in writing, 'relating English skills to students as more than reading books', and the 'soft skills' of working on and carrying the momentum of a long-term project. For this beginning teacher, the project was 'a totally win/win situation', for her own professional development as well as for her students:

> Georgina: You get to learn about new aspects of the English curriculum and harnessing creativity and technology and they get a rewarding opportunity to showcase their work in a public environment with prestige and pride.

Our focus here, however, is specifically on the ways in which the ITE film project has provided the opportunity for the beginning teachers and their pupils to represent themselves and the communities in which they live and learn, and the potential for such collaborative work in English classrooms to engage creatively with identities in place. We turn now to discussing three aspects of the films in relation to this focus. First, we consider how the films have engaged with the topic of place in relation to school. We then consider how the learners see English, and the potential for the subject represented by both the process and the products of the film project. Finally, we consider the transformative potential of collaborative working to disrupt the framing of learners as passive recipients of static knowledge suggested by currently mandated curriculum and pedagogy.

The place of school

Trajectories and negotiation (Comber 2016) are strong themes in each film. We see characters involved in transition and movement across time, and the physical and emotional negotiation of 'my place', both individually and as a wider community of young people. There is a strong message communicated in each film that their place is a place for all. This is represented in the High Bridge film by the focus on the celebration of different subjects, including the practical and creative, rather than merely a focus on classrooms as the sites of reductive models of knowledge. For the High Bridge pupils, their place is also constituted by different people, across generations and hierarchies. In telling the story of their school, the young film-makers had to arrange to interview senior teachers, writing emails and holding meetings where they were the experts who knew what they wanted to achieve.

The films also represent the negotiation of place across time. Each has a sense of the school as a place that exists and that is joined by new members of the community who negotiate their place. School is also a place that remains after they leave, and this is directly addressed by the group at the Kingsville School, who expressly locate the history of their school within a wider context, but who also represent the way the school will stay with them as their 'place' when they have moved on in their own lives and find themselves as prime ministers and doctors. One of the teachers interviewed in the High Bridge film was herself a former pupil and makes connections to her own experience in terms of how the school has changed, but also what has, for her, stayed the same about this place.

The place of the subject

The subject of English is represented *in* each of the three films we have examined. English teachers are presented as an untouchable other, be they the 'wild creature' of High Bridge's wildlife documentary, or the stern gatekeeper standing at the door to greet her late students in Kingsville's film. In Silver Hill's film, the isolated protagonist is shown sitting alone in his English lesson, with the teacher framed by an over-the-shoulder shot as a distant figure writing on a whiteboard populated by wordy learning objectives.

The English classroom is represented in each film by doors and corridors, students sitting alone at desks facing the front, and an infrastructure of whiteboards, paper and pen.

However, the subject as represented *by* the films, and the process of making them, challenges the reduced model so prevalent in the experience of learners and teachers negotiating the mandated curriculum in contemporary classrooms. Each film is the result of drawing on a range of resources, not all of which are directly represented by the official curriculum. Pupils involved revealed themselves to have sophisticated understanding of the grammar of film, and were supported to develop this within the focus of the project. There is clever use of devices to show the passing of time, for example, or the movement between locations. Stairs and doors are used to good effect in each of the films to represent advancement of the narrative.

Kingsville is an excellent example of playfulness with genre, with the shift from historical documentary to a narrative representation of the future. The pupils' sense

FIGURE 2.3 The English classroom as represented in Silver Hill's film

FIGURE 2.4 Movement between locations as depicted in Kingsville's film

of genre is exemplified in their choice to include a 'blooper reel' to accompany their end credits. Such a device is usually reserved for light-hearted films, and its inclusion suggests attention to the conventions of the genre. However, we can also infer that the pupils feel the end product should include the playfulness and fun of the process itself. The 'blooper reel', where we can hear the laughter of Lisa alongside that of her pupils, reminds us that the process and product of the film-making project not only allow for mistakes to be made, but celebrate them as key parts of the story about place and identity.

The place of pupils

The young film-makers represent their place through the broad range of skills and knowledges that Comber (2016) sees as inherently engaged by place-based pedagogies. Among the 'literacy repertoires' drawn upon are documentary, autobiography, public speaking, self-evaluation and interviewing, as well as the 'new hybrid genres' evident in the films themselves. The knowledge of place engaged in making these films is demographic, geographic, historical, sociological, cultural and linguistic (such as the use of the local term 'swirling') (see Comber 2016: 64).

Ella outlined the roles undertaken by her pupils in making their film at High Bridge. The class consisted of eight Year 7 students who were placed in this group because of a range of issues, from diagnosed special educational needs to behavioural difficulties and disaffection elsewhere in the school. She described the way the project gave opportunities for each of the participants to develop in their own ways:

> Ella: Each one of these students requires something different in order to progress and the different tasks involved allowed them to each face their own challenges. Whilst they all reached their end point of creating a film, they made achievements along the way and these were a key part of the process.

Ella feels that the interview process involved in the project significantly 'contributed to the confidence' of High Bridge's film-makers in 'dealing with people in a position of authority – key skills for life after school'. Within the classroom environment, during the process of making the film, 'the relationships between students have strengthened so they felt reassured around each other to put themselves in more vulnerable situations'. The project also improved the social interaction between pupils about their English lessons: 'Their parents attended the premiere where before they would have had limited involvement in a unit of work.' Ella's description of the impact of the project on her class suggests that their involvement gave them an opportunity for the focus to be on 'learning to do and be, rather than what they will be learning about' (Lankshear and Knobel 2011: 232).

Georgina, another beginning teacher involved in the project, reflects that the project 'allowed the students to show pride in their school and in the group. A project like this is brilliant for getting seemingly disparate students to work together effectively.' The collaboration that is a central feature of the project reframes power relationships in relation to knowledge and place. Learning is taking place in the relationships between pupils and their peers, with sharing of knowledge and skills about film as well as their lived experiences of place, as well as teachers learning from their pupils and from creative professionals. The film project has seen many examples of hierarchies disrupted by the process, with senior teachers cast in different roles on camera, and also incorporating the finished product into the narrative they themselves present of their school, as in the case of High Bridge, where the film has been shown to prospective pupils and their parents, and to teachers outside the school in a presentation given by its head teacher.

Connecting community through film: the possibilities of place

The collaborations that emerged from the film project led to powerful learning in several ways. At a time when education is narrowing, particularly in the case of mandated schooled literacies, we argue that there is all the more need to recognize and to encourage opportunities for learning where 'students are not to be seen as objects to be moulded and disciplined, but as subjects of action and responsibility' (Biesta 2013: 1). This agency is central to the film project. In making films about what they saw as 'their place', young people were able to do more than merely *connect to* knowledge through a curriculum based on the fixing of meanings. Rather, they were provided with the means *to connect*, across time and space, a wider repertoire of resources drawn from both within and outside their English classrooms, in an act of what Comber (2016: 64) describes as 'reciprocal knowledge building'.

These young film-makers have actively re-appropriated elements of the dominant narratives that exist within and about their communities and use these to present their own alternatives. The process and the product of collaborative film-making has exposed the structures experienced by learners in English classrooms, and, to use Massey's image, 'cracked them open to reveal the existence of new voices' (2005: 42). Education systems dominated by new market discourse can be stifled by aversion to risk. The participants in the film project, both pupils and beginning teachers, have been able to work within a space where they can learn from taking risks, with what they learn, where and how, and, as Biesta (2013: 1) notes, 'if we take the risk out of education, there is a real chance that we take out education altogether'. We would argue that this facilitated a disposition towards risk-taking that extends beyond the time and place of the project itself.

In this film project, young people have been able to represent how they fit into a story of their community. These stories can stretch back in time, and across spaces far wider than the boundaries of the school campus and those imposed by mandated curriculum. We hope we have been able to demonstrate too that the films, and the process of making them, also represent new possibilities for the future.

Note

1 Pseudonyms are used for schools and beginning teachers.

References

Allard, A. and Doecke, B. (2014) Professional knowledge and standards-based reforms: learning from the experiences of early career teachers. *English Teaching: Practice and Critique* 13(1), 39–54.

Ball, S. (2003) The teacher's soul and the terrors of performativity. *Journal of Education Policy* 18(2), 215–28.

Barton, D. and Hamilton, M. (1998) *Local Literacies*. London: Routledge.

Bazalgette, C. and Buckingham, D. (2013) Literacy, media and multimodality: a critical response. *Literacy* 47(2), 95–102.

Biesta, G. (2013) *The Beautiful Risk of Education*. London: Routledge.

Comber, B. (2012) Mandated literacy assessment and the reorganisation of teachers' work: federal policy, local effects. *Critical Studies in Education* 53(2), 119–36.

Comber, B. (2016) *Literacy, Place and Pedagogies of Possibility*. Oxford: Routledge.

Cresswell, T. (2004) *Place: An Introduction*. Oxford: Blackwell.

Department for Education (2014) *National Curriculum in England*. Retrieved from www.gov.uk/government/publications/national-curriculum-in-england-english-programmes-of-study.

Garcia, A. and Morrell, E. (2013) City youth and the pedagogy of participatory media. *Learning, Media and Technology* 38(2), 123–7.

Gonzalez, N., Moll, L.C. and Amanti, C. (2005) *Funds of Knowledge: Theorising Practices in Households, Communities and Classrooms*. London: Routledge.

Jones, S. and Chapman, K. (2017) Telling stories: engaging critical literacy through urban legends in an English secondary school. *English Teaching: Practice and Critique*.

Jones, S. and McIntyre, J. (2014) 'It's not what it looks like. I'm Santa': connecting community through film. *Changing English* 21(4), 3220–333.

Jones, S., Hall, C., Thomson, P., Barrett, A. and Hanby, J. (2013) Representing the 'forgotten estate': participatory theatre, place and community identity. *Discourse: Studies in the Cultural Politics of Education* 34(1), 118–31.

Lankshear, C. and Knobel, M. (2011) *New Literacies*, 3rd edn. Milton Keynes: Open University Press.

Leander, K. and Sheehy, M. (eds.) (2004) *Spatializing Literacy Research and Practice*. New York: Peter Lang.

Locke, T. (2008) English in a surveillance regime: tightening the noose in New Zealand. *Changing English* 15(3), 293–310.

Massey, D. (2005) *For Space*. London: Sage.

McIntyre, J. (2016) Riots and a blank canvas: young people creating texts, creating spaces. *Literacy* 50(3), 149–57.

McIntyre, J. and Jones, S. (2014) Possibility in impossibility? Working with beginning teachers of English in times of change. *English in Education* 48(1), 26–40.

Parry, R. (2014) Popular culture, participation and progression in the literacy classroom. *Literacy* 48(1), 14–22.

Ravitch, D. (2010) *The Death and Life of the Great American School System: How Testing and Choice Are Undermining Education*. New York: Basic Books.

Sandretto, S. and Tilson, J. (2015) Discursive constructions of literacies: shifting sands in Aotearoa New Zealand. *Discourse: Studies in the Cultural Politics of Education* 38(2), 222–34.

Turvey, A. and Lloyd, J. (2014) Great Expectations and the complexities of teacher development. *English in Education* 48(1), 76–92.

Vasudevan, L. and Campano, G. (2009) The social production of adolescent risk and the promise of adolescent literacies. *Review of Research in Education* 33, 310–53.

3

MUSLIM YOUTH IDENTITIES THROUGH DEVOTIONAL SONGS AND POETRY IN SOUTH YORKSHIRE COMMUNITIES

Andrey Rosowsky

Introduction 1: creative language study as etiolation

Ever since Austin (1962) dismissed the importance of creative literature for the study of language as 'etiolation' or 'parasitical', the importance of literary and poetic forms in the study of language more generally has had a relatively subservient role in contrast to studies using natural settings especially those featuring spoken interactions (Labov 1972; Gumperz and Hymes 1986). As a result, even the sociolinguistics of writing is a relatively recent research field (Lillis 2013). The extensive research now available on multilingualism, too, focuses largely on spontaneous oral language and interactions. In matters of language variation and language maintenance among minority groups, the transmission of language from one generation to the next is usually an oral one with written forms either absent or supplementary, so this focus on speech is hardly surprising. In recent studies in multilingualism (Blackledge and Creese 2010) focusing on institutional sites such as complementary schooling, data are often predominantly oral in nature and foreground analysis of teacher–pupil and pupil–pupil interactions rather than on texts that may be present. In some multilingual settings, however, the place of creative literature can play an important part in language practices, with song, poetry, stories and play all serving as contexts and opportunities for language learning, language maintenance and language identity (Rosowsky 2011, 2016). This chapter, then, considers an example of creative language practice within a multilingual setting that has implications for both the language maintenance of minority codes and language identity among young people. In addition, these multilingual settings can often be religious ones where young participants manage and navigate their lives through several language forms for both secular and sacred purposes.

Introduction 2: faith-based complementary schooling and language heritage

Complementary schooling is a growing dimension within the UK educational system (DCSF 2010). Much of this growth is down to recent, and relatively less recent, periods of immigration to the UK resulting in the emergence of a highly multicultural and multilingual society. Minority communities have sought to create ways to preserve and transmit their cultural and linguistic heritage to new generations. There has been greater interest in this sector from governments in recent times as they have sought to extend centralized control and regulation of all educational sectors more generally. This interest, aided by local authority monitoring, has sought to harness the growth of this predominantly community-led emerging sector that has been more intense for certain types of complementary school than for others. One type of complementary school which predates the current regulatory purview is the religious complementary school. In the UK the Sunday School, although not as ubiquitous as it once was, is still functioning as a complementary school providing religious instruction and often extra support for literacy. The cheder within the Jewish community fulfils a similar role, as do equivalent schools attached to the places of worship of other minority faiths in the UK (Rosowsky 2013). Most UK mosques have a mosque school associated with them (Rosowsky 2008). This subsector of complementary schooling has had less attention paid to it in recent times in an academic sense. However, greater media and political attention of late, linked with the ever-increasing securitization of the UK, has cast a suspicious glance at these community-run Islamic schools in the UK and in other Western countries.

Introduction 3: Islamophobia and youth identity

This Islamophobia context (Allen 2010; Runnymede Trust 1997) is perhaps encouraged by interventions that focus on language as a problem within Muslim communities in the UK. In 2002 the then home secretary, David Blunkett, linked civil unrest and potential terrorism to the failure of Muslim communities to speak English in the home (Blunkett 2002). Research into language practices of these and similar communities reveals the opposite to be the case, with parents often dismayed that their children were not maintaining their heritage languages of Punjabi and Urdu. Fast forward to 2016 and the then British prime minister resumes this theme by claiming that 'not speaking English' might mean a young Muslim is 'susceptible to the extremist message' (Cameron 2016). The current prime minister, Theresa May, in a speech when home secretary regarding 'British values', made no mention of multilingualism and focused rather on 'the way we help people to learn the English language' (May 2015). This preoccupation with language is an interesting yet somewhat sinister one, which demonstrates a certain 'folk' linguistic notion that certain languages might be more easily associated with violence and extremism than others. Recent events highlighted in the media demonstrate how Arabic script overseen on mobile phone screens or overheard spoken Arabic on aeroplanes can instil suspicion and fear among fellow passengers or airline staff, which shows how pervasive the meme of Muslim-related language use has penetrated UK and Western society (Suleiman n.d.; Beydoun n.d.).

The language practices shared in this chapter will contribute to a counternarrative which reveals a more dynamic and fluid, and hopefully less essentializing, linguistic profile than that shared by many political and media commentators.

Poetry and 'song' in the Islamic world and among Muslim youth in the UK

Poetry and Islam have been intimately linked since the faith's beginnings in seventh-century Arabia (Nicholson 1921). His contemporary, Ibn Thabit, composed poetry for the Prophet Mohammed and the 'Golden Age' of Islam (roughly ninth to thirteenth centuries CE) gave birth to many of the poets now known as part of the faith's poetic heritage (Nicholson 1921; Schimmel 2001). Poets such as Ibn Farid, Rumi, Hafez, Jami, Saadi and Attar are all considered among mankind's poetic heritage, not just Islam's. Poetry has been a regular feature of various Islamic cultures throughout its history.

The heading to this section of the chapter uses the words 'poetry' and 'song' rather ambivalently. The performance of devotional poetry in the Muslim world might be seen, from a Western observer's perspective, as a way of circumventing some of the more stringent objections to the performance of 'music', which, in some interpretations of Islam, is considered unlawful (Karim 1982) and is a regular item on Islamic discussion boards (Nadir n.d.). Much performance of Islamic poetry, around the world, to a Western-attuned ear would be considered 'singing'. Emically, the type of language used, however, to describe such performance studiously avoids words that might be interpreted as 'music' per se. Therefore, in the Arabic-speaking world, the terms *inshad* and *nasheed* are often used when poetry is being performed, which, by strict definition, are more related to the English 'intoning' or 'chanting' and 'ode' or 'anthem' respectively. The Arabic words for 'singing' (*alghana*') and 'song' (*aghnia*') are generally avoided. In the heritage languages of the young people in this chapter, the word 'read', or 'recite', is used even when 'sing' seems to be the most ready comparison to Western ears. This may also explain why many young Muslims in the UK retain *nasheed*[1] or *naat*[2] as loan words for much of their poetic performances despite their affinity with Western notions of music. Some *nasheeds* are indistinguishable from Western pop or folk songs in terms of melody and instrumentation. In this chapter, in deference to my young participants, I employ the terms they use, *nasheed* or *naat* when they are referring to the poetry that they 'recite' and 'read', regardless of how such performances might appear to Western notions of music and singing.

In South Yorkshire, for many young Muslims, there is a discernible enthusiasm for the performance of poetry in the range of languages available to them: mainly English, as their increasingly common first language; Arabic as the language of both the Islamic liturgy, which is acquired in a restricted decoding sense in the complementary school; and Urdu, the community's heritage language. A variety of spoken Punjabi is also found in the home, although this has less to contribute to performances. Each of the languages is indexical of certain social and historical trajectories, which will be explored in the analysis later. Elsewhere, I have explored how this practice may have potential for reversing language shift or for language maintenance (Rosowsky 2016). There is the possibility that regular recitation of the poetry supports at least a lexical and phonological awareness of the respective languages. This, if complemented by vestigial bilingualism in the home (only in respect of Urdu, however), and accompanied by a linguistic environment that strongly features the heritage languages, might lead to a greater staying power of the languages involved. However, it cannot be overstated that English has already in most cases become the first language of the young Muslims in this community. The vestigial bilingualism of the home just mentioned mostly refers to passive or unidirectional bilingualism (Baker 2001) when conversing with parents and, increasingly, only grandparents. It remains to be seen what the lasting linguistic outcome will be of this interest and practice. Outside the sub-group of young Muslims interviewed for this chapter, there is already a strong surge of interest in Islamic poetry composed in English and were this trend to become dominant, the effect of performing in Arabic or Urdu might diminish.

On an almost daily basis, but certainly weekly, poems are discovered, listened to, downloaded, recited, memorized and performed, both individually and collectively. Unsurprisingly, most of the repertoire is sourced from and rests on the internet, with mobile devices used for accessing and storing favourite *naats* and *nasheeds*. Public performance can take place in the mosque, at formal gatherings or informally in the home. The poems come from the dual heritages of Arabic and Urdu (occasionally literary Punjabi) devotional literature and are themselves performed, in the case of Arabic, throughout the Islamic world, and in the case of Urdu, in South Asia and its diaspora. The poems performed can be accompanied by minimal or extensive instrumentation (a key consideration for the discussion board mentioned earlier; Nadir n.d.) or performed by the voice (or voices) alone. Older members of the community serve as role models and are supported by the occasional invitation to professional performers from 'back home' who are prepared to perform in modest local gatherings in people's houses (often for a small fee). This transnational process adds to the dynamic and fluid way in which these young Muslims develop their multilingual repertoires and identities. Influences can be closer to home, with many UK-based young performers becoming known via YouTube performances and websites offering downloads. It is a vibrant cultural scene and in many ways is not dissimilar to how many young people of all cultural backgrounds engage with artistic practices such as music and lyrics.

This study

In previous studies (Rosowsky 2010, 2011, 2016), I worked with slightly older members of the Muslim youth community (young men in their late twenties) with the aim of tracing the trajectory of their interest in Islamic poetry through their youth and its impact on identity. For this study, thanks to these pre-existing contacts, I was able to work with younger boys (UK Years 6, 7 and 8). Linked to an Arts and Humanities Research Council-funded symposium focusing on religion and performance, I had arranged a public event showcasing performances linked to various faith traditions. In liaison with my older informants, it was decided to feature some of the boys in a choir at the performance event. Poems were selected, time set aside in the complementary school for their rehearsal, and the boys performed their multilingual poetry at the University of Sheffield on 11 September 2015. A video was made of the event by the university's media unit and an edited version of this video including interviews with performers, was uploaded to iTunesU shortly afterwards. This video forms the first part of the data for this study. Later I returned to the complementary school and interviewed six members of the choir in order to explore their experience of the event and, more broadly, their interest in the performance of Islamic poetry. Extracts from the transcripts of these interviews are presented as data for the discussion in the second part of this section.

Any analysis of this video must start with the observation that this type of performance outside its cultural and religious context is rare. Although children's choirs are common and heard frequently both in schools and more widely in much of the UK, they often tend to sing the regular school repertoire focusing a lot on Christmas and usually performed monolingually in English. Sing Up, a nationwide scheme for encouraging children to sing in school and elsewhere (Sing Up, n.d.), is focused, by and large, on mainstream schooling and its publicity material, online and offline, suggests strongly that the expectation is for school choirs to sing monolingually and predominantly in English (in the song bank only seven out of 500+ songs refer to Arabic, Urdu or Punjabi). Even more monolingual in outlook is the UK nationwide poetry memorization and recitation competition Poetry by Heart. It is self-evident from everything on its website (Poetry by Heart, n.d.) that poetry in English is what is meant. The persistent monolingualism of British society, particularly in the educational context, has been well documented (Martin-Jones et al. 2012). The validation and incorporation of linguistic and poetic practices from minority ethnic communities would go some way to removing this monolingual straitjacket. An 'elephant in the room' in respect of the practices in this chapter, however, may be the link to religion. The fact remains that persistent and pervasive Islamophobia in UK society and elsewhere may be responsible for both overt and covert policies that recoil somewhat at the visibility, and audibility, of religion and religious practice in secularized public spaces (Allen 2010; Jouili 2013).

The boys performed three poems, in Arabic, Urdu and English respectively. The Arabic poem was composed in the thirteenth century by Al-Būsīrī (Murad 2009) and is recited throughout the Islamic world almost exclusively in the original Arabic regardless of its geo-linguistic context. Although the boys recited only a few verses (the original consists of 160 rhyming couplets), the language of the poem, to an expert, is sophisticated and composed in the technical poetic style of the *qasidah,* a rich poetic tradition in the Arabic-speaking world predating Islam (Arberry 1965). The second poem in Urdu was a *naat*, another specialized poetic form sometimes compared to the English 'ode'. The language of the Urdu poem, like the Arabic, is in a specialized register that the boys would find hard in places to follow (regardless of their knowledge of Urdu). In addition to the presence of many lexical items in Urdu being of Arabic origin, particularly in the prestigious variety used for the *naat*, well-known Arabic words and phrases are often used as well to form refrains. Finally, the boys performed a *nasheed* in English, 'Blessed are you, O Mustafa', composed by a contemporary singing ensemble from Birmingham, Aashiq Al-Rasul. The lyrics are in English, although the level of poetic language is not quite up to the quality of poetry evident in the Arabic and Urdu poems. These English *nasheed*, out of the three genres, more resemble songs in a popular sense than poetry. However, similarly to the Urdu poetry, Arabic words and phrases are again used for refrains. The Urdu and the English poems, on that basis, constitute a form of textual or performance code-switching (Sebba et al. 2012).

The boys, therefore, performed their poems in a variety of languages from their linguistic, cultural and religious heritage. We will see later in their own words how these languages, albeit part of a restricted performance mode, contribute to their linguistic repertoires and identities.

Language as performance in its 'full' (Bauman 1977) or 'high' (Coupland 2011) sense has been usefully theorized by Richard Bauman and others who have developed a conceptual framework with which one can approach the analysis of language within performance settings. Bauman proposes a continuum for identifying and analysing creative language performance where word-for-word fidelity to a written text (actual or memorized) sits at one end and improvised and spontaneous language performance is at the other. The performance of the poems by the boys is very much at the verbatim end of this continuum and is similar to their experience of liturgical literacies where recitation of the Qur'an is likewise performed but with even greater fidelity to the sacred text. Lexical meaning in both contexts is a secondary concern and attention is rather focused on language externals such as accurate articulation of sounds, correct intonation and authentic expression. Meaning in both a lexical and semantic sense takes a back seat to these aural/oral considerations.

In a previous study (Rosowsky 2001), it was observed that reciting or reading in this way does not appear to be disconcerting or unsettling for the young readers concerned. A common experience of struggling readers in mainstream settings is 'giving up' once a level of non-comprehension is reached (Smith 1994). Young Muslims who experience reading in the mosque school regularly, and perhaps others used to reading in a performance way, can read or decode in their mainstream settings, and quite often well beyond their level of comprehension, without reaching that point of frustration where they might quit reading. Their concentration on the aural decoding of the written symbols on the page appears to be enough motivation for them to read in this way even in English, their first language. The boys in the choir are happy to recite in the same way. The Arabic of the first poem is beyond their comprehension as is a significant amount of the Urdu *naat*. Only the English poem is understood in a referential way. This aural performance, like their recitation of the Qur'an, is not a disconcerting experience and forms part of their generally aural experience of their religion and of their linguistic heritage.

Bauman (1977: 17–21) lists a number of features characterizing language 'full' performance. None of these are exclusively performance-orientated either on their own or in combination. They can all co-exist in other language genres. However, in certain configurations, a language event becomes a performance in the full sense. This 'keying in' of a performance might include 'special codes', 'special paralinguistic features', 'special formulae', 'appeal to tradition' and 'parallelism'. The boys' choir begins with an opening address from one of the boys who announces what is to be performed and that the first item will be not a poem but a recitation in Arabic from the Qur'an. This prefacing ('appeal to tradition') situates the performance that is to follow in its religious context. It, in a sense, signals the sacredness of the performance regardless of its context and location. It also, importantly, serves as an authorization. The sacred and central nature of the Qur'an in Islam is presented as something that is pre-eminently superior to what follows but simultaneously acts as a licence for it. The classical Arabic of the recited Qur'an presents a 'special code' that is readily associated with performance even for those for whom Arabic is their native language. Its register is archaic and replete with linguistic and literary traits of seventh-century Arabic, which is far removed from the spoken varieties of Arabic speakers today (and even of previous eras) (Versteegh 2001). Special codes here, of course, do not just mean different languages. The poems, as mentioned before, are composed in certain styles and registers, often with a syntactic and lexical complexity beyond the general language user. Think Chaucer for most English speakers. Parallelism is a constant feature of the language performance in all three languages with repetition and rhyme common to all three texts recited. Chorus repetition is very important to the boys as it provides all of them with the opportunity to perform, even if the verses are sometimes beyond many of them. The choruses in this performance are in Arabic in the English poem also. How the boys stand, how they dress and how they hold their facial expressions are all key paralinguistic features of the performance. Schechner (1988: 120), in his extensive work on performance, uses the metaphor of a 'braid' to denote a continuum between 'efficacy' and 'entertainment' as a way of accounting for the range of contexts ritual performance may span. At the university, the boys' choir is veering towards the 'entertainment' strands of the braid but, on other occasions, perhaps at a celebration in the mosque, the performance may have more in common with ritual devotions and therefore sit more comfortably towards the 'efficacy' end of the braid. A group of mystics with a secure grasp of the language of the poems performing for their love of the divine would be at the extreme efficacy end of the braid.

A 'special formula' used by the boys to signal the close of each recitation was performed in Arabic. In the heritage community of the boys, this is somewhat unusual in the sense that their grandparents would never have used such a formula on similar occasions. This formula comes from the heritage of Arabic performance poetry and expresses a request to God to bless and grant peace to the Prophet Muhammed. This formula is emblematic of transnational multilingualism engendered by a linguistic orientation to the Arabic language spearheaded by many of the young people in the community. This embracing of Arabic as a language of performance (beyond its traditional role in the liturgy, which would have been shared by grandparents) is a growing element in this youth revival. Not only is Arabic poetry being performed but the tropes and formulae of poetic performance in the Arabic-speaking world are being adopted too.

In talking with the boys sometime after the university event it was evident that this had been a memorable moment for them and for their families. The posting of a video of the event on iTunesU and YouTube helped with this (YouTube n.d.). Its availability online allowed it to be brought into school on mobile devices. At the time of writing this had had 1,000 views. As a point of comparison, other videos linked to this event had fewer than 100.

> After we went to the university it was on YouTube and as we were talking about it. Some of the teachers got to know about it. I don't know if they watched it or not.
>
> *(Akhtar, 11)*

One perhaps surprising outcome from the interviews was the boys' evaluation of the role the different languages play in their performance repertoires. With Urdu commonly associated with the heritage of the Pakistani community in the UK,[3] it might be natural to assume that Urdu would be, after English, the language most favoured for performance. Instead, almost unanimously, the boys claimed Arabic to be their favourite language for performance.

> Author: Which language do you recite in that means the most to you?
>
> Rafiq (10): I'd say Arabic because of the Prophet. And most people recite Arabic as well.
>
> Faiz (10): I listen to Arabic *nasheeds*.
>
> Ali (11): I only know Arabic ones.
>
> Sajid (12): But in performing, Arabic is before Urdu.
>
> Ahmed (11): I think Arabic would be before Urdu.

The reasons for this are complex but link to notions of identity. On one level, there is the natural affinity any Muslim would feel towards Arabic, the language of the faith at its origin and, in theory, the lingua franca of the Islamic world. In practice, the latter has never happened on a major scale. However, in the limited sense of the liturgy, the Arabic language *is* universal in the Islamic world with prayer, recitation, litanies and even stylized sermons performed in Arabic. The boys, already attuned to Arabic through their learning in the complementary school, would find it straightforward to transfer their skills in decoding and reciting to the poetry. The awareness of Arabic's special position in Islamic tradition would reinforce such a transfer. There is here a positive identity with the Arabic language, albeit in specialized modes and registers, and this affinity is manifested most strongly in respect of performance practices such as those used for devotional poetry and the liturgy.

However, there was a certain ambiguity in their preferences. Asked directly about which *poems* they prefer to perform, they all said English, even though for some of them their experience of reciting in English was limited.

> The poem we did at the university was one of my first English naats.
>
> *(Tanveer, 10)*

This preference, of course, reflects the reality of the community's shift to English as their first language and spoken language of choice. Their lack of experience of English poems, however, possibly reflects the traditional non-English heritage of the community and its institutions, although there is plenty of evidence that this non-English environment is changing, and among the boys' generation, changing swiftly and significantly. On the one hand, it represents a clear and obvious sign of linguistic integration that would be welcomed by those sharing monolingual ideologies and who see multilingualism as somehow segregationist and threatening (see the political quotes from the Introduction to this chapter). On the other hand, there is a clear risk of linguistic assimilation where not only the spoken environment favours a shift to the majority language, English, but the cultural one does too, with poems, songs and other materials increasingly available in English. A double-edged sword, linguistically.

Arabic, as a performance language, is thus preferred over Urdu, the community's literary language, by all the boys bar one. The reasons given for this choice appear to be an 'appeal to tradition' and familiarity and greater awareness of the Arabic poems. Although I have no data from the generation or two older than these boys and their teachers, I suspect it is unlikely a similar linguistic preference would be expressed. Events with poetry and speeches I have attended over the past 30 years have tended to be Urdu-exclusive occasions. Arabic has been confined to the liturgy. This 'appeal to tradition' is reflected in comments such as the following:

> Author: Why is that better in Arabic than it is in English?
>
> Ahmed: Because in Heaven they speak Arabic. Because the first ever language was Arabic. And you can read *naats* from years ago. And the Arabic language is the language of Islam. 'Talaa badru Alayna'[4] was read 1,400 years ago and we are reading it today in 2016.

This preference is bound up with not only a linguistic identity but also a religious one. The boys associate themselves with the language of their faith, which they appear to experience more immediately as linked to their beliefs. Familiarity with Arabic performance is possibly a more localized phenomenon in respect of this particular study. The older members of the youth community who acted as

informants for my previous work now work part-time as teachers in the complementary school and themselves demonstrate a preference for Arabic in their own
poetry performances. This is likely to be having an impact, with their students
becoming more familiar with the Arabic repertoire. However, outside this particular context, there is evidence of the same ethnolinguistic community also turning
to the Arabic heritage rather than the Urdu one (Abu Zahra Foundation n.d.), so
this phenomenon is not unrepresentative. The boys express their greater confidence
with Arabic poetry as follows:

> Akhtar: I'm confident with Arabic... These two are confident with it...
> They're really good at Arabic *naats*.
> Author: Do you think you'll carry on as you get older?
> Akhtar: Maybe.
> Author: In English or in ...?
> Akhtar: In Arabic mainly I think.

The one boy who said he preferred to perform in Urdu was insistent that his mother,
who had been born and educated in Pakistan, was responsible for this in the main.
An interesting linguistic dynamic within this community is where one parent has
been born and educated in the UK and the other has come from 'back home'. These
conditions often lead to a greater possibility for Urdu to be supported within the
family (Rosowsky 2008). Linguistic repertoire and identity can thus be subject to
matters such as exogamy, which in the literature of multilingualism and language
maintenance and shift has been an observation made by many (Fishman 1991).

A second important theme emerging from the data is the importance of role
models from within and outside the community. All the boys were familiar with
either local and national or international performers and mentioned how these had
made a contribution to their own growing awareness of this genre. Some of these
role models are local, as in the winner of a recent school talent show.

> In school, someone ages ago, I didn't go to the school, I saw this on YouTube,
> 'Pine Valley's Got Talent', this boy he sang like X-Factor, and he won, singing,
> like, *naats*. He's at university now.
>
> *(Rafiq, 12)*

Another boy told of how a recognized local and national performer of poetry had
visited his local primary school to perform for the children (a rare example of
mainstream school and this practice meeting).

> Yeah, Ahmed Hussain, he came to my school and started reading. He did a
> performance in my school. In assembly. In front of the whole school. Before he
> read it, he said to everybody, if you know this *nasheed* you can recite with me.
>
> *(Naeem, 11)*

I have written elsewhere on the transnational dimension of much of this role-model activity as performers disseminate their work across the borderless zone of the internet but also move physically around the diaspora, performing and inspiring their audiences (Rosowsky 2016).

The link between this poetry practice and the internet for the boys appears central. This is, of course, no surprise. I have written before (Rosowsky 2010) of how poems are transcribed into notebooks and kept as aide-mémoires to learn from and support performances. These resources have been replaced, particularly by the younger generation, by mobile phones that act as a resource for finding, accessing and listening and learning poetry. One of the boys was keen to share with me a performing artist he liked called 'Harris J' who performs in English and other languages:

> Tariq: I listen to this one a lot [showing me a YouTube video of Harris J]. Harris J is a *naat* reader.
>
> Author: Do you know of any other English ones?
>
> Tariq: No. I only know Arabic ones.

Whereas once poems were downloaded and stored on their phones, with the expansion of mobile technology and roaming high-speed internet this was no longer necessary as poetry was searched for and accessed on demand whenever it was required.

Finally, a crucial site for the validation of personal identity for young people is the mainstream school. On a number of occasions, the boys' words revealed a significant gap between their personal language and performance practices and their school's monolingualism. Despite their performance at the university, their regular performances in the mosque and elsewhere, there was little recognition or accommodation of this cultural activity in their schools. I wrote some time ago (Rosowsky 2008) of how teachers in mainstream schools serving catchment areas with Muslim children often had little or no awareness of the cultural and religious, or even linguistic, practices of their pupils. The phenomenon of middle-class teachers driving into schools in socially deprived areas and then leaving these areas at the end of the school day is not an unfamiliar one (Cochran-Smith 2004). The social class dimension of this lack of familiarity is not missing from this situation either but it is added to by dimensions of language and culture. The consequences of this refusal to admit the languages and identities of their pupils into the classroom are significant.

> I'd like to do it in school because then they'd get a chance to know about what we have been doing and the languages we know. So they would know more about us. That we know Arabic (Rafiq, 12).
>
> In school we have a music lesson, and they said once we could recite anything. Most people recite English songs. We ran out of time so couldn't do it. The other children took all the time. I was going to sing 'Blessed are you, O Mustafa'.

Would you like to recite in school?

Yeah. But only if they were positive about it. Some people wouldn't understand it and they'd be thinking what you are saying and that… or be laughing at you when you sit down. Taking the mick out of you.

The Sing Up and Poetry by Heart campaigns mentioned earlier would be perfect vehicles for such a rapprochement were they orientated differently. As it is, the monolingualism (and monoculturalism) of mainstream schools leads to missed opportunities. Ironically, the most positive response from a school to this practice came from one of the boys who related how he had been in trouble and assigned special staff to mentor his behaviour.

Yeah. You know when you have a behaviour problem. I had that and then I had two teachers who mentored me and when we were sitting down they made me laugh and we had a chat. They told me to read and then I read an Arabic *naat*. Only to those two because I felt positive about it. I told them about the university event and that I read over there.

A link here between positive validation and behaviour, although only one case, appears obvious.

Conclusion

The practices described and analysed in this chapter are a rarely mentioned dimension of the lives of thousands of British schoolchildren (and indeed children throughout the Islamic world). In other religious contexts, the performance of religious poetry takes place regularly and enthusiastically by young people. The Sikh community and the Hindu diaspora are experiencing similar change in terms of language and practices (Rosowsky 2013; Pandharipande 2013) If we widen the scope further, Haredi Jews performing religious rap (Vick n.d.) or Malaysian youngsters singing classical Arabic odes (Huda n.d.) are all elements of young people's dynamic involvement in music, poetry and song with a devotional content or purpose. The linguistic aspects of this vibrant and rich practice are indexical of wider linguistic processes evinced by transnational and globalizing processes. To exclude them from consideration when accounting for linguistic change, as once advised by Austin, would be a significant omission from language study.

Notes

1 An Arabic word denoting 'song', usually in religious contexts.
2 Strictly speaking, an Urdu word for a particular type of devotional poem but now used for other types of devotional poems as well.
3 In the most recent census (ONS 2012), Urdu was nominated as the second largest minority language spoken after Polish.
4 A very famous Arabic poem sung throughout the Islamic world.

References

Abu Zahra Foundation (n.d.) The Keighley Munshids. Retrieved from www.abuzahra.org/keighley-munshids.

Allen, C. (2010) *Islamophobia*. Farnham: Ashgate.

Arberry, A.J. (1965) *Arabic Poetry*. Cambridge: Cambridge University Press.

Austin, J.L. (1962) *How To Do Things With Words*. Oxford: Clarendon.

Baker, C. (2001) *Foundations of Bilingual Education and Bilingualism*, 3rd edn. Clevedon: Multilingual Matters.

Bauman, R. (1977) *Verbal Art as Performance*. Illinois: Waveland Press.

Bauman, R. and Briggs, C. (1990) Poetics and performance as critical perspectives on language and social life. *Annual Review of Anthropology* 19, 59–88.

Beydoun, K.A. (n.d.) Speaking Arabic while flying. Retrieved from www.aljazeera.com/indepth/opinion/2016/04/speaking-arabic-flying-160420051548323.html.

Blackledge, A. and Creese, A. (2010) *Multilingualism: A Critical Perspective*. London: Continuum.

Blunkett, D. (2002) *Integration with Diversity: Globalisation and the Renewal of Democracy and Civil Society*. London: Foreign Policy Centre.

Cameron, D. (2016) *Today*. BBC Radio 4. London.

Cochran-Smith, M. (2004) *Walking the Road: Race, Diversity, and Social Justice in Teacher Education*. New York: Teachers College Press.

Coupland, N. (2011) Voice, place and genre in popular song performance. *Journal of Sociolinguistics* 15(5), 573–602.

DCSF (2010) *The Impact of Supplementary Schools on Pupils' Attainment: An Investigation into What Factors Contribute to Educational Improvements*. London: DCSF.

Fishman, J.A. (1991) *Reversing Language Shift: Theoretical and Empirical Foundations of Assistance to Threatened Languages*. Clevedon: Multilingual Matters.

Gumperz, J.J. and Hymes, D. (1986) *Directions in Sociolinguistics*. New York: Blackwell.

Huda (n.d.) Raihan albums. Retrieved from http://islam.about.com/od/arts/tp/Raihan-Albums.htm.

Jouili, J. (2013) Rapping the republic: utopia, critique and Muslim role models in secular France. *French Politics, Culture & Society* 31(2), 58–80.

Karim, M.F. (1982) *Imam Gazzali's Revival of the Religious Learnings, Volume 2*. Lahore: Kazi Publications.

Labov, W. (1972) *Sociolinguistic Patterns*. Philadelphia: University of Pennsylvania Press.

Lillis, T. (2013) *The Sociolinguistics of Writing*. Edinburgh: Edinburgh University Press.

Martin-Jones, M., Blackledge, A. and Creese, A. (eds.) (2012) *The Routledge Handbook of Multilingualism*. London: Routledge.

May, T. (2015) *A Stronger Britain, Built On Our Values*. The Home Office. Retrieved from www.gov.uk/government/speeches/a-stronger-britain-built-on-our-values.

Murad, A.H. (2009) *The Mantle Adorned*. Cambridge: Quilliam Press.

Nadir, E. (n.d.) Listening to music is a sin? Retrieved from https://qa.islam.com/s/12242/listening_to_music_is_a_sin#gsc.tab=0.

Nicholson, R. (1921) *Studies in Islamic Poetry*. Cambridge: Cambridge University Press.

ONS (2012) *Language in England and Wales, 2011*. Office for National Statistics. Retrieved from www.ons.gov.uk/ons/dcp171776_302179.pdf.

Pandharipande, R.V. (2013) The language of Hinduism in the US diaspora. *World Englishes* 32(3), 417–428.

Poetry by Heart (n.d.) Retrieved from www.poetrybyheart.org.uk.

Rosowsky, A. (2001) Decoding as a cultural practice and its effects on the reading process of bilingual pupils. *Language and Education* 15(1).

Rosowsky, A. (2008) *Heavenly Readings: Liturgical Literacy in a Multilingual Context.* Clevedon: Multilingual Matters.

Rosowsky, A. (2010) 'Writing it in English': script choices among young multilingual Muslims in the UK. *Journal of Multilingual and Multicultural Development*, 31(2), 163–79.

Rosowsky, A. (2011) 'Heavenly singing': the practice of *naat* and *nasheed* and its possible contribution to reversing language shift among young Muslim multilinguals in the UK. *International Journal of Sociology of Language* 212, 135–48.

Rosowsky, A. (2013) Faith, phonics and identity: reading in faith complementary schools. *Literacy* 47(2), 67–78.

Rosowsky, A. (2016) The role of Muslim devotional practices in the reversal of language shift. *Journal of Multilingual and Multicultural Development.* Retrieved from www.tandfonline.com/doi/full/10.1080/01434632.2016.1177062.

Runnymede Trust (1997) *Islamophobia: A Challenge For Us All.* London: Runnymede Trust.

Schechner, R. (1988) *Performance Theory.* New York: Routledge.

Schimmel, A. (2001) *As Through a Veil: Mystical Poetry in Islam*, 2nd edn. London: Oneworld Publications.

Sebba, M., Mahootian, S. and Jonsson, C. (2012) *Language Mixing and Code-Switching in Writing.* London: Routledge.

Sing Up (n.d.) Retrieved from www.singup.org.

Smith, F. (1994) *Understanding Reading.* Hillsdale: Lawrence Erlbaum.

Suleiman, Y. (n.d.) After Islamophobia comes the criminalisation of Arabic. Retrieved from www.aljazeera.com/indepth/opinion/2016/03/islamophobia-criminalisation-arabic-160320073445033.html.

Versteegh, K. (2001) *The Arabic Language.* Edinburgh: Edinburgh University Press.

Vick, K. (n.d.) Shyne-ing in Jerusalem. Retrieved from http://world.time.com/2011/12/14/shyne-ing-in-jerusalem-how-one-rapper-saw-the-light-and-converted-to-ultra-orthodox-judaism.

YouTube (n.d.) Heavenly acts. Retrieved from www.youtube.com/watch?v=Oolcsvei3EM.

4

CREATIVE SPACES FOR DEVELOPING INDEPENDENT WRITING WITH ENGLISH TEACHERS

Lorna Smith

Typically, English teachers come into the profession because they are voracious reader with English literature degrees and wish to share their love of books (Blake and Shortis 2010); far fewer join because they are voracious writers. English teachers often present themselves to their students as book-lovers (with many an English teacher's email footer announcing what they are currently reading), but it is rare for them to promote themselves as authors. Yet it goes without saying that a balanced classroom English curriculum depends upon the warp of writing as much as the weft of reading. Young children make connections between reading and writing very early as they experience literacy in the world around them (Heath 1982). Britton asks why we should see reading and writing as separate entities any more than speaking and listening, since each is fundamental to the other (1989; cited in Smith and Wrigley 2016), and goes on to remark, 'The world about the child waits to be written about' (1994: 110). The current national curriculum states that the purpose of English education is teach students 'to speak and write fluently so that they can communicate their ideas and emotions to others, and through their reading and listening, others can communicate with them' (DfE 2014a). However, despite the interdependence of reading and writing, practising English teachers have cited their own lack of confidence as writers as a reason for their resistance to developing their pedagogy in writing (NAWE 2010).

Why do we need to develop teachers as creative writers?

There are various reasons why individual teachers may not identify themselves as writers, leading to this collective lack of confidence in the profession. One problem might be concerned with the act of writing itself. Writing is a journey of discovery for a writer, just as exploring a text can be for a reader. Indeed, since the act of production necessarily precedes the act of consumption and interpretation of a text, it could be argued that writing is the logical way to prepare for the 'adventure' of reading. The hermeneutic scholar Gadamer (1986) discusses the creation of a piece of writing, encouraging us to think about the making of meaning, or how meaning comes to be *even before the text exists for us as reader to decipher*. Gadamer suggests that the author does not have a preconceived idea of where they are writing to; the act of writing is itself an act of investigation. He argues that even if a writer has a plan and works towards it, they are actually discovering their direction as they go. This suggests, building on Rorty (in Ramberg and Gjesdal 2006), that the writer, as the creator of a text, is altered through the writing process, as well as – subsequently – the reader. For those who identify themselves as writers, all this can be very exciting, even liberating; for those who do not, however, it can spark fear – writing is a journey into the unknown, including the 'unknown' of oneself.

A connected concern is the fear of being judged, a fear of failure. Ironically, partly as a consequence of having read so much 'good' writing throughout their lives, earning a degree in English literature and identifying themselves as experts in reading, English teachers are anxious about writing because they doubt that they will come up to a self-imposed mark ('I don't choose to write creatively, probably because I'm worried it wouldn't be any good'; 'I was paralysed by wanting it to be good' (Trainee[1] responses, 2016)). It is all very well for A.S. Byatt to point out that good reading makes good writing possible (in Smith and Wrigley 2016) but one can imagine a 'she would, wouldn't she?' style of response: for many, there remains a disconnect between advice from an established, critically acclaimed best-selling author and the actions of a novice teacher-writer. Yet studies that have shown that teachers' beliefs in their own writing capacity has an impact on the success of their students (Bifuh-Ambe 2013), and thus it is particularly important to help teachers themselves identify as writers.

A third reason for teachers not viewing themselves as writers is that they identify *instead* as professional practitioners: they do not see room for the writer in the teacher. Trainees and established teachers alike report feeling guilty if they spend time on their own writing; they feel that time could (and should) be better spent doing other things that they perceive as more immediately relevant to their role and so do not prioritize writing: 'There can be so much school paperwork… There is often a feeling of being overwhelmed' (Buckinghamshire teacher in Smith and Wrigley 2016); 'There is so little time to do this on top of everything else that I found it difficult to write' (Trainee responses, 2016). Writing can be seen as an egotistical activity (which is hard for altruistic teachers to accept), or a selfish luxury to be completed 'when time permits' or 'maybe when I… feel I can "afford" the time' (Trainee responses, 2016). The current 'high-stakes learning environment' (Bifuh-Ambe 2013: 137) cannot but exacerbate the situation.

Further, that same national curriculum that requires both reading and writing to be taught at Key Stage 3 is remarkably light on detail when it comes to the type of writing that students are required to undertake – is creative writing even encouraged? The writing orders are condensed to fewer than 200 words, in which 'grammar' appears four times, 'accurate' and 'spelling' twice each, with their cousins 'punctuation', 'knowledge of literary and rhetorical devices', 'plan, draft, edit and proofread' jostling for attention (DfE 2014a); on top of this is an *additional* 170 words that detail the grammar and vocabulary that 'should be taught' (DfE 2014a): the shininess of a finished written product appears perhaps more important than the messy processes that go into making it. The list of suggested writing genres begins with the rather uninspiring 'well-structured formal expository and narrative essays' (DfE 2014a). There is no reference to 'creative' or 'creativity' and only one to the related concept of 'imagination' (Smith and Foley, 2015) in contrast to the previous version, where 'Creativity' was one of the four underpinning concepts of the English National Curriculum (QCA 2007). We grant that the concept of 'creativity' is a complex one, so much so that the noun 'creativities' has been coined to indicate how it means many things to many people (McCallum 2012) – for instance, that 'well-structured formal expository essay' could be said to be 'creative' both because it is a piece newly created (it did not exist before) and because it may be written in an original or imaginative style. Yet even if we are not all Big C 'genius' creatives (Craft 2001), creativity is fundamental to human development and should be nurtured. So, while it could be argued that the paucity of detail in the current curriculum might be liberating for teachers (and students) in that it frees them to write in any way they like, the danger is that creative writing in the sense that most readers would understand – the opportunity to write freely and expressively – now appears to be almost absent from the national curriculum. Accordingly, a teacher hard-pressed to ensure that their classes make the required 'progress' in the technicalities of writing may now feel obliged – or even mandated – to do so through dry formal writing activities dressed up as 'Literacy' and avoid creative writing altogether. With children thus deprived of creative writing opportunities, it is not surprising that today's authors are wondering where tomorrow's writers will come from (Rosen 2015).

Finally, it may be that teachers often do not see themselves as writers because they were not trained as writers. Although the idea of teachers writing themselves, even alongside their students, is not new – indeed, active modelling of writing was encouraged in guidance to English teachers almost a century ago (Board of Education, 1924) – reference to such an approach as part of teacher education programmes is relatively rare. The Post Graduate Certificate of Education (PGCE) course that I followed at an esteemed university nearly 30 years ago did not encourage my cohort of trainees to write, nor did the PGCE course I inherited when I first became a lecturer. Further, despite wishing to promote writing as 'a contribution to various forms of social and cultural dialogue' (Moss 2009: 139), explicit advice for teachers to write themselves remains absent from well-respected and commonly used texts for English trainees (e.g., Sutherland and Wilkinson 2010; Green 2011; Gordon 2015) – the implication is that writing is something that *students* do, not teachers. However, I would suggest that it is incumbent on teacher educators to help develop trainees as confident, sensitive, critical writers to support them when teaching writing in schools.

The role and influence of the National Writing Project

One approach to developing established teachers' confidence as writers and address some (or even all) of these issues is through teachers' writing groups, in which there has recently been heightened interest and awareness through the work of the National Writing Project (NWP). The NWP, established in the UK in 2009 – inspired by the National Writing Project that had begun in the US in 1974 (nwp. org) – was established to explore the question, 'What happens when teachers gather together to write and share their writing?' (nwp.org.uk). The groups are supported to develop into communities of practice, with teaching and writing conjoined as the 'shared domain of interest' that enables the community to learn together from each (Wenger-Trayner and Wenger-Trayner 2015). This shared domain means that members come to explore their multiple identities: 'meetings are not simply about writing but about *who we are* as people and as teachers' (Smith and Wrigley 2016: 16, emphasis added). Testimonies from both the US and UK projects demonstrate that a community of practice provides companionship and a sharing of experience that 'strengthens and extends learning' (Smith and Wrigley 2016: 3) and makes risk-taking increasingly possible, leading to teachers' enhanced confidence. I set up a group in 2012 called Teachers as Writers, open to both established teachers and PGCE trainees as a voluntary enrichment activity (Smith 2014); I also promote the NWP's ethos and approach with all my trainees as core to their practice.

Accordingly, this chapter focuses on developing the identities as writing teachers of two recent PGCE cohorts, each of around 25 trainees (a combination of Core and School Direct). All trainees were involved: the writing opportunities described below were not bolt-on enrichment activities attended by writing enthusiasts, but central to the programme. Writing of various descriptions takes place throughout the PGCE English year: trainees are recommended to keep a weekly blog or journal in which to record and reflect upon their professional learning and there are the inevitable assignments, but from the start they are also encouraged to write creatively, and it is some of these opportunities that I focus on here.

I draw below in particular from two sources of evidence – the trainees' weekly blogs or journals from both cohorts (focusing on trainees' impressions of the writing they had personally undertaken and creative writing lessons they had taught), and paired questionnaires from the most recent cohort that focused on trainees' writing identities before and after a specific creative writing activity. In all cases permissions were sought and obtained in the approved manner (BERA, 2011) and all responses referred to are anonymized. Because of the relatively small numbers involved, I am aware that it is not possible to draw conclusions of any statistical significance: however, I offer comments and observations that are of interest.

The first questionnaire was undertaken just after Easter, by which time the trainees had experienced – after a fortnight's introductory observation in a primary or secondary school – a total of six weeks of the university-based programme wrapped around 18 weeks of teaching practice across two different secondary schools. In order to provide parity and simplify the analytical process, the questions were a combination of Likert scale tables with options for further comment and requests for short prose responses.

The writing identities of trainee teachers

It was immediately striking that despite the various creative writing activities that they had already engaged in (in and around) university – with time built into the programme to enable them to write and reflect, and a lot of encouragement to do so – and the creative writing that they had led with their classes (with three-quarters of the cohort having taught at least one such lesson), the majority of the trainees did not identify themselves as creative writers (with nine responding 'not really' or 'to some extent', against seven 'yes, fairly' and only one 'very, definitely'). Those who did not identify themselves as writers did not express a dislike of writing – on the contrary, it was a lack of time or a perceived lack of talent that prevented them seeing themselves so; it was not that they did not *want* to write, but a sense that they could not or should not (with some of their comments cited above). Yet when asked about a creative writing experience they remembered, 'whether positive or negative', every single response was positive, either because the writing activity fulfilled a personal or emotional need, or provided an opportunity for recognition. Examples included a GCSE creative writing assignment to write Bertha Mason's diary ('It allowed for absolute freedom and I really relished the chance'), keeping personal diaries that allowed for exploration of thoughts and feelings, success in competitions and the publication of poetry, and 'writing a story… about something that came into my head when listening to a song and it affecting someone else' (Trainee responses, 2016).

Further, despite the trainees' insecurity about whether they did or did not identity as writers personally, all of them agreed that 'it is important that English teachers write creatively' (with four 'to some extent', nine 'yes, fairly' and four 'very, definitely'), with several adding statements to the effect, 'we cannot teach the processes of [writing] if we don't understand them ourselves' and that a writing teacher 'inspire[s] and motivate[s]' (Trainee responses, 2016). In other words, although the trainees were more than two-thirds of the way through their PGCE, with most having already met the Teachers' Standards and attained a post for the following year, and despite having taken part in and taught creative writing sessions and considered their own positive recollections of the creative writing experience, their individual images of the complete English teacher each aspired to be included a creative-writing-shaped jigsaw piece that a number had not yet found. Even one of the highest attaining trainees who had secured an NQT post in her placement school and had taught several post-16 creative writing lessons noted, 'My concerns are that I don't feel I am a naturally creative writer and I will find this task [as described below] difficult' (Trainee responses, 2016).

Accordingly, the writing activities here described aimed to encourage the trainees to become more confident writers, foster their own personal, aesthetic development, and provide them with the ways to model creative practice for their own students. Aware that going out of class can be 'liberating' and 'fertile' for students (NAWE 2010: 62) and that they 'respond very positively' (Smith and Wrigley 2016: 65) to different settings, I wanted to prompt the trainees to consider the value of writing outside the confines of our teaching room. One trainee wrote that she hoped that writing outside would give her 'another new discovery... about something/somewhere new, as well as myself' (Trainee responses, 2016).

Further, I hoped that the experience of writing beyond the classroom would prompt the trainees to look at and question things past the obvious, and to consider whether – just as being a writer can help us understand the writing process in a different (arguably deeper) way than 'just' reading (Nabukov 1980) – being writers *in a context* helps us understand that context in a far deeper way than 'just' visiting it. It was through being *in* nature, not just reading about it, that Wordsworth gained the power to 'see into the life of things' (1798). Through writing intimately about the identity of a place, could the trainees develop their own writing identities?

Writing in creative spaces

We are fortunate in Bristol to have access to inspirational places close by. Within a few minutes' walk from the Graduate School where the PGCE is based is the Georgian House, a large house now owned by Bristol City Council and open to the public as a museum. It was built around 1790; 11 rooms across four floors are presented as they might have been when it was newly constructed, enabling visitors to imagine what life might have been like both above and below stairs (www.bristolmuseums.org.uk/georgian-house-museum). Five minutes in another direction there is the history-seeped Brandon Hill – a high point giving views across the harbour and generations of city towers. At the top of the hill is the dramatic Cabot Tower, a Gothic-inspired edifice built more than 100 years ago to commemorate the 400th anniversary of the landing of John Cabot in Newfoundland in 1497. The tower is itself built on the site of an important Civil War fortress; round about the hill is parkland and a nature reserve.

I had prepared a short booklet of nineteenth-century literary extracts for the trainees to accompany them to these settings, with the objective of supporting the trainees' appreciation of nineteenth-century literature in an appropriate context, given the emphasis of the current national curriculum on this period (DfE 2014b). The booklet for the Georgian House visit included, for instance, an excerpt from *Pride and Prejudice* to be read in the Breakfast Parlour, another from *The Secret Garden* for the Housekeeper's Room, another from *Jane Eyre* by the steps to the attic. The booklet for Brandon Hill included, among others, several stanzas from Poe's *The Raven* and Browning's *Childe Roland to the Dark Tower Came*, and an atmospheric passage from *Barnaby Rudge*. The booklets were intended to be used as prompts for the trainees' writing if necessary. The trainees were told that the tangible outcome would be an anthology to be published at the end of the PGCE programme, to include at least one piece of writing from each trainee, possibly but not necessarily written in response to this stimulus. No other instructions were provided: the trainees were simply asked to immerse themselves in either setting, to be quiet and to write. They could work in small friendship groups or alone. They could write in any genre. They were encouraged to take notes and photos or record sounds if they thought that would be helpful. They were given four hours, and were asked to return to our teaching room with a piece that they were happy to share at the end of this time. I accompanied the trainees and wrote alongside them.

When the groups reconvened, they were asked to form pairs or groups of three with trusted peers. As has been illustrated by working with the Teachers as Writers groups (Smith 2014; Smith and Wrigley 2016), it is important that participants have confidence in those with whom they are working in order to forge effective communities of practice, not only because the writing they are sharing may be on a sensitive or personal theme, but because of the intimacy of the writing process itself and the revelations of self that are exposed (Gadamer 1986). In these safe twos and threes, trainees' writing was discussed, honed and developed. We followed a process offered by a colleague[2] who had led a previous Teachers as Writers session: trainees were encouraged to read a peer's work carefully, offering i) general praise, ii) marginal notes and suggestions on form and content, iii) one criticism; and then identify one frisson-inducing 'real toad in the imaginary garden' (after Moore, 1924). While trainees enjoyed sharing their work in this way, some found it 'valuable but vulnerable': despite recognizing how helpful it can be, 'you feel slightly shy about your own work' (Trainee journal extracts, 2015). This whole process led on to a useful discussion about how to prevent peer assessment that students might undertake in class becoming at best, an empty gesture, at worst, a barrier to writing: trainees began to consider how to develop a supportive community of practice in their own classrooms.

Subsequently, the trainees worked up their pieces for their respective anthologies; some excerpts are featured here. Reflecting on the writing produced from the visit to the Georgian House (see examples at the end of this chapter), it is striking how many pieces were inspired by its history. The house was originally owned by John Pinney, a merchant made rich through slavery – and thus the house is central to the identity of the city itself. A small bedroom at the top of the house contains an exhibition with illustrations of the plantations Pinney owned, alongside further information about the triangular trade and the slaves' working conditions. Several trainees incorporated their impressions of what life must have been like for the Pinney family and their servants with their horror of how the wealth had been generated. They produced poems and narratives that blended imagined descriptions of the rich, genteel household with a condemnation of the slave trade; 'It got us thinking about how life and culture has changed and what we now expect from society' (Trainee journal extracts, 2015). In doing so, they both discovered more about themselves and considered the type of teacher they wished to be.

Like the two extracts presented at the end of this chapter, much of the writing produced on Brandon Hill was inspired by the historical and cultural significance of the site as well as its natural beauty; a number of pieces focused on the relationship between human actions and nature. Again, there was a sense of exploration of self as well as place. Trainees variously described being 'inspired' and 'engaged'; the 'calm tranquillity' provided 'creative freedom' that enabled them to experience a 'very natural writing process', as if the organic setting prompted something effort-less and uncontrived (Trainee responses, 2016). A reluctant writer noted that it was a 'fantastic setting, *even for people like me*, to take part in creative writing' (Trainee responses, 2016, emphasis added), which suggests that while she still did not imme-diately identify herself as a writer, she *had* felt impelled to write. The place explored and the trainee's writing identity had become invariably intertwined.

Trainees completed a second questionnaire at the end of the PGCE, once they had had an opportunity to read the anthology of their work and reflect upon the process. When asked again whether they identified themselves as writers, a third of the cohort responded more positively than they had previously and several admit-ted to being pleased and proud with what they produced. This time, almost the whole group identified themselves as a writer at least 'to some extent', with most 'fairly' or 'definitely' doing so (Trainee responses, 2016). The fact that the balance had shifted so dramatically could perhaps be due to the collaborative spirit engen-dered by the communal writing, sharing and reflecting in the manner promoted by the National Writing Project – trainees felt in it together, prepared to take risks that they might not have done before. All remained convinced that teachers should be writers, with four indicating they now placed an increased significance on this. All plan to incorporate creative writing into their teaching, for a variety of rea-sons including '[students'] increased engagement and enjoyment'; it affords students 'greater ownership' of their learning and 'teaches students to reflect on themselves as writers'; and, crucially, it helps students respond to a text and understand how authors 'work' because it 'provides opportunities to think about and engage with texts differently' (Trainee responses, 2016). The trainees understood that they devel-oped as readers themselves and they saw the value of ensuring that their students write creatively to help them develop as readers too.

Creative writing has become a tenet of the trainees' professional identities. It is something they will use in their teaching to help their students develop a sense of *their* own identities, true to the child-centred practice described by Britton (1994). Further, almost all expressed a commitment to continue as writers – those who were 'lapsed' writers vowed to do so more regularly, with one expressing her joy at rediscovering something she loved and promising not to lose it again; another undertook to go back to a part-finished novel; several realized that writing could be as an 'outlet' from work and simultaneously the opportunity to help them develop as professionals. Even the two of this cohort who responded that they would not write creatively for their own purposes stated that they would do so to provide models for students (Trainee responses, 2016).

Some conclusions: writing teachers in creative spaces

I do not wish to claim that we have uncovered anything new about the value and importance of English teachers' practising writing (in the sense that doctors practise medicine). The need for teachers to be 'accomplished writers in themselves' (DCSF 2008) is central to our personal identities as well as our professional identities, and to the identities of the students it is our responsibility to nurture – and particularly so, given research suggesting that students 'use their literacy practices to form their identities in, and sometimes in opposition to, the figured worlds of school, work and family' (Lutrell and Parker, 2001: 245). However, this project has reinforced some points that I believe are important, especially in a political context that is suspicious of creativity (Gibb, 2015).

1. We must foster teachers' identities as writers in order to develop their pedagogy and help them better support their students.
2. Developing teachers' writing identities is time-consuming. There is no quick-fix way to turn a non-writer or a lapsed writer or an unconfident writer into a regular, committed writer, and established writers need to protect time to continue writing.
3. It is important that teacher training courses include opportunities for creative writing so that it is established as part of a trainees' professional identity from the beginning, 'as anything else is simply playing catch up' (NAWE 2010: 67).
4. Organizations such as the National Writing Project that encourage teachers to build communities of practice are effective in inspiring and supporting writing teachers at any stage of their career.
5. An individual's writing identity can be developed through exploring the identities of new places. A fresh context may become not simply the backdrop for writing processes and products, but core to the endeavour. Discovering the new beyond the confines of the classroom (even if simply the outer reaches of the playground) enables the discovery of the new in oneself.
6. Confident, imaginative, critical writers make confident, imaginative, critical readers.

For both writer and readers, interpretation is not about finding an end point but being led in a direction towards an 'open realm' (Gadamer 1986: 68) that can be explored in various ways. The process of the writing and the reading might be different, but the result is similar: anyone who partakes in a text, whether producer or consumer, broadens their horizons. While 'open' has connotations of danger and exposure, which may be apposite, I think that Gadamer is also referring to its sense of unrestricted freedom, particularly as 'realm' suggests a demesne over which the owner has influence. The writer and readers might end up in different realms (even opposing realms), but this does not diminish the authority of their interpretations. Taking Gadamer literally and encouraging the writing to take place in a new realm simply emphasizes this idea.

Meek famously claims that 'Literacy begins with writing' (1991: 18), on the chicken-and-egg principle that one cannot read if the text has not been written. I hope it would not discredit her if we adapt her statement: teaching literacy begins with teachers writing.

Writing from the Georgian House

Georgian House – an acrostic

Stone cold captivity
Lost in translation
Aristocrat Africans
Valuable possessions
Empty regret
Reflections distorted
Yesterday preserved

Helen Conway

Pinney: Returning to Britain from the West Indies (*excerpt*)March 7th 1795

I am most excited to be returning to Bristol this season; the past year on Nevis has been so stifling and I have succumbed to a number of fevers that have significantly weakened my constitution.

Of course I couldn't contemplate returning to England without Pero, my most beloved slave. Without him I would be quite lost and my daily routine would simply fall apart.

My fondness for Pero must be described like one's best snuff box or pet lapdog. The comfort that Pero provides me is tantamount to my very existence... of course Madeleine does not understand this particular requirement of mine and finds it quite distasteful that I should return with a negro slave to attend about my person; she has even threatened moving to the bedroom in the west wind that overlooks the garden and doesn't get any air at all.

The business however has profited most greatly from the recent acquisition of 50 new slaves on the plantation. Pero was most helpful at the market in singling out the fittest – he definitely knows how to measure human stamina, for my recent purchase has created a 3 fold increase in profit compared to last year.

I must admit that I do not look at Pero in the same way... he seems to have a certain refinement about his features and a manner which almost allows me to perceive him as an equal. At these times I must check myself, for God has given me no sign or symbol that slavery should not be continued: I must continue to see them as placed here for my purpose.

Josephine Close

Dust (*excerpt*)

Margaret stepped slowly between the dust motes as they swam in the light of the soft May morning. The east-facing drawing room, with its pleasant view across College Green, was usually a favourite spot for the family at this time of day: the master frowning over his newspaper, Lady Pinney raising an eyebrow at the various social engagements she would not attend, and the children, briefly tolerated to chase each other through pools of sunshine. But today the house was silent. The family were blurred images, crossing an unknown ocean to the West Indies; a place so distant and unimaginable to Margaret as to render them non-existent.

Laura Wyles

Writing from Brandon Hill

The Cabot Tower (*excerpt*)

Life surrounds
the tower's skeleton.
Viewed from its skull,
weaving up its bones,
scampering through its concrete veins.
It stands a rare tranquillity
in a bustling city.
Looking with a steadfast melancholy
onto a changed world.

Jennie Amer

The Tower (*excerpt*)

I built this tower three score years ago
– when I say built, I mean had built
by other folk of lesser birth
whose grey hands roughened were by nature's power,
and thus were suited to such baser tasks.
It was, by design, mine.
I dreamed its form; each balcony
and chiselled stone is placed where I willed.
It is grand, is it not? Four strong stones
hold each corner straight and represent
the noble blood coursing down and through
my veins from my great ancestors.
I shall not name them, for there is no need.
All the Empire knows their deeds, and mine.

Bethany Arnott

Notes

1 The term 'trainee' is used here as that currently used by the Department for Education, although 'student teacher' or 'beginning teacher' are possibly more helpful appellations.
2 David Briggs, the Head of English at Bristol Grammar School and published prize-winning poet: http://poetrysociety.org.uk/poets/david-briggs.

References

BERA (2011) *Ethical Guidelines for Educational Research*. London: British Educational Research Association. Retrieved from www.bera.ac.uk/wp-content/uploads/2014/02/BERA-Ethical-Guidelines-2011.pdf.

Bifuh-Ambe, E. (2013) Developing successful writing teachers: Outcomes of professional development exploring teachers' perceptions of themselves as writers and writing teachers and their students' attitudes and abilities to write across the curriculum. *English Teaching: Practice and Critique* 12(3), 137–56. Retrieved from http://education.waikato.ac.nz/research/files/etpc/files/2013v12n3art8.pdf.

Blake, J. and Shortis, T. (2010) Who's prepared to teach school English? The degree level qualifications and preparedness of initial teacher trainees in English. Retrieved from http://clie.org.uk/wp-content/uploads/2015/12/pgce-report-2010.pdf.

Board of Education (1924) *Some Suggestions for the Teaching of English in Secondary Schools in England*. London: His Majesty's Stationery Office.

Britton, J. (1994) *Prospect and Retrospect*. London: Heinemann.

Craft, A. (2001) Little c creativity. In A. Craft, B. Jeffrey and M. Leibling (eds.) *Creativity in Education*, 45–61. London: Continuum.

DCSF (2008) *Getting Going: Generating, Shaping and Developing Ideas in Writing*. Nottingham: DCSF. Retrieved from http://webarchive.nationalarchives.gov.uk/20130401151715/http://www.education.gov.uk/publications/eOrderingDownload/00283-2008BKT-EN.pdf.

DfE (2014a) *National Curriculum in England: English Programmes of Study*. Retrieved from www.gov.uk/government/publications/national-curriculum-in-england-english-programmes-of-study/national-curriculum-in-england-english-programmes-of-study.

DfE (2014b) *English Programmes of Study: Key Stage 4 National Curriculum in England*. Retrieved from www.gov.uk/government/uploads/system/uploads/attachment_data/file/331877/KS4_English_PoS_FINAL_170714.pdf.

Gadamer, H.G. (1986) *The Relevance of the Beautiful and Other Essays*. Cambridge: Cambridge University Press.

Georgian House Museum (n.d.) www.bristolmuseums.org.uk/georgian-house-museum.

Gibb, N. (2015) *The Purpose of Education*. Retrieved from www.gov.uk/government/speeches/the-purpose-of-education.

Gordon, J. (2015) *Teaching English in Secondary Schools*. London: Sage.

Green, A. (2011) *Becoming a Reflective English Teacher*. Maidenhead: Open University Press.

Heath, S.B. (1982) What no bedtime story means: narrative skills at home and school. *Language and Society* 11, 49–76.

Lutrell, W. and Parker, C. (2001) High school students' literacy practices and identities, and the figured world of school. *Journal of Research in Reading* 24(3), 235–47.

McCallum, A. (2012) *Creativity and Learning in Secondary English*. Abingdon: Routledge.

Meek, M. (1991) Literacy. In *On Being Literate*, 13–48. London: Bodley Head.

Moore, M. (1924) Poetry. Retrieved from www.slate.com/articles/arts/poem/2009/06/marianne_moores_poetry.html.

Moss, J. (2009) Writing. In J. Davison and J. Dowson (eds.), *Learning to Teach English in the Secondary School*, 134–57. London: Routledge.

Nabakov, V. (1980) *Good Readers and Good Writers*. Retrieved from www.ohs.rcs.k12.tn.us/TEACHERS/isheem/documents/Nabakov_Readers_Writers.pdf.

NAWE (2010) *Class Writing: A Research Report into the Writers-in-Schools Ecology*. York: NAWE/Paul Hamlyn Foundation.

QCA (2007) *The National Curriculum: Statutory Requirements for Key Stages 3 and 4.* London: DCSF/QCA.

Ramberg, B. and Gjesdal, K. (2006) Hermeutics. In *The Stanford Encyclodpedia of Philosophy.* Retrieved from http://plato.stanford.edu/entries/hermeneutics.

Rosen, M. (2015) Good writing; well-edited writing; teaching, assessing, helping pupils write, publishing. Retrieved from http://michaelrosenblog.blogspot.co.uk/2015/12/3-blogs-as-one-articlegood-writing-well.html.

Smith, J. and Wrigley, S. (2016) *Introducing Teachers' Writing Groups.* London: Routledge.

Smith, L. (2014) Diving into writing: reflections on the first year of my involvement in the National Writing Project. *The Use of English* 66(3), 10–19.

Smith, L. and Foley, J. (2015) Talking together, learning together: the story of English PGCE student teachers' adventures in classics. *Changing English* 22(1), 47–58.

Sutherland, J. and Wilkinson, J. (2010) Writing. In S. Clarke, P. Dickenson and J. Westbrook (eds.) *The Complete Guide to Becoming an English Teacher,* 2nd edn. London: Sage.

Trainee journal extracts (2015) redacted.

Trainee responses to pre/post creative writing activity (2016) redacted.

Wenger-Trayner, E. and Wenger-Trayner, B. (2015) *Introduction to Communities of Practice: A Brief Overview of the Concept and its Uses.* Retrieved from http://wenger-trayner.com/introduction-to-communities-of-practice.

Wordsworth, W. (1798) Lines written a few miles above Tintern Abbey. In *Lyrical Ballads.* London: J. & A. Arch.

5

DURHAM CITY AS AN EDUCATIONAL RESOURCE IN INITIAL TEACHER EDUCATION FOR ENGLISH

Seeing the city with new eyes

David Stevens

The experiences of beginning teachers – specifically the Post Graduate Certificate in Education (PGCE) English student teachers at Durham University – lie at the heart of this chapter. The venue chosen as the basis of the exploration is geographically convenient, but – more significantly – is also a place of note and fame: a major tourist destination generally seen as an attractive venue, with the cathedral and its immediate surroundings designated a World Heritage Site. This, of course, is only part of their story: Durham lies at the heart of a now defunct coalfield with many deprived areas surrounding it, including within the city boundaries. The research at the heart of the chapter looks at how identities of places may vary significantly through the eyes of people in different roles – including, crucially, teachers and (by implication at least) their pupils – using as a practical/professional basis the project of seeing aspects of places as potential teaching resources to foster a telling combination of critical and celebratory learning. In so doing, the exploration plays with notions of how a particular place may lend itself to diverse educational projects focusing on ideas of identity as both liberating and extending.

Context

One of the first activities undertaken by the Durham University Partnership PGCE English group each September is to explore the city of Durham, in which the School of Education is conveniently situated, through the lens of beginning English teachers starting to reflect on the nature of resourceful teaching that attempts to combine critical awareness of both word and world. There are several purposes at work here, some of which are directly relevant to the nature of this chapter and to the overarching project of the book. First, the nature of the activity, as can be seen from the brief issued to them, gets the student teachers working together quickly, thus breaking the 'new-course, new-people' ice. Second, the idea is to encourage a notion of teaching and learning that is not classroom-bound: they will inevitably very soon have enough experience during their teaching practices of classes of pupils focused on IT-presented sequences, window blinds closing off awareness of the world outside, invariably culminating in some version of 'point – evidence – explanation' stereotypical response to texts. The activity in question attempts to suggest a different idea of teaching and learning; at once more outward-looking and more critically reflective. Perhaps most significantly, however, the activity seeks to inspire an approach to English pedagogy that is fundamentally both celebratory and critical. The brief (replicated below) should, I hope, give enough information about the nature of the activity itself.

As appropriate to this book's theme, we need also to consider the place itself: Durham city, and, contained within it, Durham University. There are several peculiarities here, all of which – potentially at least – may have a bearing on the students teachers' activities and presentations, and thus to their early development as beginning teachers. Durham city may be seen as a microcosm of a wider world, as indeed may all places, with a particular relevance to current social relationships and conflicts, as well as an idiosyncratic place with its own unique particularities. Such a realization chimes with Charlton et al.'s suggestion that,

> Rather than a sense of place defined by a close connection between place and a singular form of identity, and a need for a clear sense of boundaries around a place separating it from the world outside, place is a process, it is defined by the outside, it is a site of multiple identities and histories, and it is unique as defined by its interactions. Reflection on all places can offer insight into the individual power-geometries through which particular places are constructed.
>
> *(Charlton et al. 2011: 65)*

The city of Durham sits in the midst of a region once dominated by coal mining and associated industries, with shipbuilding, steel and chemical industries (among others) surrounding it. To a large extent, these industries have now either disappeared or been severely curtailed, leaving an area of considerable social deprivation in search of new social, industrial and economic identities. And yet Durham University, spread across several colleges within the city, has a national reputation, deserved or not, as a place for the education of elites, with many links to independent schools. The contradiction is readily apparent, I suspect, even to a casual visitor. As I write this, for example, I am uncomfortably aware of the very recent referendum on Britain's exit from the EU, with the resulting social and cultural fissures. Nowhere in the UK has the division been more stark than in the north-east, with largely working-class communities voting decisively for 'Brexit': Hartlepool, for example, close to Durham city and containing several of our partnership schools, has been held up nationally as the place with the largest margin in this respect. In Durham itself, meanwhile, a relatively small city dominated by its university, a much more professionally orientated, cosmopolitan and often academic population, with a significant number of young people, the position is markedly different and much more Eurocentric.

A couple of further examples may serve to give a more vivid flavour of the inherent contradictions associated with the place Durham, closer to the actual experience of the student teachers at the heart of this exploration. The situation and history of the magnificent cathedral and almost adjoining castle, dominating the cityscape from its imposing position above the River Wear, epitomize conflict and contradiction: places of worship and impressive beauty on the one hand, and military domination on the other (compare the architecture and siting of Durham Cathedral, for instance, historical seat of the often warlike Prince Bishops, with those of York Minster, a short journey southwards). The castle now functions as a university residential college, and indeed has the reputation as the college most sought-after by students arriving from prestigious independent schools. Beneath this imposing hill lies the Department of English, from where, every year, a few graduates join the PGCE English course at the centre of the current exploration. The architecture and position of the department exemplifies the town–gown conflict: it turns its back resolutely on the town, whose people can only see its arguably ugly, largely windowless, concrete walls, while opening up on the other side to the splendid vista of the river and its far bank. The social and cultural distinctions hinted at above are further suggested by the nature of the PGCE group each year, invariably comprising a full range of socio-economic backgrounds (and correspondingly wide-ranging educational contexts) much more diverse than those found throughout the rest of the university – and, incidentally, with a much more local flavour.

The activity

I include here the brief given to the student teachers, and largely adhered to (at this very early stage of the course, everyone seems very willing to do exactly as requested, to the point of showing anxiety about what precisely this may be):

Guide for students: the city of Durham as an English teaching resource

The general idea here is to get everyone working together in groups with the aim of seeing a particular location – in this instance the city of Durham – as a potential teaching resource for secondary English. As well as considering the practical/professional side of this project, you should also reflect critically on the complex notions of place and identity that may both underpin and destabilise such an exploration: what, for example, may be the key tensions in the identity of a city like Durham as seen by various inhabitants and visitors? And how may these tensions be encapsulated in the aspect of the city you decide to investigate?

During the first session of this project, groups will scour the city, disturbing its serene equilibrium, to research and consider what aspects could lend themselves to productive English teaching. For example, it may be fruitful to focus on literary associations, or on examples of local dialect, or on the city as a backdrop for creative writing, or the planning of instructional/persuasive writing. The possibilities are in fact endless. To give this work a slightly sharper focus, each group should collect one relevant artefact or image which somehow encapsulates the teaching idea: a photograph, for instance, or a leaflet, or a tacky souvenir, or a piece of the historic cathedral. Each group will determine the age/ability level of its work, across the 11–18 spectrum. During the second session groups will present their findings in general terms to the rest of the English group, focusing on resources available (and particularly the representative artefact) and an outline of teaching possibilities. Each group will have around 15 minutes for their presentation.

A summary of the work of two such groups, both during recent years of the course, may suffice to give a fuller, more detailed impression of what exactly was undertaken and achieved. All names have been anonymized.

The first group in question comprised four students – two women and two men – of varying backgrounds and prior experiences: one Durham English graduate with an independent school background (Jack), one slightly older Scotsman with an intense interest in educational creativity (Peter), one young woman from a relatively local comprehensive school who had subsequently spent time teaching abroad (Michelle) and a middle-aged mother of three who had decided to enter teaching later in life than the others (Lois). All had first degree backgrounds predominantly in English literature, although creative writing options had also been followed by two of the group (the two women, as it happens). This sort of mix, I should say, is not untypical of the PGCE English groups I have known. This is their summary of work undertaken:

Durham as a teaching resource

Our group initially discussed the different environments that Durham offers; the Cathedral, the old town square, the river and the newer developments of bars and shops. We decided that Durham would be a good example of diversity, and might serve to problematize for pupils some of the assumptions about places we all live with.

We then decided to focus on the River Wear in Durham. Our chosen artefact was a picturesque postcard of the river with the cathedral in the background. As a starter activity we thought we could present this postcard to the class and read out a traditional poem about a river. We chose Robert Wadsworth Lowry's poem 'At the River' – almost, in fact, a hymn – which overly romanticizes the river and links it to religion. It opens with the lines 'Shall we gather at the river,/Where bright angel feet have trod,/With its crystal tide forever flowing/by the throne of God?' and continues much in that vein. We thought that most children would not relate to this poem at all and thus we hoped to elicit a critical reaction.

Then, taking a trip to see the river (having first cleared all health and safety rules, naturally!) we would refer back to the poem and postcard asking various questions…

- Is the River in Durham really like the perfect postcard? Where are the carrier bags floating down stream? Why are there no people in the picture? Does the river always look so peaceful? – what about after a flood or during winter?
- Does the poem give a good description of a river? If not – why not?
- What about the River Wear in other places? The once thriving but now virtually moribund ship-building industry on Wearside, Sunderland?

The activity: writing poetry about the River Wear

For lower ability pupils we decided that a highly structured form of poetry such as Cinquains would be appropriate. Working with a framework and perhaps even discussing useful adjectives in small groups would help them get started.

For higher ability pupils we envisaged a task focusing on not only writing a poem but choosing different poetic forms to match the situation. For example the students could compose a Sonnet about the River (inspired by Wordsworth's Sonnet to the River Duddon).

As an extension the pupils would be asked to write a poem about the market square in Durham using a different form. For example, a limerick describing all of the characters who pass through the square. Students would be asked to think about how different poetic forms are appropriate for different subjects.

The work carried out by my second exemplar group contrasts quite strongly, focusing sharply on aspects of language change and, critically, how such change may both reflect and influence social relationships based on power. This emphasis reflected the particular interests and academic backgrounds represented in the group: of the four, three (all women) had as undergraduates studied English language or (in one case) linguistics, interestingly exemplifying the breadth of the subject we know as English. These three were in their early twenties, locally educated, and had relatively little professional experience behind them (Jane, Rochelle and Emma). The fourth member of the group had a rather different history: previously a successful solicitor, he had decided in his mid-thirties to change career direction and return to his first loves, English and teaching, through further studies at Master's level (Paul). Table 5.1 shows the schemes of work developed by the group.

Implications

As mentioned, one of the basic purposes of setting up such an activity so early in the course is to underline the potential of the subject English in terms of an

TABLE 5.1 The schemes of work created by the group

Subject: Creative Writing/Creating Atmosphere	Subject: Language Change
Target age: Year 7–11 (lower ability groups)	Target age: Year 11–13
Purpose: For students to: a) understand and harness descriptive linguistic techniques in order to create atmosphere in their own writing b) recognize where these techniques are used in other works c) focus on how language is used to depict the same/similar building in different ways → the power of language	Purpose: For students to: a) understand how the English language has changed over time b) understand some of the reasons for language change, e.g. French influence c) be able to better understand texts from earlier periods of history such as Chaucer and Shakespeare
Durham resources: a) Durham Cathedral as depicted in tourism-promoting material (innocent, calm, spiritual, etc.) compared with creepy depiction of the inscribed stone. b) Compare with depictions of other local landmarks, such as Whitby Abbey, e.g., in Dracula → secondary English text.	Durham resources: a) Headstones and plaques situated in and around Durham Cathedral from various centuries →η evidence of language change is all around us.
Potential classroom activity: a) Write own descriptions of the cathedral in the context of a story, trying to depict it in an original way through vividly descriptive language.	Potential classroom activity: a) Write a section of publicity text for Durham in a critical historical context to demonstrate understanding of the particular location and its problematic history. b) Prepare and perform short drama performance to show the relevance of this text to modern concerns, in the form of a dialogue between modern and historical characters. c) Highlight syntactic and morphological differences from modern English in a given passage.

imaginatively resourceful approach to world and word, before the invariably harsh culture of assessment-driven curricula in schools hits home. In my oral introduction to the activity, I was completely honest about this aim, and the attendant need to set up a tension (if possible, of course, a creative tension) between what is pedagogically desirable from an ideal English-teaching point of view, and what is actually possible in the context of classroom reality. With this in mind, I asked the student teachers involved to discuss the project in their reflective journals (a key component of this and many other PGCE courses), both at the time and again towards the end of the course, looking back and considering their possible personal, professional and academic development. Some of the comments are significantly illuminating, not least for me as their tutor concerned with developing the course appropriately, and many touch on the key areas of creativity, criticality, openness to the world, resourcefulness and teacher collaboration. A sample of comments may help to give a more vivid flavour of the enterprise.

> It certainly came as a surprise to me, and others on the course, that so early on we were given the freedom to wander around Durham, exploring it with so much flexibility. I had thought everything at the start would be geared to detailed lesson planning on a set curriculum, and at first several of us wondered what the point of the session was. Once we got started, though, it became clear – we really got to grips with what English teaching could be all about, and how it could relate creatively to environmental factors – as well as just enjoying the freedom of working together, getting to know each other, and really thinking about the subject.
>
> *(Lois, immediately after the initial session)*

> The quality of the presentation, including our own, I think surprised all of us – it certainly surprised me! With a literature background like mine, I'd always regarded setting and place as key elements in any text, and we were encouraged to take this view at university, but until now I hadn't really made the link to my own ideas about teaching. I suppose we're just beginning to question assumptions about teaching and learning, and how we as teachers think about the places we happen to be in is just one of these assumptions. It was certainly good to do this not just by talking about it, or reading/writing about it, but by actually doing something active together. I do wonder, though, having spent some time working in schools before the course started, how much real scope we'll get for this sort of thing on teaching practice. Time will tell I suppose.
>
> *(Michelle, soon after the initial session)*

> The whole Durham as a teaching resource project opened my eyes to several things right at the start of the course. Coming from a working class background in a County Durham ex-mining village with high unemployment and quite a lot of social deprivation, I'd always thought of Durham city as just a place for loads of students from private school backgrounds in the south of England. None of my family had even been to university, and I wasn't expected to either. So my whole identity was based to some extent on my position outside the sort of 'expected' Durham University experience. The exercise has challenged all this, partly through working with PGCE students from very different backgrounds, which is challenging my identity-stereotypes (including my own), and partly by investigating the place itself in much more detail. Seeing the city with new eyes really.
>
> *(Ruth, at the start of her first teaching practice some six weeks into the course)*

What has struck me in two schools, on both teaching practices, is how little students say they know about where they live and the language they speak. Familiarity breeds contempt I suppose. But when we probe these areas through the subject English – trying to open their eyes to the world and what it can mean through language – it soon becomes pretty obvious that they know and feel a lot more than they let on at first. It's not always the sort of knowledge or feeling that's sought and taught by the 'official' curriculum though – that's the point. As I get a bit more experienced in English teaching, and maybe a bit more confident and courageous, it seems to me all the more important that in English we get to explore such things (as well as what we have to do for exams of course – the trick is to do it together, and a few of the teachers I've got to know seem to achieve this). This is my aim anyway – it's really why I've become a teacher.

(Paul, mid-way through his second teaching practice)

Although I've always been interested in environmental matters, and even fairy committed, I'd never really made any connection between this field of interest and my professional commitment to English teaching. I don't know why not, really, as now the relationship seems clear, and even urgent. Things we've done during the PGCE course, such as the Durham as a teaching resource project early on, and the session on ecocriticism later in the year [the whole group had enjoyed a visit from a visiting academic with a focus on the whole area, and subsequent creative activity], have certainly opened my eyes to the great potential English has not just to relate a sense of place to language and literature, but also to foster in pupils a greater sense of valuing wherever they happen to be as important to their lives.

(Rochelle, towards the end of the course)

I came to do my PGCE in Durham from well outside the area, and I knew nothing about the city or its university. Coming from north of the border [Scotland] I didn't even share the common assumptions about Durham – its 'poshness' for example! So when one of the first things we did on the course was to explore the city, it helped me enormously, both personally in getting to know the place (and some of my fellow students), and professionally in preparing me for the sort of pupils – their backgrounds and identities – I was about to teach. More than that, though – I spent quite some time thinking about the whole subject of place and identity and their relationship to teaching, and decided that it could be one of the main areas of English teaching where I could actually get pupils to teach me. After all they know so much more of these things, locally, than I do as an alien Scot! And it has in fact worked out that way, especially in a Year 8 [12–13-year-olds] project I set up in my main teaching practice school based on language, place and identity which has now become a standard theme in that school's English department.

(Peter, towards the end of the course)

Looking back over my journal, re-reading what I wrote after the first Durham as a teaching resource activity, I feel both optimistic and pessimistic at the same time. In fact that's what teaching has done to me! In one of my schools, the first one, we were encouraged by the department to be flexible and adventurous in our planning and teaching, at least with younger pupils, and in fact I did a whole scheme of work on 'A Sense of Place' with a lively Year 7 [11–12 year olds] group which went well and produced really interesting work – the display that came out of it was much praised by other teachers and my tutor, which pleased me no end and gave me much more confidence after a tricky opening couple of weeks on TP. On the other hand, in my second school, the approach was much more exam-orientated, with a fixed curriculum we all had to follow and very little wriggle-room. When I asked about doing the sort of creative work I'd done previously, I was told that it might be OK right at the end of the year when assessments had been completed, but not before. I suppose it's all taught me to look very carefully at the schools/departments I apply for!

(Michelle, towards the end of the course – and happily she was appointed to a school where her adventurous spirit would be given plenty of scope)

I hope that these quotations do some justice to the imaginative breadth and reflexive insights displayed by the beginning teachers in question; the quality of insight manifest here, as well as the lucidity of expression, I think, speaks for itself. For the purposes of this chapter, and the theme of the entire book, however, it may be instructive to tease out some of the key ideas and (sometimes) tensions. Notions of place and identity permeate all of the accounts, in different ways of course, but with a unifying sense that the project, in its broader philosophical and professional context, can enable teachers to explore the often bewildering complexities of English teaching and learning through an appropriately focused lens. In particular, the relationship between critical and celebratory aspects of English pedagogy is vividly highlighted, as well as the tension between what may be desirable and what is actually allowed (especially during the PGCE year, with its limited professional autonomy).

Viewing the whole area from a very different educational and geographical viewpoint (surely appropriate in an exploration of place and identity): from a Far-Eastern/Australian perspective, McInerney and colleagues have made some interesting points concerning the relationship between education and location, from the standpoint of a broadly critical pedagogy – points that echo the experiences of Durham student teachers and their concerns (and those of their tutor). The quotation itself, read collaboratively by the students and myself, became a significant part of the exploration, as incorporating a series of potentially provocative prompts for reflection; as such, it is worth full citation:

A critical perspective in PBE [place-based education] encourages young people to connect local issues to global environmental, financial and social concerns… It invites teachers and students to question the established order, to view how things are from the position of the most disadvantaged, and to work for the common good rather than self-interest. A critical pedagogy of place not only interrupts the insular and prejudicial views of people but more importantly involves students in a political process of understanding and shaping communities. When teachers and students view their schools and communities through a critical lens they are prompted to ask such questions as:

- What are the best features of our community? What could be done to make it a better place for all?
- What do monuments and public architecture tell us about the heritage that is most highly valued in this community? What groups are under-represented or rendered invisible?
- What might we do to ensure a more inclusive and accurate record of community heritage in our school and community?
- What is the quality of our local environment – the air, water, soil, native flora and fauna? What might we do to conserve our environment and resources to achieve a more sustainable future?
- To what extent does our school model and promote good environmental practices?
- What are the social, economic and cultural assets of our community? How fairly are they distributed? What can we do to work for a more just community?
- Who gets to make the decisions in our community? Whose voices are largely unheard? What might we do to achieve a more democratic society?

There is always a danger that focusing exclusively on what is wrong with the world will engender feelings of hopelessness amongst young people rather than imbuing them with a sense of agency and possibility. Hence, a critical approach to PBE must combine a respect for, and a critical reading of, the social institutions, histories, cultures and environments that constitute students' lifeworlds. In this context, the question of what needs to be conserved and protected may be just as crucial as the question of what needs to be transformed.

(McInerney et al 2011: 12)

It seems to me that the sentiments expressed here are entirely appropriate, even illuminating, in the context of the entire project described in this chapter. Indeed, when I introduced this necessarily lengthy quotation to the participants close to the end of their respective PGCE course, a vivid sense of recognition emerged, despite (or perhaps a little because of, in the sense of opening up a different perspective) the very much contrasting social and educational contexts.

One of the key emerging themes, however, is that of creativity (and its enemies). As can be seen even in a cursory glance, student teachers' comments, some of which I have cited above, often mention the importance of creativity in teaching, and there is an interesting exploration to be had here in looking at the relationship between creativity and place/identity. Certainly, without going into a lengthy discussion about the problems of what exactly it might or might not be, creativity – if it is to mean anything significant in practice – needs a place from and about which it may thrive. As ever, the language we use in this context is highly suggestive. The noun 'place' implies a fixed site: there seems to be something definite, permanent, even immovable about the term. Where precisely this place may be is another matter: could it be the physical base of the classroom? Perhaps the wider school? Or the still wider geographical context? Or, more abstractly, might it be found in the curriculum, or in the particularities of the various subjects which make up that curriculum, or especially in the discipline of English studies? All of these are interesting, even provocative, possibilities. Michel Foucault has elaborated further on such matters, at once presenting complexity and possibility:

> The space in which we live, which draws us out of ourselves, in which the erosion of our lives, our time and our history occurs, the space that claws and gnaws at us, is also, in itself, a heterogeneous space. In other words, we do live in a kind of void, inside of which we could place individuals and things. We do not live inside a void that could be coloured with diverse shades of light, we live inside a set of relations that delineates sites that are irreducible to one another and absolutely not superimposable on one another.
>
> *(Foucault 1986 in Blundell 2016: 45)*

However, as the form of the English language requires, it is the accompanying verb that qualifies, amplifies and clarifies the noun, thus making fuller exploratory sense of the issues. And the crucial adverb 'critically' adds yet another important dimension. Thus it is possible to speak of discovering, recognizing, exploring and celebrating the place – and all of these emerge as key elements of the project at the heart of this chapter. After all, a place remains just a place without the verb denoting human social action to make – create, in effect – sense and meaning out of its latent possibilities. Our approaches to 'place' as teachers and learners need not be limited, clearly, by the four verbs suggested above. Nevertheless, they seem to me vital in realizing the creative potential of the educational places we find ourselves in – in both abstract and concrete terms – and should inform the theoretical and practical exploration of which this book is a small part. To pursue the linguistic connotations just a little further, it is interesting to explore the word 'place' as a verb. If indeed we find as teachers that creativity is not in place, despite our attempts to discover, recognize, explore and celebrate, then it is up to us as active participants to 'place' (or perhaps 're-place'?) it there. By envisaging the word as an active force in itself, its radically participative and transformational possibilities may be released: teachers and learners creating and developing the appropriate conditions for ourselves.

Creativity as placed or as place is not without its tensions and difficulties, of course, as is hinted at throughout the present book in diverse contexts, and yet it seems to me to be an absolutely vital – in all senses – part of our work as teachers and teacher educators.

References

Blundell, D. (2016) *Rethinking Children's Spaces and Places*. London: Bloomsbury.

Charlton, E., Wyse, D., Cliff Hodges, G., Nikolajeva, M., Pointon, P. and Taylor, L. (2011) Place-related identities through texts: from interdisciplinary theory to research agenda. *British Journal of Educational Studies* 59(1), 63–74.

McInerney, P., Smyth, J. and Downs, B. (2011) Coming to a place near you? The politics and possibilities of a critical pedagogy of place-based education. *Asia Pacific Journal of Teacher Education* 39(1), 3–16.

6

SHAKESPEARE, TURGENEV (AND KALASHNIKOV) IN SIBERIA

Nicholas McGuinn and Amanda Naylor

Introduction

What issues emerge when young people from very different cultural and national backgrounds meet to share their responses to classic texts of international literature? In this chapter, we describe a project which involved students from the University of York in the United Kingdom and their counterparts from the Buryat State University at Ulan Ude, capital of the Republic of Buryatia in the Russian Federation. We took a group of five University of York undergraduates from different subject disciplines for a two-week visit to the Buryat State University, where the York undergraduates worked with Buryat and Russian students of English and their tutors from the Foreign Languages School.

Although the population of Buryatia is small (just under one million according to the 2010 census) it is rich in ethnic and cultural diversity. Two-thirds of the population are Russian – Russia began to colonize the country in the seventeenth century – and only 30 per cent are Buryat. This imbalance has placed particular pressures on the indigenous language and culture: Russian is the dominant mode of communication. Buryatia is also home to a range of religious faiths: Tibetan Buddhism, Russian Orthodox Christianity and both 'Yellow' and 'Black' versions of Shamanism.

Taking this contextual information into account, we chose to study one classical text from each of the main cultural groups involved in the project: William Shakespeare's *King Lear* (English), Ivan Turgenev's *A Lear of the Steppes* (Russian) and Isay Kalashnikov's *Cruel Century* (Buryat). One of the reasons we chose these particular texts – more on this later in the chapter – is that they share a common concern with what we considered to be universal themes of power, identity and family relationships. We also felt that the three texts provided fruitful opportunities to explore issues of representation and narration.

The project yielded a wealth of rich and fascinating data – far too much to cover within the space constraints of a single chapter. We have decided to focus therefore on one area of particular relevance to the concerns of this book: how we as tutors and students worked with classic literary texts from our respective cultures to establish a 'meeting place' where we might explore together the editors' assertion that 'the language arts' are 'crucial to enhancing understanding and empathy' in a 'pluralistic… social context'.

Literature review

Our preparatory reading for the project focused on two major and contrasting concepts: *nationalism* and *cosmopolitanism*. Words like 'them and us', 'narrative', 'representation' and 'difference' featured prominently.

Writing almost 20 years ago, Elshtain described nationalism as the 'great political passion of our time' (1998: 25). Today – as the United Kingdom's recent experiments with referenda have demonstrated – its 'bewitching power… continues to help sculpt the contours of global power relations' (Bell 2003: 63–4). Bell describes four conceptual models of nationalism. *Primordialists* (see, for example Geertz 1972; Van den Berghe 1990) emphasize ties of blood and kinship. *Perennialists* (for example, Smith 1999) conceive of nationalism as an historic constant – the product of a continuous dynamic between cooperation and conflict. For *Modernists* – whose views, according to Bell, dominate contemporary thinking – the nation-state is a political enterprise, forged by elites from the furnace of capitalism and industrialization (see, for example, Hobsbawm 1990; Nairn 1997). The fourth model described by Bell is that of the *Ethno-symbolists* who attempt to synthesize the positions of *Primordialists* and *Modernists* by drawing upon the kinship ties of the former to reinforce the claims to legitimacy of the latter (for example, Smith 1986, 1999).

Particularly pertinent to our purposes is Bell's identification of 'representation and narration' – the 'construction of stories about identity, origins, history and community' – as 'crucial' to all four conceptual models of nationalism (2003: 68, 69). Nations attempt to invest their members with a common sense of identity by employing what Bell calls 'a governing myth' (2003: 74) to tell a particularly potent and self-affirming story about themselves. (One has only to consider how the United Kingdom was mediated through the opening ceremony of the 2012 London Olympics.) In Bourdieusian terms, nationalist norms inform the individual *habitus* by means of the dissemination of governing myths and thus "society becomes deposited in persons in the form of lasting dispositions, or trained capacities and structured propensities to think, feel and act in determinant ways, which then guide them" (Wacquant 2005: 316).

What engaged us especially was Bell's observation that the primary role of 'representation and narration' in the construction of national identity and individual habitus necessitates 'an interest in the modes and mediums in which such narratives operate and through which linguistically and symbolically mediated communities

are formed and dissolve'. Central to this concern is the 'pivotal' role of 'film, literature, folk rituals and the media' (Bell 2003: 69).

Choosing to work with a major work of literature such as Shakespeare's *King Lear* meant an engagement with one of the most potent of all the 'governing myths' that have been used to construct a particular narrative about what it might mean to be 'English'. Such is the talismanic power that the name Shakespeare exerts over the English educational system that, when invited almost 30 years ago to construct a National Curriculum for English in England, Brian Cox felt able to declare 'almost everyone agrees that [Shakespeare's] work should be represented' and that 'even those who deny his universality agree on his cultural importance' (Cox 1991: 82). Buttressed by the force of law, Shakespeare remains, today, 'the ultimate citadel to be protected' (Burnett 2007: 16) with pupils in English schools being expected to study at least three of his plays between the ages of 11 and 16 (DfE 2013: 83, 85). The reach of this governing myth extends beyond Shakespeare's homeland. In *Filming Shakespeare in the Global Marketplace*, Burnett cites as an example the 2003 television drama *Indian Dream* in which two Indians – Surender, a teacher of English literature, and Rajiv, a doctor – describe what Shakespeare's *A Midsummer Night's Dream* means to them. Surender declares that he loves the play 'and per-forming it on a mid-summer night's eve in an English village is like a dream'. For Rajiv, the village in which the performance is set is 'everything that's great about England… civilized, polite, and with a long and rich history' (in Burnett 2007: 11).

These readings gave us much pause for thought. Our concerns centred on three of the other key words mentioned in the opening paragraph of this literature review: 'them', 'us' and 'difference'. Writing about ethnical tensions in the post-Soviet Ukraine, Janmaat observes that 'the promotion of one language and culture automatically leads to the demotion of another' (2007: 307). 'The governing myth of the nation,' Bell writes, 'usually gains its ascendancy at the expense of other dis-sident voices.' Governing myths threaten to create a 'totalizing mnemonic' (Bell 2003: 73, 74), an 'historically internalized national gaze' (Beck and Sznaider 2006: 10) which, at the very least, is indifferent to difference and, at worst, creates a sense of 'double consciousness' (Du Bois and Edwards: 1903/2007: 8). Writing 113 years ago about his experiences as a black American, his words are as depressingly relevant now as they were then. Du Bois puts it most tellingly:

> Between me and the other world [of White America] there is ever an unasked question: unasked by some through feelings of delicacy; by others through the difficulty of rightly framing it. All, nevertheless, flutter round it. … How does it feel to be a problem?
>
> *(Du Bois and Edwards: 1903/2007: 7)*

Du Bois' response to this unspoken question is significant: 'I answer seldom a word.'

Du Bois articulates here something that, more than a century later, Tomes was to describe as a fissure between 'self-identity' and 'social identification' – the difference between how one sees oneself and how one is seen by society (2013: 16):

> It is a peculiar sensation, this double-consciousness, this sense of always look-ing at one's self through the eyes of others, of measuring one's soul by the tape of a world that looks on in amused contempt and pity.
>
> *(Du Bois and Edwards: 1903/2007: 8)*

It is more even than a matter of exclusion. As Du Bois' 'problem' question indi-cates, the dominant 'us' can also engage actively in what Lyons et al. (citing Manne 2004) describe as 'othering' (2012: 364) – by creating its own narratives and representations of 'them' (Snee 2013). At one extreme, these can be as nega-tive and destructive as those described above by Du Bois. At the other extreme, as Wang has cautioned, they can encourage a way of positioning difference as a kind of 'romanticized exoticism' (2000: 140–1). In terms of our project, it is interest-ing here to consider the following extract from the writer and director David Kaplan's account of his 1995 production in Buryatia of *A Midsummer Night's Dream*, the play that exercised such a hold over the protagonists of the film *Indian Dream*:

> The Buryat language is melodic and sounds like running water. The play was translated by an 80 year-old blind poet who recited his Buyrat verses stand-ing up while his peppy 70 year-old wife read a flowery 19th century Russian version aloud to him.
>
> *(Kaplan 1995)*

These issues of difference – of 'othering' – pressed heavily upon our thinking about how we might follow in Kaplan's footsteps. Were we to steam into Buryatia (liter-ally, on the Trans-Siberian Railway as the University of York students did, travelling third class), hauling *King Lear* like some cultural juggernaut designed to proclaim 'Englishness' to a grateful population? Or, ignoring Wang's warning, were we to opt for the 'romanticized exoticism' approach – traces of which can be detected here in Kaplan's account:

> The Buryat production of *A Midsummer Night's Dream* was staged with Siberian motifs: shamans, forest lovers, the Swan Goddess as Titania, The Grandfatherly God of Lake Baikal as Oberon. Hippolyta was an Eskimo, Theseus a Soviet General who spoke in Russian.
>
> *(Kaplan 1995)*

Certainly, Shakespeare – whose own acting company was known as the King's Men – was not averse to supporting 'governing myths'. Noting for instance that *Macbeth* was 'written in 1606 for performance before James I and his royal guest, King Christian IV of Denmark', Hunter comments that the 'play seems to catch at several of James's obsessive interests' (1967: 38). Perhaps the most extreme example of Shakespeare's work being drafted in to support what Albrow describes as the 'overreach of the nation-state' (1996: 111) occurred during the era of the Soviet Union. Writing shortly before the death of Stalin, Gibian notes that Shakespeare 'played such an important part' in what he describes as a 'great Soviet Battle of the Books' that the 'ideological system of Marxism… supported by the might of the Soviet state and its cultural organizations' led to the imposition of a univocal critical response to the plays which was dedicated to the dissemination of propaganda. 'It was no wonder,' Gibian adds, 'that such teleological class interpretation resulted in violent distortions of Shakespeare' (1952: 30, 29, 29).

And so to *cosmopolitanism:* an alternative way of thinking about the world so challenging of nationalism that it marks nothing short of a 'mnemonic'' (Bell 2003: 78) or 'cultural' (Delanty 2011: 638) *turn* in the social sciences – a dramatic shift in vision that 'entails the systematic breaking up of the process through which the national perspective of politics and society… confirm and strengthen each other in their definitions of reality' (Beck and Sznaider 2006: 5)

There are numerous ways of refining the concept of cosmopolitanism (see, for example, Hannerz 1990; Giddens 1991; Savage et al. 2005; Beck and Sznaider 2006; Nowicka and Rovisco 2009; Snee 2013) but, for reasons of brevity, we just wish to note that a definition that spoke to us particularly is this from Delanty:

> The key underlying characteristic of cosmopolitanism is a reflexive condition in which the perspective of others is incorporated into one's own identity, interests or orientation in the world. This is what distinguishes it from global culture, internationalism, transnationalism, which may be preconditions of cosmopolitanism: it is less a condition expressed in mobility, diversity, globalizing forces than in the logic of exchange, dialogue, encounters. Cosmopolitanism requires that some degree of self or societal transformation take place as a result of the interaction of different groups.
>
> *(Delanty 2011: 634–5)*

What distinguishes cosmopolitanism here from other ways of thinking beyond the confines of nationalism – *universalism* or *globalization,* for example – is that whereas universalism sacrifices 'the particularity of others' to 'an assumption of universal equality', cosmopolitanism 'assumes that there is not just one language of cosmopolitanism, but many languages, tongues, grammars' (Beck and Sznaider 2006: 19, 14) and regards the 'exploration of difference' as 'central' (Delanty 2011: 635). A second key feature is that, while 'globalization is something taking place "out there", cosmopolitanization [*sic*] happens "from within"' (Beck and Sznaider 2006: 9). Both the habitus and the act of culture in which it is engaged are inwardly transformed through a series of critically reflexive encounters with difference – encounters that, rather than suppressing or 'othering', seek to '*articulate* and *sustain* conflicting interpretations of the world' (Arnason 2003: 151, emphasis added). Du Bois, stung by his first childhood experience of racism, recalls that he felt 'shut out from their [his white classmates'] world by a vast veil' and that he had 'no desire to tear down that veil, to creep through' (Du Bois and Edwards 1903/2007: 8).

Cosmopolitanism seeks not only to pierce the 'veil' but also to understand how the habitus and the culture within which it operates have been shaped by and may be changed by the encounter with the 'veil'.

Relating these points specifically to our Shakespeare project, we were particularly encouraged by Beck and Sznaider's (2006) comment about the 'many languages' of cosmopolitanism. We could see a connection here with Bell's assertion that the 'governing myth' of nationalism can be 'constantly contested' by what he calls 'subaltern myths':

> capable of generating their own traditions and stories, stories as likely to be concerned with past oppression and suffering at the hands of the dominant groups as by tales of national glory.
>
> *(Bell 2003: 35–6)*

Our earlier questioning of Kaplan's approach to *A Midsummer Night's Dream* was partly tongue-in-cheek. We understand that his inclusion of shamans, Soviet generals and the rest in the production was an attempt to create a bracingly cosmopolitan cultural space in which the *particular* might engage with the *universal* and where 'governing myths' of Shakespeare – whether they be what Hoffman calls the 'tyranny of the "Hey Nonny Nonny" Elizabethan cliché' (in Burnett 2007: 36) or of Shakespeare as 'passport' to 'assimilation' (Burnett 2007: 12, 11) – might be challenged by a range of answering Buryatian voices. By thus creating opportunities for 'liminality' (Turner 1974) – behaviour involving 'inversions or reversals from the norm' (Snee 2013: 144) – the habitus can be shaken into the critical reflexivity so essential to the cosmopolitan vision.

As Burnett's (2007) account of contemporary film versions of the plays around the globe demonstrates, Shakespeare is robust enough to embrace 'liminality', to sustain and to enrich reflexive, cosmopolitan encounters. By taking *King Lear* to a nation within the Russian Federation, we were entering a cultural network that already possessed a long and sophisticated tradition of engagement with Shakespeare – and an engagement that, far from signalling an 'attempt to colonize through art, to assume control via the commercial and transnational power embodied in Shakespeare's world' (Burnett 2007: 12), was played out confidently on its own cultural terms. Gibian, noting that the works of Shakespeare were introduced into Russia as early as the eighteenth century, concedes that even during the Soviet era, there were periods of powerful collaboration between scholars, translators and directors to the mutual benefit of 'theatre and scholarship' (1952: 31). At the height of the Second World War, a major Shakespeare conference was held in Erevan, the capital of Soviet Armenia. Gibian observes:

> This festival of 1944 was greeted in Russia as a testimonial to the domestication of Shakespeare in the non-Russian sections of the country and to the diffusion of knowledge of Shakespeare in the entire country.
>
> *(Gibian 1952: 31)*

The experience of Armenia provides a particularly telling example of how Shakespeare can counter the power of a governing myth and, literally, encourage 'many languages, tongues, grammars'. Alexander (1958) observes that Shakespeare's work was introduced to the country in the eighteenth century by Hovsep Emin, freedom-fighter and friend of the famous Shakespearean actor David Garrick. Citing Shakespeare as a 'major source of inspiration' three decades before the country achieved independence from the former Soviet Union, Alexander suggests two main reasons why this should be so:

> The English poet [sic] dealt in elevated manner [sic] with events removed perhaps chronologically and geographically from the Armenian scene but spiritually very much akin... Shakespeare could be read in a series of translations of the utmost purity, economy, and beauty of language, devoid of the forcibly injected Russian words with their reminders of the present.
>
> *(Alexander 1958: 387)*

Choosing the texts and modes of engagement: issues and possibilities

Bell's account of the 'pivotal' role of literature in determining how narrative can mould and position the *habitus* within a particular social context influenced our thinking, not only about text selection, but also about how we intended to engage with the chosen works. In order to acknowledge the rich dramatic, cinematic and academic Shakespearean heritage already established within the republics of the former Soviet Union, we quickly agreed with our counterparts in Ulan Ude that we would pair *King Lear* with Turgenev's short story *A Lear of the Steppes*. Comparing English and Russian versions of the same story offered a fruitful opportunity for helping our respective students to explore Beck and Sznaider's (2006) assertion that 'there is not just one language of cosmopolitanism, but many languages, tongues, grammars'. Selecting a text that might not only 'speak' for Buryatia but also link to our chosen themes proved far more problematic. The fate of the Buryat language provides a stark example of Janmaat's (2007) observation that 'the promotion of one language and culture automatically leads to the demotion of another'. With only 353,113 speakers recorded in the 2002 national census, Buryatian is one of almost 30 endangered Siberian languages. It is significant that, in its written form, it is based largely on the Russian Cyrillic alphabet – and equally significant that the text we finally settled on was Isay Kalashnikov's 1978 novel *Cruel Century*, a work written in Russian. In making this choice, we were influenced by the work of Van Hook who, having explored how images taken from advertisements and television commercials might evoke 'transcultural resonance' (2011: 7) in respondents from different cultures, suggested that his study might be replicated using works of literature as stimulus material. *Cruel Century* provided opportunities to explore 'transcultural resonance' in that, through its depiction of the twelfth-century Mongolian emperor Genghis Khan, it engages with the themes of power, patriarchy and family tension found in *King Lear* and *A Lear of the Steppes*. Moreover, by focusing upon the life of Genghis Khan, the novel speaks to one of the 'governing myths' – to use Bell's term – of Buryatian identity.

In choosing to work with literary texts that explore similar themes from different cultural, linguistic and historical perspectives, we hoped to examine the tensions between the 'assumption of equality' which Beck and Sznaider (2006) describe as a key characteristic of 'universality' and the 'exploration of difference' that Delanty (2011) argues is 'central' to the concept of cosmopolitanism. Crucial, also, to Delanty's interpretation of cosmopolitanism is the encouragement of critical reflexivity, which Snee argues arises from situations involving inversions or reversals from the norm. We hoped that our planned engagements with the texts would provide opportunities for the students to experience 'liminality' so that their sense of *habitus* might be shaken into the critical reflexivity so essential to the cosmopolitan vision.

Tensions between universality and cosmopolitanism surfaced immediately in our discussions about the language through which the activities would be mediated. Once again, Janmaat's presence loomed. Although the University of York contingent comprised only five students and the Buryat State University group consisted of more than 20 in an almost equal ethnic mix of Buryats and Russians, English was selected as the common language of communication, partly because neither we nor the University of York students speak Russian but also because one of the main reasons why the students and tutors from the Foreign Languages School at Buryat State University wanted to participate in the project was so that they could interact with native speakers and thus improve their own speaking and listening skills in English. This decision suited our pedagogical aim of encouraging critical reflexivity through exchanges of perspective and viewpoint: we insisted that the students worked on the chosen activities in mixed ethnic groups. On the other hand, our decision raised issues of linguistic hegemony and 'othering'. Although the Buryat State University students were extremely proficient in all four modalities of English, none of them had spent time in an Anglophone country and they did not possess the idiomatic fluency of the University of York students. In their written reflections on the project particularly, they demonstrated a tendency that Snee (2013) has identified as characteristic of people writing in a second language: their choice of words could sometimes seem anachronistic and imbued with a 'flowery' and even exotic quality that they would not have exhibited had they been communicating in their mother tongue. We were conscious that these linguistic issues impacted on ethnic Buryat students particularly. Although not many of them were proficient speakers of the indigenous language, they were obliged to work in a second language on texts written in English and Russian: there seemed little space here to explore and even celebrate their home culture.

One of the ways in which we tried to address these challenges was by selecting shared activities that were not too heavily language-dependent. We invited the students, for example, to dramatize key scenes from the texts, to summarize their responses in no more than five words, or to design a theatre poster for a performance of *King Lear.* At the same time, we needed to acknowledge the concern – noted by an American teacher of Shakespeare in China (Berry 1988) – of foreign language students to use engagement with literature primarily as a means of improving their proficiency in the target language. Consequently, we encouraged students and tutors to deliver a series of formal lectures, in English, on issues germane to the three texts: the role of the Fool in *King Lear* and *A Lear of the Steppes*, for example, or the challenges posed by reading a text in translation. The lecture series provided a particularly fruitful means of encouraging critical reflexivity. To take the experience of the York students as an example: only one of the five was studying English literature: the others were, respectively, a chemist, an economist, a historian and a philosopher. Inviting a chemist, for instance, to talk about *King Lear* from her subject perspective provided an unexpected and fascinating example of 'liminality'.

Striking a balance between encouraging explorations of difference while heeding Wang's warnings about 'romanticized exoticism' proved a complex challenge. We were pleased that the University of York students chose to journey to Ulan Ude on the Trans-Siberian railway. They took five days to travel from Moscow, so their introduction to the Russia that lies east of the Urals was a gradual one. The first communal activity involved staff and students from both institutions in visits to a Buddhist monastery and to the Ethnographic Museum on the outskirts of the city. Our intention here was to try to balance the dangers of 'exoticizing the other' against the need for the University of York students to gain a sense of the richness of the new context in which they found themselves (none of them had ever travelled east of the Urals before). Conscious of Bell's comments concerning 'the construction of stories about identity, origins, history and community' (2003), we wanted the University of York students to experience at first hand the kinds of 'official' stories Buryatia chooses to tell about itself. The Buryat State University students acted as guides and interpreters during both visits – an experience that not only enhanced their proficiency in mediating between informal and formal modes of spoken English, but also established them in a position of authority and expertise from the outset. Both sets of tutors made several other attempts to encourage what Snee (2013) calls 'inversions or reversals from the norm'. For example, the York students were housed with local families and met up with their Buryat State University counterparts socially and informally in the evenings. Perhaps most significantly in terms of linguistic hegemony, identity and liminality, we agreed that the project would culminate in a theatre production of scenes from each of the three selected texts, performed by the students in either English, Russian or, in the case of *Cruel Century*, Buryat. Tutors from both institutions felt it important that the indigenous language be given a textual 'voice' alongside English and Russian; and to this end, our Buryat State University colleagues translated an extract from the novel into a play script written in Buryat. The stakes of 'liminality' were raised particularly for the York students here: not only were they required to act before a public audience in two languages with which they were unfamiliar; they also had to take instruction from a professional theatre director who spoke no English.

Commonality or difference? Three critical incidents

Both during and after each workshop session, we invited the participants to reflect in writing or through taped discussion, in English, on their responses to the issues explored and to the chosen activities. We can do no more here than give a flavour of those responses and have, therefore, chosen to focus on three particularly significant encounters and exchanges – one from each text. All the names of the respondents have been anonymized. Where appropriate, the home institution of the students is indicated by parentheses containing either the letters UY for University of York or BSU for Buryat State University.

The first critical incident we want to describe provides some idea of the ways in which students' encounters with the three literary texts highlighted issues of commonality and of difference. In consultation with our fellow tutors from Buryat State University, we selected three pivotal scenes from *King Lear* that focused on the presentation of Lear as a father and patriarch: his portrayal at the opening of the play, when he sets his love test and divides his kingdom; his encounter with Poor Tom on the Heath, and the harrowing moment towards the end of the play when he enters with Cordelia dead in his arms. At the end of the *King Lear* workshop, we invited the students to reflect upon the work we had done. Whereas the University of York students tended to comment on how the workshop activities had enhanced their thinking about different interpretations of the play, their Buryat State University counterparts were more focused on the actual pedagogy used to stimulate those encounters with difference. In the extract below, both students have chosen to comment on the 'five word' exercise mentioned earlier:

> James (UY): Thinking of *Fate* [one of the five words he selected] was the first opportunity to widen the discussion to consider different approaches to Fate in Western and Eastern cultures.

> Yelena (BSU): Five words written on the paper helped me see other people's perspectives and look at the play in a new way.

As in our work on *King Lear*, so in our exploration of Turgenev's *A Lear of the Steppes* we chose to focus upon key moments where we felt issues concerning parents and children were foregrounded. For example, we concentrated on a particularly dramatic scene towards the end of the story where Turgenev's Lear figure, Harlov, having gone mad and destroyed the ancestral home, addresses his daughters on his deathbed. Turgenev does not make it clear if the dying Harlov curses the daughters or forgives them. Asking the students to consider whether they thought Harlov had cursed or forgiven his daughters revealed interesting differences between the responses of the University of York and the Buryat State University students. Most of the latter felt that the father forgave his daughter. Yelena, for example, commented:

> Harlov forgives [his] daughters to let them free to be free himself for his soul to be calm. Forgiveness is part of Russian and Christian nature – a crucial necessity like rain in dry weather.

The University of York students' responses, on the other hand, were less sanguine. Eva, our chemistry undergraduate, commented:

> I think that [at] this particular stage of Harlov's life he would [not] have forgiven. His destruction of the house shows his intent to affect the daughters' life in the future. The moment was also quick and therefore he would not have had time to become calm and realize that he is at his very last moment.

Even allowing for what Snee (2013) says about the constraints of writing in a second language, there are noticeable differences between the responses of Yelena and Eva, not least in their use of the English word 'calm'. For Eva, it is Harlov who is or is not 'calm'; for Yelena, it is his 'soul'. Where Eva interprets Harlov's behaviour as an all too human act of spiteful revenge and suggests that it would have been practically impossible, given the time constraints, for him to act in any other way, Yelena ignores the pragmatics of the situation and locates her response within a timeless religious context that references a touchstone of Russian culture – the concept of 'soul' or *dushá*.

As noted earlier, Kalashnikov's *Cruel Century* was selected as our third text with the intention of providing our students with opportunities to encounter one of Buryatia's 'governing myths' in the person of Genghis Khan. Attempting to remain true to the literary themes explored during our explorations of *King Lear* and *A Lear of the Steppes*, the scripted extract from *Cruel Century* prepared by our Buryat State University tutor colleagues focused particularly on a domestic scene from the novel. In order to challenge received Western opinion about Genghis Khan, the scene selected for translation was one in which, unlike Lear or Harlov, he is portrayed in a positive light. Following the workshop, the students were invited to reflect upon whether or not their views about Genghis Khan had been altered by their experiences. Kasenia, a Buryat State University student, noted:

> Genghis Khan is a genius. He [has] perfect will[power]. He made such an army that frightened the whole world. For me he is a very controversial person because he was very good at wars but I don't like his cruelty in the army. Judging by this somebody can think he was like a 'stoneman' [*sic*]. But as we all know he loved his wife very much (and he proved it several times!). Also we know that he was an obedient son (that sounds even stranger) but nevertheless he was not a very good father... I think English people know a lot about the wars [of Genghis Khan] but very little about the family, love relationships, wives, sons. But today's discussion tells them a lot about it.

Kasenia remains conflicted in her views. While Khan is perceived to be a 'genius' who demonstrates strength of leadership ('perfect willpower') as well as familial virtues (he loves his wife and is an obedient son), Kasenia recognizes that he can nevertheless be regarded as 'controversial' and a 'stoneman', particularly by 'English people' from the West. She acknowledges the darker aspects of Khan's personality, but nevertheless feels that her University of York counterparts are not in possession of what Bell might call the full story and she is therefore pleased that 'today's discussion tells them a lot about it'. Just as Yelena located her reflections upon Harlov within a religious and nationalistic context, so here Kasenia, through her use of the personal pronoun *us*, stakes what Bell would call a *Primordial* national claim to Khan. The use of parentheses suggests that her feelings remain, however, ambivalent:

> Moreover, for us (I mean the Buryats) Genghis Khan means more than a wonderful will. We feel (at least, we want to) his blood flowing in us. So, it is in some way a feel [*sic*] of being proud of him

The responses of the University of York students reflected something of the conflicted approach voiced above by Kasenia. Eric noted that, as Kasenia suggested, the governing myth regarding Genghis Khan to which he had previously subscribed positioned Khan as 'a fearsome barbarian warrior'. Like most of his York companions, Eric felt that the workshop activities had persuaded him to take a more nuanced view, summed up by his colleague Eleanor's suggestion that Genghis Khan was a more 'complex character' than she had previously thought. Only one of the University of York students – perhaps significantly the historian trained in the interpretation and validation of written evidence – was not prepared to accept this revised version of the Western 'governing myth' regarding Genghis Khan. Jeremy writes:

> The main way my opinions have been challenged relates to the glorified persona with which [*sic*] he holds in Buryatia. He was, while often calm in demeanour, ferocious with enemies and responsible for some acts which when put in comparison with modern population sizes could equate to genocide.
>
> Stories such as those about his wife and the feel[ing] he was not the best warrior but could easily command respect unfortunately cause me to react with cynicism as to the reliability of these sources (as much of Mongolian history was written after the time which calls first hand description into question. I fear this may be an attempt to rather glorify his character without proper analysis).

When we reflected upon the student responses to our work on *Cruel Century*, we wondered what our reaction might have been if the name *Genghis Khan* had been replaced by *Adolf Hitler*. In the extract from the novel that we studied together, Khan showed compassion to his wife and acted as a dutiful son. Hitler was a vegetarian and, apparently, kind to little children. Do those qualities compensate for the fact that both men were mass murderers? We felt uneasy that all but one of the University of York students – perhaps acting out of an understandably polite desire to respect the views of their hosts – had shown themselves so willing to concede that Genghis Khan might not have been as bad as they had been led to believe.

We felt we had witnessed at first-hand what Bell describes as the 'pivotal' role of literature in the construction of national identity through 'representation and narration'. We left the project with a fervent belief in the importance of making the teaching of historical enquiry a compulsory part of the curriculum for all pupils. Our encounter with *Cruel Century* also obliged us to think hard about the extent to which we are willing to, as Arnason (2003) put it, 'articulate and sustain conflicting interpretations of the world'.

Concluding remarks

We opened the chapter by referring to the editors' assertion that 'the language arts' are 'crucial to enhancing understanding and empathy' in a 'pluralistic… social context'. Although we would by no means wish to make overblown claims for a project based on such a small research sample, we do feel that the encounters we shared in Ulan Ude raise some interesting points that are worth noting here. As the quotations from the respondents cited in the previous section suggest, we found that our selected literary texts did indeed provide a meeting place where students from all three ethnic backgrounds were able to exchange ideas about fundamental issues. Thinking of the tensions between 'universalism' and 'cosmopolitanism', we felt that the University of York and the Buryat State University students did establish a sense of community across their respective national and cultural boundaries; the mixed working groups functioned well and the drama activities – particularly the shared experience of rehearsing and performing on stage together – really helped the participants to bond. We all came away from the project with an enhanced understanding and appreciation of each other's cultural heritage. For the two of us particularly, the encounter with *Cruel Century* obliged us to engage with a 'governing myth' about nationalism that we found difficult to accommodate. Genghis Khan: hero or mass murderer? It was Kalashnikov, the least globally known of our three selected authors, who highlighted for us a dilemma that, Delanty argues, is of central concern to the future of democracy:

> With the growing diversity of contemporary societies as a result of transnationalism, be it tourism or migration, and more generally multiculturalism, democracy has been both enhanced and at the same time challenged … Democratization has everywhere led both to more rights and to greater consciousness of rights. This has been enhanced by opportunities for networking and when combined with social interests it leads to an increase in contestation and conflict. The more groups and perspectives that are mobilized, the greater the dissensus and contestation… The nature of the relation [*sic*] between the groups is the key problem for democracy.
>
> *(Delanty 2011: 635)*

If the 'nature of the relation' between groups is 'key', then surely the fact that engagement with the 'language arts' allowed us to explore commonality and difference within the safe space of a fictional text through discussion, laughter and the excitement generated by shared creative endeavour, has got to be a powerful safeguard against 'dissensus and contestation'?

References

Albrow, M. (1996) *The Global Age*. London: Polity Press.

Alexander, E. (1958) Shakespeare's plays in Armenia. *Shakespeare Quarterly* 9(3), 387–94.

Arnason, J. (2003) *Civilizations in Dispute: Historical Questions and Theoretical Traditions*. Leiden: Brill.

Beck, U. and Sznaider, N. (2006) Unpacking cosmopolitanism for the social sciences: a research agenda. *The British Journal of Sociology* 57(1), 1–23.

Bell, D.S.A. (2003) Mythscapes: memory, mythology, and national identity. *British Journal of Sociology* 54(1), 63–81.

Berry, E. (1988) Teaching Shakespeare in China. *Shakespeare Quarterly* 39(2), 212–16.

Burnett, M.T. (2007) *Filming Shakespeare in the Global Marketplace*. Basingstoke and New York: Palgrave Macmillan.

Cox, B. (1991) *Cox on Cox: An English Curriculum for the 1990s*. London: Hodder & Stoughton.

Delanty, G. (2011) Cultural diversity, democracy and the prospects of cosmopolitanism: a theory of cultural encounters. *The British Journal of Sociology* 62(4), 633–56.

DfE (2013) *The National Curriculum in England: Framework Document*. London: Department for Education.

Du Bois, W.E.B. and Edwards, B.H. (1903/2007) *The Souls of Black Folk: Essays and Sketches*. Oxford: Oxford University Press.

Elshtain, J. (1998) *New Wine and Old Bottles: International Politics and Ethical Discourse*. Notre Dame: University of Notre Dame Press.

Geertz, C. (1972) *Myth, Symbol and Culture*. Cambridge, MA: American Academy of Arts and Sciences.

Gibian, G. (1952) Shakespeare in Soviet Russia. *The Russian Review* 11(1), 24–34.

Giddens, A. (1991) *Modernity and Self-Identity: Self and Society in the Late Modern Age*. Cambridge: Polity Press.

Hannerz, U. (1990) Cosmopolitans and locals in world culture. In M. Featherstone (ed.) *Global Culture: Nationalism, Globalization and Modernity*. London: Sage.

Hobsbawm, E. (1990) *Nations and Nationalism since 1780*. Cambridge: Cambridge University Press.

Hunter, G.K. (ed.) (1967) *William Shakespeare: Macbeth*. Harmondsworth: Penguin Books.

Janmaat, J.G. (2007) The ethnic 'other' in Ukrainian history textbooks: the case of Russia and the Russians. *Compare* 37, 307–24.

Kaplan, D. (1995) *A Midsummer Night's Dream*. Retrieved from http://davidkaplandirector. com/1995/01/02/a-midsummer-nights-dream.

Lyons, K., Hanley, J., Wearing, S. and Neil, J. (2012) Gap year volunteer tourism: myths of global citizenship? *Annals of Tourism Research* 39(1), 361–78.

Manne, R. (2004). Howardism triumphant. *The Age*, 1 November. Retrieved from www. theage.com.au.

Nairn, T. (1997) *Faces of Nationalism: Janus Revisited*. London: Verso.

Nowicka, M. and Rovisco, M. (2009) Introduction: making sense of cosmopolitanism. In M. Nowicka and M. Rovisco (eds.) *Cosmopolitanism in Practice*. Farnham: Ashgate.

Savage, M., Bagnall, G. and Longhurst, B.J. (2005) *Globalisation and Belonging*. London: Sage.

Snee, H. (2013) Framing the Other: cosmopolitanism and the representation of difference in overseas gap year narratives. *The British Journal of Sociology* 64(1), 142–62.

Smith, A. (1986) *The Ethnic Origins of Nationalism*. Oxford: Blackwell.

Smith, A. (1999) *Myths and Memories of the Nation*. Oxford: Oxford University Press.

Tomes, Y.I. (2013) *Social Issues, Justice and Status: Cross-Cultural Interaction and Understanding: Theory, Practice, & Reality*. New York: Nova.

Turner, V. (1974) *The Ritual Process*. Harmondsworth: Penguin.

Van den Berghe, P. (1990) *State Violence and Ethnicity*. Niwot, CO: University of Colorado Press.

Van Hook, S.R. (2011) Modes and models for transcending cultural differences in international classrooms. *Journal of Research in International Education* 10(1), 5–27.

Wacquant, L. (2005) Habitus. In J. Becket and Z. Milan (eds.) *International Encyclopedia of Economic Sociology*, 316. London: Routledge.

Wang, N. (2000) *Tourism and Modernity: A Sociological Analysis*. Oxford: Elsevier Science.

7

POETRY, PLACE AND IDENTITY

Karen Lockney

The ideas at the heart of this chapter are inspired by contemporary debates relating to the nature of place and people's relationship to place. Such debate spans popular culture as well as academic discourse. Step into any decent bookshop and there is likely to be a table arranged with books exploring our relationship with place. Recent successful titles include, for example, Tim Dee's *Four Fields*, Jean Sprackland's *Strands*, and Paul Farley and Michael Symmons Roberts' highly influential *Edgelands*. Popular interest in place is not merely literary: a glance at TV schedules will reveal programmes such as *Coast, Countryfile, Britain's Secret Places*. Such programmes explore places explicitly, and on some level question our changing relationship with them. In academic discourse, the term 'spatial turn' is often used to describe the focus on an investigation of place and space across inter- and intra- disciplinary contexts, something that is becoming increasingly visible in academic debate.

This chapter relates to work carried out in primary and secondary school classrooms, using poetry to support pupils' consideration of places in which they were currently living, as expressed through their creative writing. Consideration of pupils' responses to a current cultural debate is interesting, but the aims of the project stretch beyond aesthetic responses to place. The work also takes place in a socio-political context where our consideration of national and local identities has become an increasing concern. As people move across and within countries and continents more than ever before, and the fabric of communities develops into something new, there is arguably more reason than ever for children and young people to be supported in reflecting on what place means to them, and how they see themselves in relation to the places to which they currently – for however long or short a time – belong.

Place-based identity: some key ideas in contemporary discourse

'Place-based identity' is a term used across a range of disciplines to describe the ways in which personal identity might be bound up with a place. A key voice in this debate is that of cultural geographer, the late Doreen Massey who notes that, 'just as personal identities are said to be multiple, shifting, possibly unbounded, so also… are identities of place' (1994: 7). Another influential commentator, Tim Cresswell, suggests that, 'When humans invest meaning in a portion of space and then become attached to it in some way… it becomes place' (2004: 10). Massey's seminal work on place centres on her view of 'identities of place [as] unfixed, contested or multiple' (Massey 1994: 5), and she is concerned that a static view of place can be viewed as 'almost necessarily reactionary' (1994: 151). While Massey was writing more than 20 years ago, her words have become increasingly relevant. Recent years have seen political upheaval in many countries – the Scottish independence referendum, the election of Donald Trump as US president, and the outcome of the UK Brexit referendum being some of the most striking examples. The reasons for and effects of such upheavals are, of course, extremely complex, and will be debated for decades to come. However, one of the factors often examined is that of people's responses to immigration, to community cohesion, to changing perceptions of nationalism and patriotism. Some people worry that the rise of UKIP (UK Independence Party) is due to a rise of English and/or British patriotism, and many more feel that the left has lost a claim on patriotism, increasing its alienation from voters: 'the affective power of England and Englishness is being taken by the conservative, Eurosceptic, xenophobic end of the spectrum, all the way from the extremist English Defence League to mild middle English Brexitism' (Garton Ash 2016). Whether or not issues of national identity can simply be explained by left and right wing differences is open to question; nevertheless it is important to acknowledge that political allegiances are a feature of this debate.

Given the strong presence of such interrogations of place within various contemporary discourses, there seems to be much scope – and potentially significant benefit – in asking similar questions about place and identity within school classrooms, incorporating children and young people's voices into our understanding of changing relationships with place in the modern world.

Contemporary rural experience

It is important to note that the school-based work discussed in this chapter is contextualized within a specific awareness of, and interest in, issues of contemporary rural experience. Clearly there are significant socio-economic inequalities in urban centres, but it is crucial that the countryside is not viewed as somewhere immune to problems stemming from inequality, nor to other stresses and pressures of modern life. Recent research pointed out that 700,000 children in rural UK areas live below the poverty line, while almost a quarter of 16-year-olds in rural areas do not attain a GCSE pass above grade D (ATL 2014). Although child poverty is lower in

UK rural areas than urban, the numbers are still significant: a quarter of all children in rural areas live in low-income households, compared to a third in urban areas (Poverty Site 2014). In 2012–2013, fewer children in rural areas left school with at least five GCSE A★–C than in urban areas, with the gap widening every year since 2010 (DEFRA 2015). There may be a danger that rural poverty and disadvantage are invisible problems, and that this makes it more difficult for rural issues to be addressed.

This is not to say that rural issues are ignored. Indeed, rural Britain has a strong presence in cultural and political debate. Ian McEwan noted that,

> We are nearly all descended from people who, only a few generations back, worked on the land. The countryside is our final link with them, and with a past which seems from here to have been more ordered and possessed with deeper certainties.
>
> *(in Barnett and Scruton, 1998: vii)*

Such a view may chime with the fact that *Countryfile* is one of the BBC's most popular programmes, part of a swathe of nature-related features (Midgely 2016), or that tourism plays such a vital role in the rural economy, contributing around £17 billion per year (UK Parliament, 2015).

A personal view is that, while a focus on rural experience is to be welcomed, this is often characterized by seeing the rural in comparison to the urban. In his seminal work, *The Country and the City*, Raymond Williams sees the well-established nature of this view:

> the country has gathered the idea of a natural way of life: of peace, innocence and simple virtue. The city has gathered the idea of an achieved centre: of learning, communication, light. Powerful hostilities have also developed: on the city as a place of noise, worldliness and ambition; on the country as a place of backwardness, ignorance and limitation. A contrast between country and city, as fundamental ways of life, reaches back into classical times.
>
> *(Williams 1985: 1)*

These contrasts, to which Williams draws our attention, still feature in representations of the rural and urban and are embedded in our cultural response to rurality. To some extent, this is understandable: it is estimated that 92 per cent of the UK population will be living in towns or cities by 2030 (*The Guardian*, 2017) so perhaps it is not surprising that the urban may be seen as the norm and the countryside as the other. Furthermore, as the vast majority of the population live in urban environments, the countryside is often a place to visit for leisure, or to pass through on a long journey – observed rather than lived in; experienced for pleasure rather than out of necessity. Therefore, the voices of children and young people experiencing rural lives may be subsumed into wider discussions of place, possibly becoming part of an examination of rural/urban dichotomies. The aim of this project, as will be discussed in further detail later in the chapter, was simply to allow some small groups of pupils to express their response to places in which they currently live, without preconception or strict direction. This small-scale work was not intended to prove anything definitive about young people's place-based identities, and certainly was not intended to be a foundation from which generalizations could be made. Rather, the work, and particularly as discussed here, was intended to raise some questions about ways in which we can begin to listen to young people's perceptions of their place-based identities, and consider what we might learn from their views.

Role of poetry

The lasting influence of Romanticism ensures that poetry remains a key battleground for the dichotomies of urban versus rural identities. Casting perhaps the longest shadow is Wordsworth's *Michael*. Critic David Gervais notes,

> Poetry after Wordsworth was to become full of contrasts between opposing Englands in which the absent one would be the most poetically real. In *Michael*, although both Englands are still real, the difference between them is simply that Michael's England is more English than Luke's is.
>
> *(Gervais 1993: 3)*

Clearly the exploration of the rural in poetry has roots even further back than Romanticism, with the strong tradition of pastoral poetry stretching back at least as far as Virgil. This is a proud and strong tradition, one to be celebrated, and one that has produced some of the very best poetry in the English-speaking world. It is important, however, that the changing nature of rural life is considered – seeing the countryside and its traditions as a place preserved in aspic is not helpful to our understanding of relations with places in the modern world. Doreen Massey reminds us of 'temptations of relapsing back into past traditions', that 'places cannot really be characterized by recourse to some essential, internalized moment' (1994: 169). Awareness of the dangers of an unquestioning veneration of the past is relevant to analysis of any place-based discourse, whether focused on rural or urban environments – 'Modern England' says David Gervais, 'is in danger of becoming a museum in itself' (1993: 271). In a world of considerable movement of peoples, and one of shifting political landscapes, it is perhaps more important than ever that we resist any view that things were *necessarily* better in a bygone age. Listening to the lived experience of children and young people can clearly help us understand how place and our relationships with place are finding a shape in contemporary life. Where any lived experiences are more marginal, as is the case with rural life, it is perhaps particularly important to allow people to reflect on and express how they relate to the places in which they find themselves.

If, as I have suggested, the nature of place-based identity is difficult to pin down, then poetry, dealing as it does with the elusive as well as the specific, may be a particularly suitable art form through which to explore this identity. Sean O'Brien claims that 'in England, all roads lead to poetry' (2012: 57), while Owen Sheers believes that 'places define poems which define places' (2008: 174). Perhaps some of this is due to the way in which poets make use of precise observation, whether to draw the reader's eye to a specific detail, or to suggest a link between the self and place. Ted Hughes suggests that feelings experienced in a place can be 'fleeting', whereas they can be 'concentrated and purified and intensified' in poems (1967: 80). Perhaps the brevity of poetry, the economy of language allows a precise image of a feature of a place to shine through, perhaps to widen out our vision through the suggestions made by one specific image. Hughes admits that it is difficult to describe landscape in words as there is so much detail, but that 'words can render the feeling' (1967: 78), and that a successful poem can project an image 'at the same time as it defines the way you are to feel about it' (1967: 81).

Clearly it is unrealistic to expect the pupils with whom I worked during this project to create images with anything approaching the same skill as Ted Hughes or the other poets mentioned above. Nevertheless it was this idea of poetry being a perfect vehicle through which to explore our responses to places that underpinned the project.

This small-scale project involved working with pupils in two schools (one primary with Years 3 and 4, and one secondary with a Year 8 class). Both schools were in rural, northern English counties – one in a small market town, and one in a small village, drawing pupils from those places and surrounding rural locations. Quite simply the aim was to support pupils in exploring their response to places around them, and to express this through poetry. There were few limits to how these experiences might be explored, but there was a desire not to go down the route of comparing urban and rural experience, for the reasons outlined above. There was also a desire to avoid generalizations of young people's experiences or of rural identities, but to let the young people speak for themselves as much as was possible, while offering some structure for thinking and writing. It is also worth noting that there was no pressure from either school to comply strictly with any particular element of the curriculum for the short duration of the project. Although clearly I wished to support pupils' writing skills and their creative writing development, I did not have to teach explicit writing skills or 'poetic techniques' and I am grateful to the schools for allowing this freedom. This is not the place to ruminate on the possibilities that can come about when not tied so explicitly to the demands in the 'Writing' section of the current English National Curriculum, but this may be worth some reflection.

Although the project ran slightly differently in each school (to cater for the age of the pupils and the amount of time it was possible to allocate), the work was comparable in both settings and followed similar structures. There were some short writing exercises and initial group discussions surrounding the pupils' perceptions of the places in which they currently lived. Pupils were given outline maps of the British Isles and were asked to note down places they or their families live or had lived, and to note down words they associate with particular places – this was simply to generate discussion. The writing exercises were straightforward 'freewrites' where pupils were given simple prompt words (for example, 'house', 'street', 'gate') and asked to write continuously, trying not to take their pen from the page and without stopping to think about what they wanted to write – just to let the words come freely, not worrying at all about spelling or punctuation, with no expectation that work would be shared or read out at this stage. They did, however, have to identify at least one word or phrase in what they produced that interested or surprised them about their view of the place they were writing about, and to share this.

Pupils were then shown a photo slideshow I had made of their respective town and village. In both cases I had taken photos of established 'views' – the main street for example, but mostly of more particular details: a shop sign, a tree, a doorbell, an upstairs window. Simply to increase engagement, I played a quiz with them first to see if they could spot the places. After this I replayed the slides, but this time with brief lines of observation I had made about what I had photographed. (For example, there was a photo of some birds circling above a café, together with the line 'pigeons spy on cupcake crumbs'; there was a picture of the top of a lamppost against the sky, with the lines 'shapes on a lamppost/geometry and clouds').

Then it was their turn to go on walkabout with cameras around the immediate environment. In the primary school they were given a (cheaply resourced) writer's notebook in which to record their observations – this was a particularly positive move and did much to help them feel they had ownership of their writing. The aim of having shown them my slideshows first was to encourage them to focus their gaze, to zoom in literally with the lens, but more in terms of their thinking. I encouraged them to look out for the overlooked, the unphotographed.

On returning to the classrooms, they were encouraged to share their photos and refine their lines if they wished, and we discussed in a fairly unstructured but detailed way what views of their environments were emerging. Were there things several people had noticed? Were there things someone had spotted that no one else had? Frequently what was thrown up here were images that they shared with which everyone was somehow familiar, but had never quite taken the time to notice so specifically before. A simple fact that emerged from the primary school work was how much of what they saw was at their eye level, and so they were picking up on things that I myself had regularly overlooked as I had walked around their village.

This exercise was extended as a homework task, asking them to record their observations of places of their choice that they experience daily. Due to resourcing issues over cameras this was a written exercise, although ideally it would also be accompanied by photographs.

After further sharing and reflection of their observations, we then moved on to look at ways other poets had recorded reflections on place. A poem I chose to focus on in particular was Andrew Fusek Peters' 'Last night, I saw the city breathing' (1997).

In one school I used this poem as a prompt to start the children off on their writing, and in the other I used other prompts of my own as line starters (Our places are…/In them you will see…/Our places are…/One day we will go to…/There we will find…/These are our places. Our places and us.)

A further stage of the project aimed to allow the pupils to present their poems to an audience, and in the primary school – as logistics allowed this to be more easily arranged – parents were invited in for a poetry reading. The village shop also agreed to exhibit the pupils' photos and poems on their wall, so there was a very positive sense of offering the poems back to the community that had provided inspiration for them.

This is a suitable point at which to stop and let the young people's work speak for itself. For the purposes of this chapter I am going to present three poems. It is not intended that these offer any conclusive insights into pupils' perceptions of place, nor that they reveal everything that emerged from the time spent in the schools. Rather they are snapshots of some aspects of the pupils' thinking, reproduced here to allow for some issues to be considered further.

Poem 1

Us and our places

> Our places are Ripon, Knayton and Nether Silton.
> In them you will see a plasma ball on a shelf, a model boat called Kingfisher
>   and a swively chair.
> Our places are unusual, welcoming and modern.
> We are from China, Africa and Harrogate.
> One day we will go to Africa, America and the moon.
> There we will find elephants, hot dogs and fifty year old footprints.
> These are our places. Our places and us.

Poem 2

Us and our places

> Our places are Orr Crescent, Alanbrooke Barracks, Tannery Cottage, Carlton
>   Miniott.
> In them you will see men and women in army uniforms,
> a red nail varnish stain on the carpet,
> a teddy bear key ring on my main clock.
> Our places are Georgian, noisy, interesting, busy, pot holey, boring.
> We are from Belfast, Edinburgh, Chesterfield, Sheffield, Nottingham, Norby.
> One day we will go to Thailand, Indonesia, the border of America and
>   Canada.
> There we will find different cultures, American products, different music
>   and vibes.
> These are our places. Our places and us.

Poem 3

Our places and us

> Our places are Manor Lea, Flexion House, Bagby, Rest Harrow.
> In them you will see Sergeant Pepper's Lonely Hearts Club Band,
> the flamboyant record sleeve,
> an eccentric collection of books.
> Our places are musical, crazy, different, calm, amazing.
> We are from Easington, Eston, Middlesborough, Sheffield.
> One day we will go to Graceland, Liverpool, Vatican City.
> There we will find the Beatles' memorial stone, Elvis's house.
> These are our places. Our places and us.

How we as readers respond to these poems will of course differ enormously, and may be more exhaustive than could be mentioned here. Nevertheless, there are some features on which we can perhaps reflect. Pupils were encouraged to use actual place names, but the choice of which to use was entirely theirs. Clearly there is a strong tradition of poets enjoying the use of place names in their work; there is a lure of the musicality or uniqueness of many place names. Beyond this, place names exemplify ways in which a poem can provide a tight focus on a particular place, while somehow having a much wider resonance. Logically, a place name might suggest a desire to convey a geographic identity – the reader may look up the place on a map, or could even go there. For some poems in the English literary heritage, the use of a place name has endowed those places with a particular layer of identity which is projected onto the place by the existence of the poem: East Coker, Adelstrop, Tintern Abbey for example. So many places names are startlingly resonant or lyrical in themselves: Emmonsail's Heath, Innisfree. Place and experience can become linked, and the nature of the place can assume an importance in the poem at the same time as the aural qualities can shine. In the pupils' poems, I would suggest that the names do have a strong lyrical/aural quality, but that there is also something special held in the pupils' choice of these names, their enjoyment of the names through their poem; if nothing else they make for striking and unusual first lines.

The details the pupils record are entirely their own. I had to resist a temptation to direct them to observe the thoughts of things I thought would be interesting. Perhaps there is a part of me that finds some of the observations not as revealing about a place as they could be; but that would be my view and not theirs. Their nail varnish stains and plasma balls are what they notice about their homes, and as such have a touching authenticity that would be lost if I controlled their view too much. There were some surprises – the classic Beatles LP cover noticed and valued by a 12-year-old boy, the precise detail of the name on the model boat. These observations of a house are quiet, domestic, precise but not outlandish – there is something about what the young people notice that presents their thoughts as realistic, lived experiences.

If running a similar exercise in most inner city environments, we might expect to see a wide geographical spread of places from which the pupils originally come. In these schools that are situated in counties with some of the lowest representation of non-white British populations, we might assume that there would be fewer places represented in a line about where 'we are from'. Nevertheless, the list of names the pupils presented shows that there has been a lot of movement, that the population is not static. Tim Cresswell notes that, 'What we are faced with now is a point in history when more people than ever are moving. Places are rarely purely vertical… they are also horizontal… produced by "elsewhere" as much as by "here"' (in Pollitt 2013).

A traditional view of rural life might be that there is considerable population stability; a potentially more dangerous view is that outsiders are different, and often not welcome. An aspect of one perception of rural identity is that some people may have a more accepted right to claim a sense of belonging than others. In popular culture such debates are reflected in terms such as 'townies' or 'offcomers'. There are very valid concerns about second home ownership in some rural areas, which is part of a wider social issue relating to affordable housing. A relatively recent report claimed that some rural locations are now places 'for the well off to enjoy at weekends' (National Housing Association 2010), suggesting that people who want or need to live and work in such places are effectively priced out of the market. There are extremely important and pressing concerns here, but it may be worth reflecting that it is sometimes deemed acceptable to claim that 'true' rural identity stems from working the land, ideally for generations. This notion of highly stable rural populations certainly does not seem reflected in these pupils' views of where they 'are from'; their perceptions are much less static. Certainly, no sense of exclusion of themselves or others comes through in their poems (nor did it in their wider discussions).

It is also worth noting here that, although no pupils who took part in this project had recently immigrated to the UK (and none had a different first language to English), pupils with diverse backgrounds are represented in rural schools (although naturally in lower numbers). A great deal of hospitality work, for example, in hotels in rural locations is carried out by people who are relatively new to the UK. It is not uncommon for children who know little English, and with different cultural backgrounds, to find themselves in a significant minority in a rural school (perhaps the only person of non-white British or non-British origin). There is also the issue of children in mono-cultural locations finding their place in and having an effective and positive understanding of multicultural Britain. Therefore, although the exploration of place in the pupils' poems presented here does not tackle these huge social and political issues head-on, they do in their own quiet way allow young people's experiences of life in a place to be expressed, and this is perhaps the beginning of a valid interrogation of ways in which we view place and identity.

Our view of our own place-based identity is, of course, sometimes with reference to our view of other places. In the pupils' poems they were invited to write about places to which they wanted to travel, and to imagine what they might like to see or experience there. This was partly to recognize the fact the writers of the poems are young, that they may be likely to have dreams or ideas of where they want to travel in their lives, and that many of them may indeed live in different places as they grow older. It is a commonly accepted fact that the world is smaller these days – that technology and travel options have allowed many people to experience more of the world than ever before. The pupils' sense of possibilities is vast, stretching as far as the moon. However, it is also more local: Liverpool features, directly next to Vatican City. The world presented to us in the poems seems both huge and tiny at the same time – we may dream of travelling to the border of America and Canada, then in almost the same breath we notice a teddy bear key-ring or a 'swivelly chair'. It is perhaps this expansion and compression of places that is a realistic reflection of the way we may hold thoughts about local contexts and the wider world in our head at the same time, just as we may hold thoughts about the past, present and future in any one moment of time.

Interestingly, one of the features of place-based identity that was a primary impetus for the project is arguably conspicuous by its absence in the poems. The fact the pupils are writing about rural locations does not particularly come through in the poems reproduced here (although there were some aspects we might associate with rural life that did feature to some extent in other poems – animals, farming equipment, fields, etc.). Far from being problematic, this in fact highlights a crucial aspect of the investigation: it was not the intention to direct pupils' gaze to explicitly rural features of place, but to let them note whatever they noticed about the places they move through daily. Most pupils tended to focus on their homes, rather than the wider area, which is perhaps understandable, and possibly reveals something about their identity in relation to place.

Work that had influenced my thinking about this project is from a team at Cambridge University, who have championed interdisciplinary research into place-based identity in school contexts (Charlton et al. 2011), and also exploring this specifically through reading and writing (Charlton et al. 2014). (These papers are highly recommended as excellent starting points for anyone interested in reading more about this issue.) Their research is also heavily influenced by the aforementioned work of Doreen Massey, in particular in relation to the way that space is seen as a 'bundle of trajectories' (2005: 12). (It should be noted here that the terms 'space' and 'place' have some variation within academic discourse, but for the purpose of this project, and given Massey's wider work on space and place, her use of 'space' is relevant here.) Massey's work acts as a crucial touchstone, reminding us that if we accept such plurality and the idea of trajectories rather than static positions, then 'people can no longer be homogenized, with some histories privileged over others or seen as being further ahead in a single queue' (Charlton et al. 2014: 156). They also found that children's literacy practices revealed fluid place-based identities, connected strongly to other places, 'dynamic and complex' (2014: 169). These findings chime with my own and reinforce what is perhaps my lasting impression of the project: the contrast between the clarity and in some ways innocent presentation of place in the work of the pupils, and the overwhelming complexity of social and political battles over place and identity at local, national and international levels. The low-key, quiet observations of place, presented simply and without too much adornment or analysis through poetry, is what makes the exploration of place-based identity so rich in potential.

The pupils' poems can either speak for themselves as snapshots of their responses to places around them, or can be seen as starting points for a wider discussion of place-based identities. There is a great deal more potential in this work, and the points discussed in this chapter are intended to raise questions rather than provide answers. I view the work done with these pupils as a starting point for further explorations of children and young people's place-based identities, in both urban and rural environments, and I would contend that work of this nature has benefits not only for pupils' creative expression, but for their growing understanding of their place in the world.

References

ATL (2014) Poverty and social exclusion in rural areas. Retrieved from www.atl.org.uk/policy-and-campaigns/policy-library/poverty-and-social-exclusion-in-rural-areas.asp.

Barnett, A. and Scruton, R. (1998) *Town and Country*. London: Johnathan Cape.

Charlton, E., Wyse, D., Cliff Hodges, G., Nikolajeva, M., Pointon, P. and Taylor, L. (2011) Place-related identities through texts: from interdisciplinary theory to research agenda. *British Journal of Educational Studies* 59(1), 63–74.

Charlton, E., Cliff Hodges, G., Pointon, P., Nikolajeva, M., Spring, E., Taylor, L. and Wyse, D. (2014) My place: exploring children's place-related identities through reading and writing. *Education 3–13* 42(2), 154–70.

Cresswell, T. (2004) *Place: A Short Introduction*. Oxford: Wiley Blackwell.

Dee, T. (2014) *Four Fields*. London: Vintage.

DEFRA (2015) Rural poverty. Retrieved from www.gov.uk/government/statistics/rural-poverty.

Farley, P. and Symmons Roberts, M. (2011) *Edgelands*. London: Jonathan Cape.

Fusek Peters, A. (1997) Last night, I saw the city breathing. In *The Moon is on the Microphone*. Sherbourne Press. Retrieved from http://childrenspoetryarchive.org/poem/last-night-i-saw-city-breathing.

Garton Ash, T. (2016) England can be true to itself, if liberals reclaim patriotism. *The Guardian*. Retrieved from www.theguardian.com/commentisfree/2016/apr/15/england-liberals-patriotism-nationalism-flag-st-george-right.

Gervais, D. (1993) *Literary Englands: Versions of Englishness in Modern Writing*. Cambridge: Cambridge University Press.

The Guardian (2015) Percentage of global population living in cities, by continent. Retrieved from www.theguardian.com/news/datablog/2009/aug/18/percentage-population-living-cities.

Hughes, T. (1967) *Poetry in the Making*. London: Faber and Faber.

Massey, D. (1994) *Space, Place and Gender*. Cambridge: Polity Press.

Massey, D. (2005) *For Space*. London: Sage.

Midgely, N. (2016) The explosion of countryside TB helping to treat our nature deficit disorder. *The Guardian*. Retrieved from www.theguardian.com/media/2016/mar/27/countryfile-bbc-nature-deficient-disorder.

National Housing Association (2010) *Home Truths Report*. Retrieved from www.housing.org.uk?page=52.

O'Brien, S. (2012) As deep as England. *Poetry Review* 102(1), 54–69.

Pollitt, M. (2013) Ozymandias has nothing on us. *Snipe.* Retrieved from http://snipelondon.com/metropolis/ozymandias-had-nothing-on-us-geographer-poet-tim-cresswell-talks-about-his-new-collection-soil.

Poverty Site (2014) Children in low-income households. Retrieved from http://www.poverty.org.uk/r16/index.shtml.

Sheers, O. (2008) Poetry and place, some personal reflections. *Geography* 93(3), 172–5.

Sprackland, J. (2013) *Strands: A Year of Discoveries on the Beach.* London: Vintage.

UK Parliament (2017). Rural tourism in England inquiry launched – news from Parliament. Retrieved from www.parliament.uk/business/committees/committees-a-z/commons-select/environment-food-and-rural-affairs-committee/news-parliament-2015/rural-tourism-inquiry-launch-16–17.

Williams, R. (1985) *The Country and the City.* London: Hogarth Press.

8

AN EXPLORATION OF IMMIGRANT-BACKGROUND CHILDREN'S IDENTITIES AND THEIR IDEAS OF PLACE IN RELATION TO THEIR GLOBAL IMAGINARIES AND LANGUAGES

Oakleigh Welply

This chapter examines the role of global representations in immigrant-background children's identities in two primary schools, one in France and one in England. It focuses in particular on the ways in which children's representations of space and place negotiated local, national and global imageries, which allowed them to transcend labels of 'Otherness' and construct new forms of intercultural engagement with peers. This chapter draws on research from a cross-national ethnographic study in primary schools in France and England, which investigated the identity narratives of 10- and 11-year-old immigrant-background children. Inspired by the work of Paul Ricoeur on social imaginary and ideology and utopia, this chapter shows how immigrant-background children's global imaginaries performed a utopian function, which allowed children to blur traditional lines of national, ethnic or linguistic differentiation in school. However, this utopian dimension played different roles in the French and English schools.

Until recently, and despite contradictions in definition, there was a general consensus around the idea that the world was becoming more global. A BBC poll published in April 2016 announced that 'global citizenship is rising' and that people around the world describe themselves as 'outward looking and internationally minded' (Grimley 2016). However, events in 2015–2016, ranging from the Paris attacks, to Brexit and the US election, strongly challenge the idea of a global sense of shared humanity (Latour 2016).

While views of the global have been widely discussed in relation to adult migrants, the views of immigrant children have been less examined (Arnot et al. 2013; Modood and Salt 2011; Tonkiss 2013). Most of the literature on children of immigrants insists on a duality between school culture and home culture (Archer and Francis 2007; Basit 2009; Youdell 2012), or the creation of oppositional sub-cultures (Youdell 2006). There are, however, fewer reflections of the way in which immigrant children engage with global representations (Ansell 2009; Blommaert 2011; Welply 2015). This chapter is interested in the way in which global represen-tations allowed children to challenge traditional categories of difference and con-struct new intercultural representations in school.

While globalization and the global have been popular concepts in the litera-ture in the past 20/30 years, there is no coherent conceptual definition of these terms (Appadurai 1996; Steger 2009; Delanty 2009; Kamola 2014; Rizvi 2008). This betrays conflicts of interpretation about the role of globalization, which are gener-ally articulated around a series of binary oppositions: local/global; homogenous/ heterogeneous; emancipatory/alienating; material/ideational (Beck 2004; Burns 2008). The ideational or symbolic aspect of globalization has gained an important place in discussions around the effects of globalization. Appadurai (1996) insists on the cultural and symbolic role of globalization, which allows citizens to imagine new, more fluid identities, across fixed categories. Banks (2016) argues that global-ization emphasizes diversity and connections, which helps imagine new affiliations and connections. Imagination takes on a strong meaning in relation to globalization, functioning as a social practice (Appadurai 1996). It confers agency to individuals and minoritized groups, allowing them to imagine new horizons and possibilities while developing new forms of interconnections with others, through 'narrative imagination' that fosters a sense of shared humanity through dialogue and conversa-tion (Nussbaum 1997; Appiah 2006).

This chapter builds on the social role of imagination to develop the concept of 'global imaginary'. Although it has not been widely used in the literature so far, this concept has roots in the concepts of social imaginary (Ricoeur 1984; Steger 2009; Taylor 2004) and cosmopolitanism (Delanty 2009; Nussbaum 2002). Here the theoretical premises of the concept global imaginary build on Paul Ricoeur's concepts of social imaginary and ideology and utopia (1986).

Social imaginary is defined as the 'range of stories and representations that societies possess' (Welply 2015). It is symbolic, and builds on collective narratives, which allow groups and individuals to build a common sense of belonging through mutual recognition. Social imaginary is underpinned by a dialectic between ideol-ogy and utopia, held together through imagination. Social imaginary is inscribed both in the integrative function of ideology and the subversive function of utopia (Ricoeur 1984:63). Ideology participates in the 'symbolic construction of social memory' (Ricoeur 1984), while utopia holds alternative and future horizons, new possibilities (Ricoeur 1984; Kearney 2004: 84). Through individual and collec-tive narratives, identities are inscribed within the wider culture, through symbolic representations.

In this chapter, the notion of global imaginary is underpinned by Ricoeur's concept of social imaginary. This emphasizes the role of narratives (individual and collective) in creating global imaginaries, which articulate both memory (past) and promise (future), with, at their heart, a dialectic between ideology and utopia. These narratives build on ideational and material representations of the global, the local and the national, across spaces and across times. The recognition of these multiple dimensions of global imaginaries helps overcome some of the dichotomies mentioned earlier in globalization theories.

Imagining the global: identity and citizenship

Imagination as a social practice is also central to conceptions of global or cosmopolitan citizenship, and to creating new ways of living in plural and mobile societies across different spaces and places. The work of Maxine Greene puts imagination at the core of dialogue in diverse or plural communities. For her, art and metaphor can extend existential possibilities and participate in the creation of new communities, through dialogue and conversation (Greene 1995). Imagination holds the potential to heal from the damage caused by silence and discrimination, by allowing people to engage with new perspectives from others. Imagination is, in this sense, transformative. It opens up new possibilities and alternative realities (Greene 1997). This is fundamental for children and young people to develop a belief in the potential of change, and reflect on their own narratives and experiences of race, gender, ethnicity; gaining in the process a stronger sense of agency (Greene 1997).

Imagination is also put forward as fundamental in conceptions of global or cosmopolitan citizenship. Nussbaum insists on the key role of 'narrative imagination' for 'cultivating humanity', by developing empathy with others and the capacity to reflect on one self (1997, 2002). Delanty (2009: 128) argues that cosmopolitan imagination allows people to emphasize common experiences, discourses, learning processes, and build a sense of belonging above national affiliations.

The concept of global imaginary and the social role of imagination offer a lens to understand the representations of immigrant children and the ways in which their narratives spawn across different spaces.

The research

Findings discussed in this chapter emerged from a wider cross-national ethnographic study which investigated the experiences of 10- and 11-year-old immigrant background children in primary schools in France and England. This study was premised on the idea that children are competent social actors, who can make sense of their own life narratives (James 2007; Qvortup et al. 2009). As such, the focus of the research was on listening to the voices of children themselves, recognizing that children's narratives can contribute to the understanding of wider social and political issues on a local and global scale (James 2007: 267; Ansell 2009).

This chapter focuses on the voices of immigrant-background children from two primary schools, one in France and one in England. Both schools were situated in average-size towns, in areas with a high proportion of social disadvantage and a significant proportion of immigrant population. The children were all aged between 10 and 11 years old, and were in their final year of primary school (CM2 in France, Year 6 in England). Children were from a range of immigrant backgrounds. They could all be classified as second-generation immigrants, being born in France or England with parents who had experienced migration from another country. All children were fully proficient in either French or English. The term 'second-generation' is problematic in many ways, not least because it assumes set categories that are rarely relevant to the multiple experiences of immigrant families. This term is thus not used as a unitary meaning, but functions as a starting point to explore the diversity of experiences of immigrant-background children.

Thirty-four children participated in the study, 17 in the French school and 17 in the English school. In the French school, 11 children self-defined as 'immigrant-background': six girls (one Laotian, one Hmong, one Indian, one Moroccan, one Algerian and one Turkish/French backgrounds) and five boys (one Laotian/Chinese, one Hmong, one Hmong/French, one Algerian and one French Réunion/Cambodian backgrounds). In the English school, 7 children out of 17 participants self-defined as 'immigrant-background': five girls (three Bangladeshi, one Russian and one Italian/English backgrounds) and two boys (one Bangladeshi and one Portuguese backgrounds). Children's parents' occupations could be defined as working class or lower professional (e.g., school cook, manual worker, lorry driver, cleaner, electrician, nursery worker, waiter) or unemployed. The researcher spent an extensive amount of time in each school (six months in the French school, four months in the English school). As a full-time participant, the researcher followed the same timetable as the children and participated in all activities. This helped build rapport with children participating in the research, by developing familiarity and trust.

Methods for this research were focused on finding ways to best listen to children's voices. To this effect, group and individual interviews were the main source of data collection. Interviews were adapted to primary-age children, integrating drawings and games to encourage children's involvement in the interview process. In addition to interviews, children were given diaries for a period of two weeks and were asked to write or draw about school. These diaries provided children with a different tool to talk about their experiences of school (Alaszewski 2006). In many cases, children found diaries to be a helpful way to talk about difference and Otherness, although they did tend to be preferred by children who enjoyed writing. The use of multiple methods did, however, allow children to use a range of forms of expression to talk about Otherness, articulating their own local experience with wider media and youth culture representations.

To ensure anonymity and confidentiality for all participants, names and identifying details have been changed. Particular attention was given to the specific ethical issues linked to carrying out research with young children (Hill 2005). Children were made aware of the issues associated to sharing information with a group during interviews. Group discussions were carefully monitored to avoid tensions or power imbalances that might emerge (Lewis 1992). The use of language was mapped to the children's understanding. Great care was given to creating an environment in which children would feel confident to share their views with their peers and the researcher.

All interviews were audio-recorded and transcribed. Data was coded thematically using a qualitative software package (NVivo). This chapter presents the themes related to children's global imaginaries and approaches to Otherness, examined in the next section.

Findings

In both the English and the French school, children's global imaginaries held a utopian function that allowed them to construct alternative representations of Otherness in school. These alternative representations challenged traditional ethnic, cultural and linguistic boundaries in children's identity narratives. In the French case, these narratives symbolically countered the dominant 'indifference to difference' approach in French schools, while in the English case, these narratives offered alternatives to stereotypes held by children's peers.

The French school: global imaginaries and belonging

In the French school, global imaginaries allowed children to reinterpret official school norms, in particular the French 'indifference to differences', which emphasizes pupils' public identity as citizens and leaves personal characteristics at the school gate (van Zanten 2000). This meant that in the French school, there was no mention of ethnic, cultural or linguistic differences in the classroom. In peer-group interactions, however, children reinterpreted these norms and redefined Otherness as a form of belonging, central to peer-group relations.

Belonging through Otherness

During interviews, most children held the view that Otherness was an important component of peer-group relationships in school. Children spoke extensively about the cross-cultural dimension of their friendships, which they articulated with reference to global imaginaries. The centrality of 'Otherness' in children's representations of peer-group relations was developed through narratives of 'intercultural connections', in an attempt to claim common belonging with others. Some of these narratives, examined elsewhere (Welply 2015) built on joint cultural creations between peers. In other cases, immigrant-background children developed a narrative of belonging that built on common identification in terms of religion or a geographical area. In other cases, non-immigrant children attempted to make connections to imagined forms of linguistic or cultural 'differences'.

Immigrant-background children developed narratives of belonging through 'sameness claims'. In some cases, these claims built on identifying peers as being of the same background (*'origine'*, a term that children used extensively to talk about identity), based on a broader view of a common geographical area of origin. These forms of identification built on global lines of pan-ethnic identification as *arabes*

(Arab) or *asiatiques* (Asian). This was the case for Ewen, Yannick, Benoît and Kenny. Ewen was of mixed Cambodian and Réunion background. Benoît was Hmong, Yannick was Hmong/French, and Kenny was Laotian/Chinese.

Although their family backgrounds were from different linguistic, cultural and geographical backgrounds, these four boys identified as being the 'same' as shown in Ewen's comment: 'Well yes, we don't really have any differences… Look Yannick, me, Benoît and Kenny… well, we are almost the same.'

This vision of common belonging built on the idea of coming from a similar geographical area, transcended fixed ethnic, linguistic or cultural categories and shows how forms of identification were multiple and shifting for these children. It was reinforced by claims of imagined family links, which reinforced the sense of common belonging. Ewen called his best friend Yannick his cousin: 'Yannick is my best friend, we feel like we are almost cousins.'

This form of common identification was not restricted to a feeling of common geographical background or '*origine*'. It also articulated symbolic references to wider global imaginaries, inscribed in youth culture and representations of global mobility. Three of the boys (Kenny, Ewen and Yannick) felt the US was an important country for them, as shown in Figures 8.1–8.3 (Welply 2015). The US was also where all four boys projected to live when they grew up. This imagined identification to the US was legitimized, in their view, through their active involvement in breakdancing outside school, which played a pivotal role in articulating local urban culture with global youth culture (Shapiro and Heinich 2012). Thus, in these boys' global imaginaries, their perceived Otherness as Asians ('*asiatiques*') in school was reimagined in their narratives through global identifications. This included the reference to the US, which occupied a higher global status, but also reference to other higher status languages. When asked what languages they spoke, Ewen, Yannick and Benoît all mentioned English (through breakdancing), Japanese (because they were fans of manga) and the language they spoke at home. This utopian function (Ricoeur)

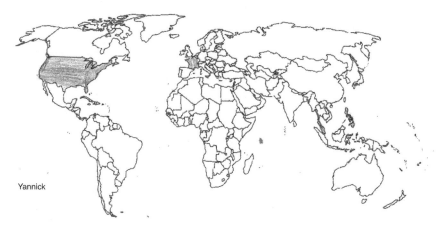

FIGURE 8.1 Yannick's map of 'important countries'

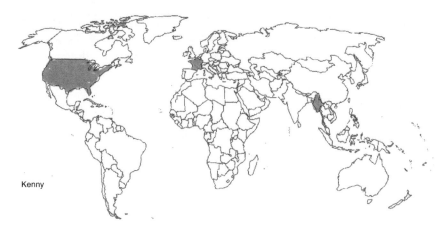

FIGURE 8.2 Kenny's map of 'important countries'

FIGURE 8.3 Ewen's map of 'important countries'

allowed the boys to transcend labels of Otherness built on traditional dichotomies between a dominant French school culture and their Other family culture, and allowed them to reimagine identities in which they presented themselves as global, cosmopolitan and multilingual citizens.

In the same vein, Clara, a girl of Indian background, spoke of living together in India with her best friend Ophélie, a non-immigrant child.

> Clara: but Ophélie, she's the worst it's not… she's a girl who wants to go live in India so much […] What does she say?… sometimes she sees houses, she says the two of us we are going to live in a house with your mother, my mother, we are both going to live there with my mother and my husband, your sons, and everything. She always says things like that. It seems like she does not want to miss me when I live in India.

Clara's narrative here carries what Ricoeur calls 'futural aspirations', an imagined life built on ideas of global mobility. Clara's friend, Ophélie, imagines living in India together in the future. In this symbolic representation, in the girls' global imaginary, India is given a desirable status, which helps transcends negative representations of Otherness that Clara felt was given to India by teachers in school. Earlier in the interview, Clara had mentioned the possible negative consequences of her speaking about Otherness with teachers, who might discriminate against her in the classroom. Thus, in her narrative, Clara constructs alternative symbolic representations of Otherness, which become central to her friendship with Ophélie.

Shared narratives

Another way of connecting with others took the form of telling stories about the linguistic and cultural 'differences' of peers during interviews. This showed a significant level of awareness of each other's cultures and languages and could be interpreted as a way of making connections and transcending differences.

This was illustrated by Ophélie and Britney, who participated in telling the story of Myriam, using the Arabic word '*ramallah*' (children's pronunciation of the word '*kmâra*' (donkey)) with the teacher in the classroom. Although Myriam was present during the interview, Ophélie and Britney were the ones to tell most of the story, in a collective narrative.

> Ophélie: [Myriam] spoke to the teacher in Arabic, she said 'You are silly like a ramallah'.
>
> *Interviewer: Oh really?*
>
> Britney/Marine: No! We had to say expressions, she wanted to say 'you are silly like a donkey'!
>
> *Interviewer: Oh really? So you said it like that! What did the teacher do?*
>
> Britney: He laughed.
>
> Myriam: He asked how to write it!
>
> *Interviewer: Actually, I wanted to ask you, are you allowed to speak other languages in school?*
>
> Ophélie: Yes, English!
>
> [...]
>
> *Interviewer: We already spoke about it with Myriam, but the others? For example when you said 'ramallah', how did the teacher react?*
>
> Britney: The teacher laughed, then he said, 'Yes, well I know how to write "silly like a ..." then I don't know'.

Imed's interjection about Yannick's languages, in the extract below, also illustrates these shared narratives. In doing so, Imed insisted on forms of common belonging between him and Yannick, through Yannick's connection to Algeria and Algerian language.

Yannick: In fact I speak three languages!

Imed: He speaks Algerian, Hmong and French.

Interviewer: Who?

Imed: Yannick! Because his mother is Algerian.

Yannick: It's my grandmother.

Telling the stories of others established a symbolic link between peers in relation to linguistic and cultural 'differences'. It shows that Otherness occupied a central place in peer-group relations and in children's social imaginaries, with the symbol of belonging as a central thread in these children's narratives.

Thus linguistic, religious and cultural differences were important in peer-group relations for immigrant-background children, not only through the creation of cross-cultural friendships, but also through forms of common identification, which built on notions of religious and ethnic belonging, claims of 'sameness' and, in some cases, family claims and telling the stories of others. These narratives drew on alternative sets of symbolic representations, which gave Otherness a high status among peers, constructing it as a form of belonging and as something towards which children aspired. Non-immigrant children also acknowledged this high status of Otherness in their narratives. Indeed, most non-immigrant children made links to Otherness by claiming they had another nationality or spoke another language.

In this utopian dimension, which offered an alternative set of symbols in which Otherness was central, children showed creative potential in filling the void left by the institutional silence around culture, language and religion in school. Forms of creation articulated global imaginaries, included joint futural aspirations about living in a different country, joint-language dialogue through singing, making connections to others through claims of 'foreignness', 'sameness' or 'family' and by telling stories about peers' 'origins'. However, these forms of creation, alternative sets of symbols and reversal of norms, were not developed in a void. Children's representations drew on the youth culture of the urban fringe and global youth culture.

Global, national and local

Children's alternative representations of Otherness in peer-group relations drew on cultural representations outside the school sphere at local, national and global levels.

The central place of Otherness in children's representations of peer-group relations reflected, to some extent, the multiethnic cultural and linguistic practices in the *banlieues* (peripheral urban areas in French cities, also referred to as *cités*) (Boubeker 2003), in which diversity represents the 'imaginative norm' (Hatzfeld 2006: 20). Many aspects of children's forms of sociability and interactions in the French school reflected the wider local urban culture, which they experienced outside school. This was apparent in children's form of speech, with its use of *verlan* (reversed speech) and words borrowed from different languages, in particular Arabic and Roma, which is characteristic of the *langage des cités* (language of the peripheral urban areas) defined as a *parler vehiculaire interethnique* (interethnic form of speech) (Begag 1997; Baillet 2001; Trimaille and Billiez 2007). Children built on this form of interethnic speech or 'language crossing' (Rampton 1995) to construct inter-cultural representations in which Otherness was central to belonging in informal school spaces, as shown in Imed's comments below.

(1) Imed: Yes, languages are different, but also it doesn't bother me, I'm used to it. I put French words in my 'rebeu' [Arabic] sentences, 'rebeu' [Arabic] words in my French sentences.
(2) Imed: They [other children] also like Arabic, sometimes they put Arabic in what they say.

Imed's description of the multilingual aspect of the *langage des cités* carries a posi-tive construction of the place of 'difference' in peer-group relations, building on the idea that children use Arabic words because they like Arabic. This shows how children's representations of other languages are inscribed in a wider representation of the place of 'Otherness' in urban youth cultural and linguistic practices.

Children's social imaginary about peer relations thus stretched beyond the school gates and drew on experiences in and representations of the local urban periphery, and on forms of youth culture within that space. These common representations and the proximity of living defined a common identity, through a sense of local place and belonging in which 'differences' were constructed as the norm.

Children experienced this urban culture both at a local level through immedi-ate experience with these practices and through media representation at a national level, as cultural and linguistic practices have been relayed extensively in national culture through their use in television shows, the multiplication of dictionaries on the *parler jeune* (youth talk) and in the use of multiethnic urban linguistic practices in other public areas (Dortier 2005).

Although the above points to ways in which informal school spaces have been 'colonized' by local and national urban youth culture (van Zanten 2000: 319), chil-dren's representations of cultural and linguistic practices cannot be reduced to a direct transposition of the cultural and linguistic practices of the *banlieue*. Children's comments also showed that their representations of 'Otherness' in informal spaces were specific to school, and were constructed differently from what they experi-enced outside school, in their local urban environment.

Children voiced a symbolic separation between an intercultural experience inside school and segregation outside school. From children's narratives, peer group relations outside school also appeared to be more ethnicized. Thus, although chil-dren's view of the place of Otherness in school built on symbolic multiethnic and multilingual dimensions of local urban youth culture, school provided a more inter-cultural experience for children, in which Otherness was constructed as 'belonging' and allowed cross-cultural friendships and interactions to develop in ways that they did not experience outside school. This points to the specificity of the school space in children's experience of Otherness, although it is inscribed in wider cultural practices and positioning within a socially disadvantaged urban periphery.

These forms of imagined global mobility and forms of common belonging gave children the capacity to symbolically challenge global hierarchies in their narratives. Global imaginaries were central to these redefinition of norms. Children's global imaginaries encompassed both their country and culture 'of origin', and other countries that they knew essentially through youth culture and media. This reflects the symbolic spatial and geographical variety that influences the local urban culture (Boubeker 2003; Hatzfeld 2006).

In the French school, children's representations of the place of language and culture in peer-group relations in school built on multiple spaces. Children's global imaginaries were located at the intersection the local (*culture du quartier*, family identifications), the national (French 'national' urban youth culture) and the global (global youth culture, forms of global geographical belonging or future aspirations). These participated in creating new forms of interculturality, which strongly contrasted with the 'indifference to difference' approach in French schools.

These different spaces were mutually constitutive of one another, and all participated in created alternative, imagined representations of Otherness for children. These 'imaginative variations' (Ricoeur 1986) show how children's lives are defined not only by their immediate local experiences but also by wider global representations (Ansell 2009; Katz 2004).

The English school: global points of imaginary encounters

The English school was marked by a contrast between the school's strong multicultural ethos and the way in which Otherness was constructed in peer-group relations. Most children saw Otherness as problematic between peers, and a justification for separation. Non-immigrant children felt that children were friends based on skin colour and religion, while immigrant-background children expressed unease at speaking about Otherness, in particular language and religion, which they felt created tension and at times projected a bad image towards non-immigrant peers.

As such, in the English school, Otherness occupied a very different place to the place it held among peers in the French school. Conversely, immigrant-background children's global imaginaries seemed to reflect these lines of division around Otherness and only included children who were also viewed as Other in school.

Although most children in the English case expressed the idea that discussions around differences were limited among peers and constructed lines of separation around Otherness, some of the children's symbolic representations countered this view. This took the form of 'points of imaginary encounter'. These imaginary projections built on immigrant-background children's 'futural aspirations' (Ricoeur 1986; Kearney 2004: 85) and the idea that children wanted to live in a different country later on because of their friends. Saalima, a girl of Bangladeshi background, wanted to live in Spain because of a Spanish friend who had moved back there; Akhil, a boy of Bangladeshi background, wanted to live in Russia, which he had heard about from Anna, a girl of Russian background. Andre, a boy of

Angolan/Portuguese background, wanted to live in Germany because of a friend from his previous school, and offers the best example of these forms of rearticulation (Welply 2015).

> *Interviewer: And where would you like to live later on?*
>
> Andre: I've got loads.
>
> *Interviewer: Really?*
>
> Andre: Um.
>
> […]
>
> Andre: New York.
>
> *Interviewer: New York, wow, why is that?*
>
> Andre: Um, I just like America and… my friend has been there […] and California.
>
> *Interviewer: Yeah.*
>
> Andre: And London… I have a friend… I don't know what school; it's somewhere in London. […] New York, California, hmmm… Washington […] Yeah, and Paris… and I think Belgium; it's in Germany.
>
> *Interviewer: Belgium is next to Germany, yeah. It's a separate country.*
>
> Andre: Berlin.
>
> *Interviewer: Oh yeah. Have you been to Berlin?*
>
> Andre: No, I have a friend […] who is from Germany.
>
> *Interviewer: Really?*
>
> Andre: He lived near Berlin.

Andre's global imaginary builds on intercultural friendships. These representations allow Andre to position himself as a globally mobile citizen, but not of one who could live anywhere he chooses. Rather, him having friends from different countries confers on him a new legitimacy in the way he defines himself: his global imaginary builds on knowing people from different places. These imagined forms of belonging through Otherness allowed children to transcend essentialist and stereotypical labels of themselves as 'Others' to construct identity narratives of cosmopolitan citizens, which stood in contrast to non-immigrant children who projected to live in England. These forms of global connecting built on 'imaginative variations' of the global (Ricoeur 1986), and positioned children as 'cosmopolitan citizens' (Delanty 2009). These projections constituted 'imaginary points of encounter' inscribed in global imaginary, and enabled the children to identify as cosmopolitans. This enabled them to symbolically transcend fixed essentialist labels that were applied to them by peers, by negotiating their perceived 'difference' with global representations. Andre, Saalima and Anna's maps (Figures 8.4–8.6) illustrate this global imaginary as a 'cosmopolitan citizen'.

Finally, for Muslim children, religious identification also drew on global representations: all Muslim children mentioned Mecca, and Taahira in a group interview

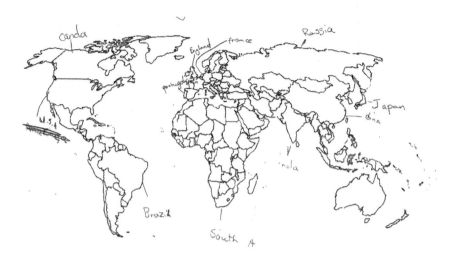

FIGURE 8.4 Andre's map of 'important countries'

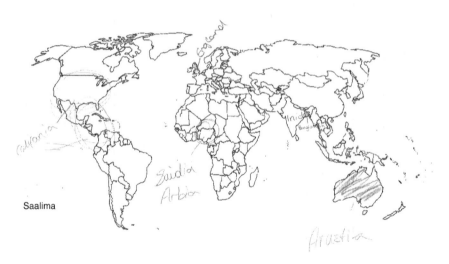

FIGURE 8.5 Saalima's map of 'important countries'

insisted on listing other Muslim countries. This reflects forms of transnational identification with the *Ummah* (Shain 2011). In their maps, Saalima (Figure 8.5), Nabeela and Taahira (Figures 8.7 and 8.8) also insisted on the importance of Saudi Arabia.

These global projections draw attention to how children articulate 'Otherness' in relation to the global and the local. The local tended to confirm the construction of 'Otherness' as separation since immigrant-background and non-immigrant children lived in different areas and did not see each other outside school, whereas future projections drew on forms of global imaginary to create representations of 'Otherness' as cosmopolitanism and belonging to the world, rather than separation

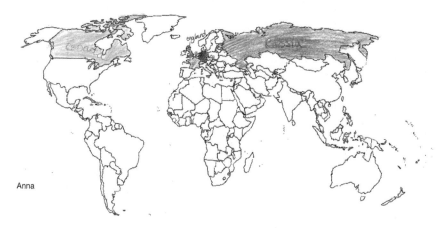

FIGURE 8.6 Anna's map of 'important countries'

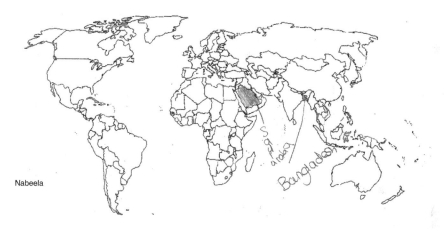

FIGURE 8.7 Nabeela's map of 'important countries'

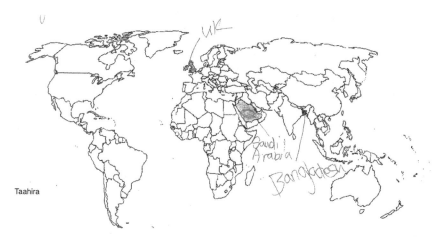

FIGURE 8.8 Taahira's map of 'important countries'

and exclusion (Delanty 2009; Nussbaum 2002). As such, in the English school, although they were less widespread, children's global imaginaries also performed a utopian function (Ricoeur 1984) that enabled immigrant-background children to transcend the fixed and stereotypical labels that were applied to them by peers.

Global imaginaries: a utopian function?

This chapter has shown how global imaginaries performed a utopian function for immigrant-background children. Although they were articulated in different ways, in both the French and the English school, children constructed alternative symbolic representations of Otherness through reference to the global. This allowed them to transcend binary lines of division in their identity narratives, which showed multiple and fluid forms of identification, where children were no longer the 'Other' within a dominant culture but reinvented themselves as global or cosmopolitan citizens (Delanty 2009; Nussbaum 2002). In the French school, this allowed children to find alternatives to the 'indifference to difference' approach, while in the English case it allowed children to move away from stereotypes given by peers.

By creating alternative intercultural symbols, children's global imaginaries performed a utopian function that challenged dominant ideologies. However, this emancipatory function should not be viewed in a simplistic way. While these imaginaries opened children to the possibility of an elsewhere, one should be cautious of not falling into what Berlant terms 'cruel optimism' (2011). Children in this research lived in conditions of social deprivation that might not afford them the global mobility they imagined. However, Ricoeur's dialectic of ideology and utopia helps us move beyond a dichotomous view of emancipatory or alienating imaginaries, by viewing them as mutually constitutive. Children's global imaginaries held both creative and restrictive possibilities. These new understandings of Otherness for immigrant-background children can help schools reflect on approaches to difference and the role of the global.

Conclusion

This chapter has examined the ways in which immigrant-background children's global imaginaries allowed them to construct alternative representations of Otherness in their identity narratives. In both the French and the English schools, children's global imaginaries performed a utopian function that participated in blurring lines of separation and Othering experienced by immigrant-background children. This offers new insights into the relationship between local and global spaces in the lived-experiences of immigrant-background children. It has shed light on the limitations of viewing children's identities through binary categories (home/school culture; local/global experiences) and stressed the fluidity and multiplicity of children's experiences and forms of identification. This chapter has offered theoretical insights into the concept of global imaginary, based on the work of Paul Ricoeur (1984, 1986) and its potential for looking at identities across place and space. It has shown the ways in which the imagination plays a social role that can help engage with diversity at different levels (global, national, local) (Greene 1997; Nussbaum 2002; Delanty 2009; Appiah 2006).

This chapter offers a new perspective on the way in which schools can approach diversity and Otherness. This is particularly important at a time when a belief in an interconnected world and shared humanity is being strongly challenged in a climate of distrust of the 'immigrant Other'. Schools need to find new ways to engage with concepts of Otherness and globalization, and challenge responses to political and media fear-mongering that has participated in reinforcing divisions in society. The notion of global imaginaries can offer ways of rethinking Otherness and nurturing common belonging rather than separation. This chapter suggests that engaging with children's own global imaginaries can offer new ways for schools and practitioners to challenge stereotypical representations of Otherness and build a more integrated approach to the inclusion of children from diverse linguistic, religious, ethnic and national backgrounds. Global imaginaries can offer schools creative solutions to reflect on new forms of diversity. They can also provide opportunities to get children to develop a more critical approach to the global, reflecting on, for example, the more alienating effects of global consumerism and the empowering potential of intercultural understanding and global citizenship.

At a time of political and social uncertainty, children's global imaginaries offer what Hannah Arendt referred to as 'illumination in dark times', a flicker of hope, the reaffirmation of small truths, as in the words of Clara:

> Everyone... for example, Kenny, he is not different from others... he's a human, isn't he? We are all humans, we are not different.

This chapter was adapted from an earlier article

Welply, O. (2015) Re-Imagining otherness: an exploration of the global imaginaries of children from immigrant backgrounds in primary schools in France and England. *European Educational Research Journal* 14(5), 430–53.

References

Alaszewski, A. (2006) *Using Diaries for Social Research*. London: Sage.
Ansell, N. (2009) Childhood and the politics of scale: Descaling children's geographies? *Progress in Human Geography* 33(2), 190–209.
Appadurai, A. (1996) *Modernity at Large: Cultural Dimensions of Globalization*. Minneapolis, MN: University of Minnesota Press.
Appiah, K. (2006) *Cosmopolitanism: Ethics in a World of Strangers*. New York: W.W. Norton.
Archer, L. and Francis, B. (2007) *Understanding Minority Ethnic Achievement: Race, Gender, Class and Success*. Abingdon: Routledge.
Arnot, M., Schneider, C. and Welply, O. (2013) Education, mobilities and migration: people, ideas and resources. *Compare: A Journal of Comparative and International Education* 43(5): 567–79.

Baillet, D. (2001). La 'langue des banlieues' entre Appauvrissement Culturel et Exclusion Sociale. *Hommes et migrations* 1231: 29–37.

Banks, J. (2016) *Global Migration, Diversity, and Civic Education: Improving Policy and Practice.* New York: Teacher's College Press.

Basit, T. (2009) White British; dual heritage; British Muslim: young Britons' conceptualisation of identity and citizenship. *British Educational Research Journal* 35(5): 723–43.

Beck, U. (2004) Cosmopolitical realism: on the distinction between cosmopolitanism in philosophy and the social sciences. *Global Networks* 4(2): 131–56.

Begag, A. (1997) Trafic de mots en banlieue: du 'nique ta mère' au 'plaît-il'? *Migrants Formation* 108: 30–7.

Berlant, L. (2011) *Cruel Optimism.* Durham, NC: Duke University Press.

Blommaert, J. (2011) *Sociolinguistics of Globalization.* Cambridge: Cambridge University Press.

Boubeker, A. (2003) Ethnicité, relations interethniques ou ethnicisation des relations sociales. *Les champs de la recherche en France. Ville-Ecole-Intégration Enjeux* 135, 40–50.

Burns, K. (2008) (Re)imagining the global, rethinking gender in education. *Discourse: Studies in the Cultural Politics of Education* 29(3): 343–357.

Delanty, G. (2009) *The Cosmopolitan Imagination: The Renewal of Critical Social Theory.* Cambridge: Cambridge University Press.

Dortier, F. (2005) Tu flippes ta race, bâtard! *Sciences Humaines* 4(159), 27.

Greene, M. (1995) *Releasing the Imagination: Essay on Education, the Arts and Social Change.* San Francisco, CA: Jossey-Bass.

Greene, M. (1997) Teaching as possibility: a light in dark times. *The Journal of Pedagogy, Pluralism & Practice* 1(1), 1–11.

Grimley, N. (2016) Identity 2016: 'Global citizenship' rising, poll suggests. BBC. Retrieved from www.bbc.co.uk/news/world-36139904.

Hatzfeld, M. (2006) *La Culture Des Cités; Une Énergie Positive.* Paris: Autrement.

Hill, M. (2005) Ethical considerations in researching children's experiences. In S. Greene and D. Hogan (eds.) *Researching Children's Experience: Approaches and Methods*, pp.61–86. London: Sage.

James, A. (2007) Giving voice to children's voices: practices and problems, pitfalls and potentials. *American Anthropologist* 109(2), 261–72.

Kamola, I. (2014) US universities and the production of the global imaginary. *British Journal of Politics and International Relations* 16(3), 515–33.

Katz, C. (2004) *Growing up Global: Economic Restructuring in Children's Everyday Lives.* Minneapolis, MN: University of Minnesota Press.

Kearney, R. (2004) *On Paul Ricoeur: The Owl of Minerva.* Aldershot: Ashgate.

Latour, B. (2016) Entre globalises et passeistes, le match reste nul. *Le Monde*, 12 November. Retrieved from www.lemonde.fr/elections-americaines/article/2016/11/12/entre-globalises-et-passeistes-le-match-reste-nul_5030081_829254.html.

Lewis, A. (1992) Group child interviews as a research tool. *British Educational Research Journal* 18(4), 413–21.

Modood, T. and Salt, J. (2011) *Global Migration, Ethnicity and Citizenship.* Basingstoke: Palgrave Macmillan.

Nussbaum, M. (1997) *Cultivating Humanity: A Classical Defense of Reform in Liberal Education.* Cambridge, MA: Harvard University Press.

Nussbaum, M. (2002) Education for citizenship in an era of global connection. *Studies in Philosophy and Education* 21(4/5): 289–303.

Qvortup, J., Corsaro, W. and Honig, M. (eds.) (2009) *The Palgrave Handbook of Childhood Studies.* Basingstoke: Palgrave Macmillan.

Rampton, B. (1995) *Crossing: Language and Ethnicity among Adolescents*. London: Longman.

Ricoeur, P. (1984) L'idéologie et l'utopie: Deux expressions de l'imaginaire social. Autres Temps. *Les Cahiers du Christianisme Social* 2, 53–64.

Ricoeur, P. (1986) *Lectures on Ideology and Utopia*. New York: Columbia University Press.

Ricoeur, P. (1990) *Soi-Même comme un Autre*. Paris: Seuil.

Rizvi, F. (2008) *Youth Moves: Identities and Education in Global Perspective*. London: Routledge.

Shain, F. (2011). *The New Folk Devils: Muslim Boys and Education in England*. Stoke-on-Trent: Trentham Books.

Shapiro, R. and Heinich, N. (2012) When is artification? *Contemporary Aesthetics* 4. Retrieved from www.contempacsthetics.org/newvolume/pages/article.php?articleID=639.

Steger, M. (2009) *The Rise of the Global Imaginary: Political Ideologies from the French Revolution to the Global War on Terror*. New York: Oxford University Press.

Taylor, C. (2004) *Modern Social Imaginaries*. Durham, NC: Duke University Press.

Tonkiss, K. (2013) *Migration and Identity in a Post-National World*. Basingstoke: Palgrave Macmillan.

Trimaille, C. and Billiez, J. (2007). Pratiques langagières de jeunes urbains: peut-on parler de 'parler'? In C. Molinari and E. Galazzi (eds.), *Les Français en Émergence*, 95–109. Bern: Peter Lang.

van Zanten, A. (2000) L'École de la Périphérie. Scolarité et Ségrégation en Banlieue. Paris: Presses Universitaires de France.

Youdell, D. (2006) *Impossible Bodies, Impossible Selves: Exclusions and Student Subjectivities*. Dordrecht: Springer.

Youdell, D. (2012) Intelligibility, agency and the race-nationed-religioned subjects of education. In K. Bhopal and J. Preston (eds.) *Intersectionality and 'Race' in Education*. Abingdon: Routledge.

Welply, O. (2015) Re-imagining Otherness: an exploration of the global imaginaries of children from immigrant backgrounds in primary schools in France and England. *European Educational Research Journal* 14(5), 430–53.

9

NEGOTIATING 'THIRD SPACE' THROUGH POPULAR CHILDREN'S LITERATURE

Creating democratic spaces

Sarah Pfenninger

In this chapter, I aim to present the literacy practices that emerged in an in-school, extra-curricular book club (McMahon et al. 1997) centred around the popular children's books by British author Jacqueline Wilson. My first experience with Jacqueline Wilson's work began as a result of finding a simple solution to a complex problem. The problem seemed to be one of an age-old dilemma: how does one get reluctant or non-readers interested in reading? In one of my first experiences in a UK English classroom this problem presented itself in a very unsettling manner. All names have been anonymised. As 60 children sat pin-straight via rows in a large room filled with various adults circulating, I observed as each child in Year 7 (aged 11–12) was asked to pull out their reading books and 'get cracking'. Out of these 60 children, only half of them were actually reading. As the register was being loudly called by one teacher, the others could be seen patrolling the room and handing out random books from a box simultaneously with demerits to the children who did not take part in the silent reading, but chose rather to giggle, send text messages to each other and generally engage in off-task behaviour. My heart leapt. As a reading teacher, one of my passions is to instil a lifelong love of reading. Love was barely evident in this regimented classroom. Where were the teachers modelling reading? Where were the comfortable reading spaces? Where were the groups of children reading together? Where were the delighted expressions and surprised reactions? Where were the signs that this was a classroom that embraced reading and found it to be an enjoyable activity? To the contrary, this part of English class was looked upon by teachers, and students alike, as a punitive measure, a crowd-control manoeuvre, if you will. One child who really caught my attention that morning was a young African Caribbean girl called Nina. As the teacher approached her to give her yet another demerit for not having her reading book in class, she stood up and protested! In a power struggle with the teacher, she was reduced to tears and stormed out of the room. As an adult in the classroom, I followed up with Nina. As tears streamed down her face, she tried to answer my question, which was simply, 'Why is it that you don't have a reading book for class?' Her answer moved me. 'I don't have any books at home and I don't know how to get any.' I quickly decided that it was time for this girl to experience reading, and English class seemed to be a very appropriate place to begin. I walked with her to the school library, which she had never entered before. After briefly assessing what her interests were, I gained the knowledge that she enjoyed books about families and relationships. The realistic fiction genre seemed a worthy place to begin, and although, as an American teacher, I was new to British schooling, I had seen many children proudly carrying Wilson's books around school, and so I gently guided Nina to the Jacqueline Wilson section. We read the book jackets and reviews, and she ended up with 'Candy Floss'. By the end of that week, she proudly came up to me and proclaimed, 'Miss! I finished the book!' That one book soon turned to two, and before long, Nina began voraciously reading many of Wilson's books, each time proudly sharing when she finished. The sense of accomplishment was real, but more importantly, Jacqueline Wilson's books allowed this child to break free of her stored notions of what reading meant, so that she could engage in the literate world of reading, free from punishment.

The power of choice

In the above scenario, the young reader felt lost, and confused as to where to begin her reading journey. Initially, reading was something that was 'done' to her, and not something that she could internalize and make her own. The punitive environment of her English classroom valued compliance over autonomy, and spaces were not created for the children to explore their reading identities. Part of the issue for children across the globe is the lack of choice present in the English curriculum. So much of what is offered lies within the traditional canon of literature (Applebee 1996) and does not present varied opportunities for children to explore their own interests relevant to modern-day living. It is invariably necessary that as educators, we begin to put value on the experiences that children not only have but that they can bring to the reading of children's literature. Andrew Goodwyn (2012) argues that literature with a 'capital L' is often a remnant of our imperialistic past, putting undue emphasis on texts with 'great worth', many times at the exclusion of readers who do not yet exhibit the habits of mind (Dewey 1997) that good readers already have as cultural capital. So, how then can we encourage all readers to develop habits of mind that will allow them to fully engage in the dialogic pedagogy of the English classroom? The International Literacy Association, in conjunction with the Canadian Children's Book Centre and the National Council of Teachers of English, have developed a position statement on leisure reading that addresses these concerns. They define leisure reading as an independent venture, that is voluntary in nature and guided by a self-selection process. While leisure reading can be done outside the home, it can also be accounted for in the formal classroom, as attempted in the above-illustrated scenario of the young Caribbean pupil. When done formally in school, 'Free Voluntary Reading' (Krashen 2004) is used to describe two types of reading, (1) Self-Selected-Reading, characterized by accountability measures and (2) Sustained-Silent-Reading, which offers no follow-up accountability, but allows for a natural exploration and immersion into reading experiences. The third space, as illustrated in this paper, blends both the self-selected reading at home with the community follow-up of the third space of peer dialogue at school. In all cases, however, successful implementation of an SSR programme entails the following eight elements, according to Pilgreen (2000): access, appeal, conducive environment, encouragement, staff training, non-accountability, follow-up activities, distributed time to read. One of the most noteworthy elements of this success formula is the appeal factor. Pilgreen found that nearly 78 per cent of all successful SSR programmes were predicated on books that will indeed appeal to children, which she defines as 'reading materials [that] are sufficiently inter-esting and provocative enough for students to want to read them' (2000: 9). The following will discuss the merits of popular fiction as an appeal factor for young children during leisure reading.

Popular fiction in the United Kingdom landscape

There is no doubt that Wilson's books are a provocative genre for young readers, holding universal appeal across the United Kingdom. Jacqueline Wilson is argu-ably the pre-eminent children's author for popular fiction, garnering such coveted accolades as the Smarties Prize and the Guardian Children's Fiction Award. Janet Evans (2005) has listed Wilson's books under most popular 'other' books as chil-dren's out-of-school and home interests for 10- and 11-year-old readers. Similarly, Cremin and colleagues (2008) found that when pre-service teachers were asked to list six 'good' writers for primary-aged children, 64 per cent named Wilson. With these staggering statistics, it is not surprising that Wilson has earned a remarkable place in British popular culture, making her one of the most borrowed authors in UK libraries.

The phenomenon of Wilson's empire is hardly unique, however. It is virtually impossible to find a young tween or adolescent today who has not come across 'Team Edward' or 'Team Cullen' at some point in the early twenty-first century. As I consider this research, I can't help being inundated by the *Twilight* series (written by Stephenie Meyer between 2005 and 2008) wherever I go. *Twilight* consumption occurs through a vast array of products that does not stop at the bookshelves, but carry well into the popular culture arena, to include social networking sites, film and media. This notion of consumption, Wolhwend (2009) argues, not only impacts teen readers, but also can start as early as kindergarten through the media images associated with book adaptations.

While *Twilight* may be a more recent literary trend among adolescent readers, it surely isn't the first. Each decade brings various series books such as *Anne of Green Gables, Nancy Drew, Hardy Boys, Babysitters Club, Junie B. Jones* and *Goosebumps* to allure primary school readers, causing some female readers in the case of L.M. Montgomery's series to 'read and re-read, generation after generation...

works have earned not only devotion, but international popularity and successful film and merchandising industries' (Miller 2010). The voracious reading of these texts and consumption of media and popular culture are largely what has taken shape among primary-aged readers in the United Kingdom with the Jacqueline Wilson series.

Often housed in the realistic fiction and modern fantasy genres, series books have not often been considered 'high-quality' literature in the eyes of teachers, librarians and the wider literary community, yet offer young readers very compelling and fruitful opportunities to engage with books in order to help build fluency and stamina, and eventually move on to different forms of literature (Kiefer and Tyson 2010) in addition to providing a solid framework for pleasure reading (Reid 1997). As children engage with texts, there is a constant interaction between the reader and text, causing a transaction that allows for the reader's experiences to be elevated to the reading, thus creating a more personal construction (Rosenblatt 1968). As a subset of realistic fiction and modern fantasy, series books have a rich history for describing the everyday struggle and experiences of young children, which make engaging with these texts viable for all readers and ability levels.

Reading researchers argue for the use of student choice in books as a part of the larger reading programme (Atwell 1998; Calkins 2000; Collins 2004), yet despite this, series and popular books still largely remain stigmatized in the formal classroom community. Some academic attention has been paid to early twentieth-century popular series books including the *Nancy Drew* books and *P.L. Travers' Mary Poppins* (Valverde 2009) and book series from the 1980s and 1990s such as the *Babysitters Club*, *Sweet Valley High* and *Goosebumps* (Mackey 1990; Lehr 2001; Dutro 2001) However, apart from the research on J.K. Rowling's *Harry Potter* series (Lehr 2001; Cherland 2008; Black 2003), there is a dearth of empirical studies dedicated to the systematic study of how contemporary children negotiate series literature in the twenty-first century, particularly outside the North American field of children's authors. This study aims to fill this gap in the literature.

The research questions

At the beginning of the twenty-first century, Jerry Harste (2003), in his piece 'What Do We Mean by Literacy Now?' challenged reading and language arts educators to thoughtfully consider how literacy is defined and honoured in classrooms across American schools, stating, 'literacy in the 21st century is not a spectator sport' (2003: 10). He argues that in order for a literacy curriculum to be rich, moving beyond the notion of children either 'having' or 'not having' literacy, teachers can and should create classrooms to support the social practices of the home literacies that children bring with them to the formal school environment. So, over a decade later, how are spaces of literacy created within the formal school environment that support the cultural and social practices that young children bring to the table in order to discover what Harste (2003: 9) calls 'new conversations'? In order to consider this, I present the ways in which one group of Year 6 pupils in Manchester, England critically negotiated and talked about popular fiction texts that they read outside school and what social practices ensued during this engagement. To explore this, the following research questions guided my inquiry:

1. How do students bring their lived experiences to the reading of popular fiction within a lunch-time book club during the formal school day?
2. In what ways, if any, can the 'third space' and popular series fiction books pro-mote critical literacy, specifically as it relates to life in the twenty-first century?

Popular fiction as third space

In an ever-changing political landscape of the United Kingdom, policies such as Every Child Matters can often lead to curriculum dichotomies that favour more traditional pedagogies and ways of viewing language and literacy. Although the UK has a broad and wide-reaching National Curriculum to provide a spectrum of literacy learning, government policies can often lead to a perceived stifled literacy programme with little room for negotiation. The current climate in the primary schools leans toward a skill-based approach to literacy, with a focus on a discrete and systematic approach to phonics instruction, throughout the Key Stages. These reduced spaces of literacy learning often value what Dyson (2003: 5) refers to as 'comfortable, tidy images of children on the literacy path (e.g. experiences with books, knowledge of letters)' often honouring a single and limited homogenized standard (Siegel and Lukas 2008). In order to move into deeper and richer lit-eracy connections, the concept of 'third space' emerges in order to bridge the gap between the official school space and the 'unofficial' cultural arena from their home. When these worlds collide, a third space is created causing not a compromise, but rather a new theoretical and pedagogical space where learning is valued over teach-ing and agency among students is created (Gutiérrez et al. 1997).

My intent for this research is not to debate the merits of the quality of writing of this genre, as it is often one of the largest critiques of popular fiction, but to encour-age the possibilities of what literacy learning and shifts might occur while children participate in these popular culture text spaces outside school.

The book club

Data for this qualitative case study-design (Creswell 2013) were collected over an 11-month academic year at an independent international school in greater Manchester. There were six pupil participants in total, to include three girls and three boys. Nationalities included children of Australian (one pupil), American (one pupil, one participant observer), Indian (one pupil), and English (three pupils) backgrounds. All of the children were in Year 6. Data consisted primarily of focus group interviews, following Raphael's Book Club method, with scaffolded semi-structured interview questions (Glesne and Peshkin 1992). Serving as a participant observer, the children and I met weekly for an hour during their designated lunch and break time. We read the Jacqueline Wilson *Tracy Beaker* series of books, but also connected to the full range of Wilson's work. The children had read each of the books prior to our session, so that the entire hour was devoted to peer dialogue. Findings from this study show that the students moved between literacy spaces of three main themes as they repositioned and considered themselves within the landscape of popular fiction. These texts impacted student's literacy practices by creating literate and social identities through the following: negotiating spaces of gender; mentor texts and curriculum connections; and lived experiences and negotiated realities. What follows is an expansion of each theme as it relates to their literacy engagement with popular fiction.

'Private book for girls': negotiating spaces of gender

In considering the challenges of the twenty-first-century literacy classroom, gender negotiations still permeate the landscape, and can sometimes become convoluted spaces in which to consider identities. For the purposes of this chapter, my theoretical perspective lies in critical literacy, and I follow Vivian Vazquez's (2004) stance of viewing texts through a lens that allows for seeing writing and images from different ways or perspectives in order to look for possibilities for change. Through this view, we make assumptions that 'literacy is never neutral' (Evans 2005) and is a space that requires careful consideration and dialogue.

Although this informal 'Jacqueline Wilson book club' took place during the formal school day, which I will consider the third space, a very large percentage of the time devoted to thinking deeply about these texts occurred during the second space, at home and in the community. As previously stated, the coverage, quantity and accessibility of these texts runs deep throughout the United Kingdom, yet unfortunately has been turned into an iconic brand quite frequently marketed towards girls. Despite Wilson's light-hearted writing approach to very deep and serious topics such as poverty, single parents, divorce and orphanages, the 'female current' has been marketed and sold to Britain's youth in a manner that clearly represents the need to critically examine unwritten symbols and images. This was evident within our conversations, and from data collected in the children's writing journals. For example, Blasa, one of the Year 6 girls, wrote about Wilson in her journal: 'Girls have a lot to say about themselves. Girls are sensitive and can do a lot more interesting things. Jacky can write amazingly but they're all about girls and that's why they're great!'

The girls in this study really connected with the female-centred characters that Wilson employs in her books. They were able to connect on a personal level, but several of the boys in the group wrote different messages in their journal. Urging Wilson to consider boys as the lead character, Jonah wrote, 'Do more boy boooooooooooooooks!'; similarly, Nevan wrote, 'It would be interesting. What would it be like doing a very different book, to do a boy book?' These private journal entries led me to ask the children, what types of books are the Wilson books?

Jonah: They are like a private book for girls. We can see inside their world.

Blasa: Boys still like reading it though. Just because there is a girl, doesn't mean that they don't want to read it.

SP: So, who reads these books generally speaking?

Jackie: Well, everyone does, but I feel that this [the book club] has made the boys more enthusiastic about Jacqueline Wilson.

Allan: I remember someone said in class that if we like Jacqueline Wilson, we must be gay.

Jackie: Nothing wrong with being gay.

Allan: I just went away because it was disturbing. I said f★★★ off.

Blasa: I think they meant that they were gay because they didn't know what to say.

Yasa: If they [the boys from outside book club] don't join [the book club] they won't understand. They should join. I enjoy it a lot.

Jackie: I feel like it [the book club] made the boys [in the book club] more enthusiastic about Jacqueline Wilson books.

Data show that despite the serious natured topics of Wilson's work, set in the realistic fiction genre, the inherent marketing campaign works against the good work in her writing, by limiting the audience through gendered marketing. For example, Wilson covers can typically be seen in shades of pink and light blue with glitter and stars dotting the cover. The book club took risks to talk about the 'othering' of masculinity, through the more traditional lens of what it means to be male. The book club provided a safe space for these conversations, while in the formal classroom space, real risks were sanitized. The containment of the club permitted all members, girls and boys, to co-construct and debate ideas and preconceived notions of gender issues. The book club additionally allowed for a natural invitation to critically examine the societal constructions of gender, and the pupil's place in that world. Tensions between conformity and culture played a role in the conversations as the children navigated the spaces created in a marketing world.

'Different stories': lived experiences and negotiated realities

In order to really live and breathe a piece of literature, pupils need ample opportunity to read aesthetically. Louise Rosenblatt (1968) describes this reading process in her transactional theory as constantly shifting between the efferent and aesthetic stances. Too often, the efferent stance of reading for detail and fact get confounded in schools to the demise of the aesthetic stance, which naturally allows for an experiential and personal connection to the reading. While all readers organically shift between the two stances, the formal school space often values the efferent reading as more viable and valid means for assessment. It is worth noting that in order to gain true meaning from a reading experience, both stances need to be integrated. The children in this study were able to take Jacqueline Wilson's work and use it to make sense of their own reality, while again finding their own way in the world.

The participants viewed these stories as 'different' from books they typically read in school. Couched in very serious modern-day issues, such as being orphaned and/or living in poverty, these stories promoted thinking beyond their own middle-class worlds, which then created understanding, empathy and curiosity into other social arenas – for instance, care homes. In this one example, the children of the book club turned to ethnographic work of investigating the lives of care homes, by interviewing neighbours, siblings, parents and family friends in regards to what it might be like working in care homes, specifically, care for the elderly. Additionally, the children trusted Wilson as an author, and because this was an inherent quality going into the reading, they were truly able to engage with not only the books, but the research of the background information also needed them to fully read these books along the efferent, aesthetic continuum. One of the boys remarked, 'It's not like Harry Potter', eluding to the fact that, although he quite liked the Harry Potter series of books, Wilson's work allowed for a deeper understanding of everyday issues that children around the world face realistically, while pushing the boundaries of their own middle-class experiences.

'You can make up what happens next': mentor texts and curricular connections

Lucy Calkins (2000) encourages literacy teachers to use exemplary pieces of children's literature as mentor texts for modelling strong writing. Although Jacqueline Wilson books are considered popular culture texts, for this group of young readers they served as traditional models of mentor texts.

> Blasa: When you get to the end, you want more.
>
> Jackie: Yeah, you get annoyed! But all of the books are evenly good.
>
> Yasa: When you read to the end… even though it's not a happy ending, you don't always want to read about good things, then you can make your own ending of what happens next.
>
> Jackie: Yeah, you can make up what happens next. If you have quite a good imagination.
>
> Blasa: Sometimes I do carry on the idea when I am done reading, I carry it on in my writing.

The pupils in this discussion were clear that when they read Wilson's books, they prepare themselves for endings that might not always be happy or complete. They used these opportunities to continue the storyline themselves, as a creative writing venture, truly embracing the aesthetic stance of living through the text and characters. This experience with the popular fiction texts have informed their own literacy learning in terms of how we traditionally view writing investigation. In addition to creative writing, as illustrated above, the children also used metacognitive strategies such as ethnographic notes during field trips. Jonah explained that he used Wilson's writing style as a mentor for him on his school field trip where they were required to keep a journal. 'When we went on our trip, we had to keep a diary. I used Tracy Beaker.' By using Wilson's character, Beaker, as an example, Jonah was able to write in a stylistic way that illustrated an observatory pattern. The pupils informed me that they used Wilson's writing style for exam papers as well, thus showing the wide range of opportunity the children had for using Wilson's work as their own writing models.

Nudging the possibilities

Concluding remarks for this chapter highlight the notion that the book club approach to literacy teaching and learning is predicated on the foundation of choice. Children's choices in literature span far beyond the traditional canon of British or American literature, and often the most powerful vehicles for change lie in the literature choices of the masses. These reading experiences are often had within the home environment, but with the inclusion of a third space, English education educators can tap into the wealth of literacy learning occurring at home. Through an accessible repertoire of books that provided availability and text familiarity, Jacqueline Wilson has paved the way for critical insight among young children who are becoming aware of their place in the world. The Book Club provides a safe space in which to entertain and discuss tensions of conformity, while also serving as a model for future literacy events such as writing and research work. Through this consumer fiction, the children navigated and negotiated conversations at school, during a third space that otherwise would have remained at home. This particular study was limited by the small number of pupils. Further work on the book club model of teaching as third space is needed in order to paint a complete picture with whole-class populations of pupils.

Findings suggest the need to re-conceptualize the role of popular fiction in the literacy curriculum. Implications for educators arising from this study may include the following areas. First, the need to create space within statutory restrictions: assessment data should be garnered from whole-text pieces that allow for a rich experience with texts, from a variety of genres outside the classics. Second, it is important to provide a safe and welcoming space for dialogic conversations around issues of critical literacy within the regular school curriculum in order to create rich visions of classroom possibilities. Finally, the study underlines the need to create an overarching school community that supports and maintains literacy practices by encouraging literate and social identities within a supportive environment that values autonomy and choice in literature selection.

References

Applebee, A.N. (1996) *Curriculum as Conversation: Transforming Traditions of Teaching and Learning.* Chicago: University of Chicago Press.

Atwell, N. (1998) *In the Middle: New Understandings about Writing, Reading, and Learning.* Westport, CT: Heinemann.

Black, S. (2003) The magic of Harry Potter: symbols and heroes of fantasy. *Children's Literature in Education* 34(3), 237–47.

Calkins, L. (2000) *The Art of Teaching Reading.* New Jersey: Pearson.

Cherland, M. (2008) Harry's girls: Harry Potter and the discourse of gender. *Journal of Adolescent & Adult Literacy* 52(4), 273–82.

Collins, K. (2004) *Growing Readers: Units of Study in the Primary Classroom.* Portland, ME: Stenhouse Publishers.

Cremin, T., Mottram, M., Bearne, E. and Goodwin, P. (2008) Exploring teachers' knowledge of children's literature. *Cambridge Journal of Education* 38(4), 449–64.

Creswell, J. (2013) *Qualitative Inquiry: Choosing Among Five Approaches.* London: Sage.

Dewey, J. (1997). *How We Think.* North Chelmsford, MA: Courier Corporation.

Dutro, E. (2001) 'But that's a girls' book!' Exploring gender boundaries in children's reading practices. *The Reading Teacher* 55(4), 376–84.

Dyson, A.H. (2003) 'Welcome to the jam': popular culture, school literacy, and the making of childhoods. *Harvard Educational Review* 73(3), 328–61.

Evans, J. (2005) *Literacy Moves On: Popular Culture, New Technologies, and Critical Literacy in the Elementary Classroom.* Westport, CT: Heinemann.

Goodwyn, A. (2012) The status of literature: English teaching and the condition of literature teaching in schools. *English in Education* 46(3), 212–27.

Gutiérrez, K., Baquwdano-López, P., and Turner, M.G. (1997) Putting language back into language arts: when the radical middle meets the third space. *Language Arts* 74(5), 368–78.

Glesne, C. and Peshkin, A. (1992) *Becoming Qualitative Researchers: An Introduction.* New York: Longman.

Harste, J.C. (2003) What do we mean by literacy now? *Voices from the Middle* 10(3), 8–12.

Lehr, S. (2001) *Beauty, Brains, and Brawn: The Construction of Gender in Children's Literature.* Westport, CT: Heinemann.

Kiefer, B.Z. and Tyson, C.A. (2010) *Charlotte Huck's Children's Literature: A Brief Guide.* NJ: McGraw-Hill.

Krashen, S.D. (2004) *The Power of Reading: Insights from the Research.* Colorado: Libraries Unlimited.

Mackey, M. (1990) Filling the gaps. *Language Arts* 67(5), 484–9.

McMahon, S., Raphael, T., Goatley, V. and Pardo, L. (1997) *The Book Club Connection.* Newark: International Reading Association.

Miller, K. (2010) Haunted heroines: The Gothic imagination of Jane Austen, Charlotte Bronte, and L.M. Montgomery. *The Lion and the Unicorn* 31(2), 125–47.

Pilgreen, J. (2000) *The SSR Handbook.* Westport, CT: Heinemann.

Reid, L. (1997) Our repressed reading addictions: teachers and young adult series books. *The English Journal* 86(3), 68–72.

Rosenblatt, L.M. (1968) *Literature As Exploration.* New York: Appleton-Century.

Siegel, M. and Lukas, S. (2008) Room to move: how kindergarteners negotiate literacies and identities in a mandated balanced literacy curriculum. In C. Genishi and A.L. Goodwin (eds.) *Diversity in Early Childhood Education: Rethinking and Doing*, 29–47. London: Routledge.

Valverde, C.P. (2009) Magic women on the margins: eccentric models in Mary Poppins and Ms Wiz. *Children's Literature in Education* 40(4), 263–74.

Vasquez, V. (2004) *Negotiating Critical Literacies with Young Children.* New York: Routledge.

Wohlwend, K.E. (2009) Damsels in discourse: girls consuming and producing identity texts through Disney princess play. *Reading Research Quarterly* 44(1), 57–83.

10

'TO SEE OURSELS AS ITHERS SEE US'

Constructions of Scotland's place and identity within a changing Scottish curriculum and context

Karen Lowing

Introduction

Scotland has recently undergone a critical shift in its political stance within the United Kingdom. The Scottish Nationalist Party rose from a fringe group in 1934 to secure, in the 2015 general election, a landslide victory of 56 out of 69 seats in Scotland. Largely left wing but now with an evolving nationalist, rather than solely socialist agenda, modern-day Scotland is increasingly distinctive in its political leanings and national identity.

Scots was acknowledged as an autonomous minority language in 2000 by the Council of Europe: European Charter for Regional or Minority Languages. In 2001 the UK government sanctioned Scots, under Part II of the Charter, as a minority language within Britain. During the past five years, with the implementation of the new Scottish Curriculum for Excellence, the subjects of Scots Language and Scottish Studies have been incorporated within Scottish classrooms. These curricular changes resonate with recent political developments in Scotland and the country's evolving national identity.

This chapter provides an introduction to national identity construction and offers an initial broad thematic analysis of Scottish history, literature and politics, as pertinent theoretical, cultural and administrative backdrops to further appreciate Scottish education policy on studying Scotland in schools. As the Curriculum for Excellence now requires Scottish schools to incorporate Scots Language and Scottish Studies in the classroom, the chapter specifically provides a preliminary study of Education Scotland's 'Studying Scotland' school resource, with reference to the Scottish Studies Scottish Qualifications Authority (SQA) award.

National identity construction

Before we consider these documents and their contextual backdrop, I would like to first define and position the concept of 'national identity', as employed throughout this chapter.

Identity is abstract, constructed and often contextual. Identity can be 'achieved' or 'inhabited' (Blommaert 2006); it can suggest 'the identity people themselves articulate or claim – and "ascribed" or "attributed" identity – the identity given to someone by someone else' (Blommaert 2006: 238). Identity through a nationalizing lens can create, as Anderson (2006) suggests, 'imagined communities', where a unity of populace exists, boundaries have some fluidity, the people have a sense of autonomy in their future and community is present through both time and place (Billig 2011; Benwell and Stokoe 2006; McCrone 1992).

A reference to Jung's theory of the 'collective unconscious' is pertinent here, where a sense of community is rooted beyond the physical and across incalculable generations of a population's psyche. This notion of a 'collective unconscious' is an enduring theme throughout many exemplars of Scottish literature; Neil M. Gunn's *Blood Hunt* (1952), for example, presents a more modern and yet, timeless Scotland, where the cry of the wolf and whisper of the forests and glens contrasts with the protagonist's harsh experiences at sea; the juxtaposition of memory (albeit elusively romantic) and experience never quite escapes the protagonist's consciousness.

Scotland displays a strong sense of national cohesion in its demonstrations of constructed identity (McCrone 1995). A clear unity of populace is often revealed through Scotland's prosaic demonstrations of national signs and symbols (Billig 2011). The Scottish heritage industry, and particularly its tourist trade, has 'commodified' Scotland, in portioning it out to be 'eaten by the other' (hooks 1992). It presents images of Highland 'noble savages', existing in a land of mystical beasts and almost fairytale-like terrain, an image readily sold to and eagerly consumed by visiting tourists.

Scotland has not only projected this construction of national identity towards and for the consumption of the 'other' but, as part of this process, created a dislocated psyche, a 'diasporic' mindset, synonymous with Scotland's notoriety for emigration and developing a global diaspora. Scattered physically, the Scots are also dispersed subconsciously from a more robust multifaceted sense of self, towards a reductionist, mythical 'ideal ego' of Scotland, by means of 'tartanry' images and 'Kailyardism' (McCrone 1995). Scotland's constructed, rather than inherent, 'collective consciousness' is therefore disaffected from any genuine notion of nationhood. A more palatable national identity would be based on a modern 'Scottish Renaissance', where 'collective' tradition and memory is reliably honoured and contemporary culture is positively acknowledged.

This said, the idea of nationalism per se must be presented with a caveat; the positioning of national identity should be a fluid and alterable process, avoiding essential and fixed outcomes to be adhered to (Kidd 2002). History reminds us that essentialist definitions of nationalism are hauntingly dangerous (Joseph 2004). Thus, when I propose that Scotland considers its 'genuine' national identity, I intend that Scotland gazes beyond its 'fixed' tartan ego and employs a credible and ever-increasing meta-awareness that supports the continual and enduring reflexive practice of positively repositioning its identity as a nation.

Scottish historical context

Before specifically investigating Scottish national identity construction in Scottish schools, it is important to first consider the main themes and rhetoric arising from the archives of Scottish history, the latter of which continue to pervade the Scottish 'collective conscious' (Lowing 2014). The historical facts here are largely a broad overview of Lynch's (2011) *Scotland: A New History*, Keay and Keay's (1994) *Collins Encyclopaedia of Scotland* and Scott's (1994) *Scotland: A Concise Cultural History*.

Historically Scotland is well known for its early 'Auld Alliance' with France in the thirteenth century; both countries agreed to support the other if the army of King Edward I of England was to invade. Such an alliance was not unusual; Scotland often gazed beyond Britain to Europe, drawing on European educational practices and also benefitting from trade links with its European cousins. In particular, St Andrews University, founded in the fifteenth century, was partly fashioned on the Parisian higher education system. Trade routes from the fifteenth century onwards with European countries such as Belgium, Denmark, France, Russia, Poland, Sweden and Norway were commonplace.

However, largely as a result of the Union of Crowns (1603) and Parliaments (1707), Scotland aligned with 'Britishness'; the Union of Parliaments principally helped to construct the institution we know today as Great Britain. Yet Burns argued in 'Sic a Parcel of Rogues' that this Union was built on the bribery of the Scottish government: 'What force or guile could not subdue/Through many war-like ages/Is wrought now by a coward few/For hireling traitor's wages… English gold has been our bane –/Sic a parcel o rogues in a nation!'

Such uneasy foundations between Scotland and England have a protracted history. In the thirteenth century, in order to allegedly avenge the death of his wife Marion Braidfute, William Wallace killed the Sheriff of Lanark. The events that followed, some of which were adapted and romanticized in the blockbuster film *Braveheart*, encapsulate the tensions between the two countries. The Wars of Independence during the thirteenth and fourteenth centuries and the Declaration of Arbroath in 1320 were significant events; the Declaration stated (in translation), 'as long as a hundred of us remain alive, never will we on any conditions be subjected to the lordship of the English'. Many of the efforts of Wallace and Bruce led to the Declaration and resulted in a renewal of the alliance between Scotland and its European counterpart France.

The tensions between and within Scotland and England continued throughout the fifteenth and sixteenth centuries with the Stuart dynasty. However the disputes between both countries were not only concerned with territory. Differing warring Catholic and Presbyterianism factions scored the landscape of what we now know as Britain. The period largely spanning that of Mary Queen of Scots and the Covenanters in the sixteenth and seventeenth centuries, and the seventeenth and eighteenth century's rising of the Jacobites and Charles Edward Stuart: 'Bonnie Prince Charlie' or 'The Young Pretender', produced much conflict between the two countries. The defeat of Prince Charles and the Jacobites at Culloden in 1746 however, led to the Act of Proscription in 1747, where tartan and weaponry was banned in the Highlands of Scotland.

Britain thereafter found itself in the midst of the eighteenth-century Enlightenment Period, when Scotland was celebrated for its scholarly ideas and inventions. Adam Smith, David Hume, James Hutton and James Watt, for example, were highly influential in the realms of trade and industry, philosophy, geology and engineering respectively. Despite this period of relative calm and optimism, the Highland Clearances befell the Scottish Gaelic community throughout the eighteenth and nineteenth centuries. The Poor Law compounded the plight of the Highlanders in 1845 and the potato famines in 1846 did little to halt the haemorrhaging of the Highlanders from their homes.

Many landlords refused to support their Highland tenants, despite this now being their obligation as a result of the new law. Landlords continued to evict native Highlanders from their crofts to fishing villages, cities or even to foreign climes such as America, Canada, New Zealand or Australia. These evictions were at best sanitary and at worst brutal acts of ethnic cleansing. A harsh enforcer of these practices was Patrick Sellar, factor of the Sutherland estate. In response to a plea from crofters attempting to stop him from burning their elderly neighbour's croft, Sellar was famously quoted as stating, 'Damn her, the old witch. She has lived too long. Let her burn.'

The Highlanders were often required to develop a different set of working skills in their new locations, while the gentry gained from the crofters' eviction through lucrative sheep farming and later, stag shooting. John McGrath's play, *The Cheviot, the Stag and the Black Black Oil*, written in the 1970s, depicts this stark demise of Scotland's Gaelic culture from the eighteenth century onwards. The text makes comparisons between the cheviot sheep, the stag and the twentieth-century oil industry in the north of Scotland. It suggests that the rich oil barons, and not the people of Scotland, benefited from the industry, just as before landowners such as the Duke of Sutherland, and the shooting gentry of Britain's elite, gained from the exile of the Highland Gaelic communities. The film *Local Hero* (1983), set in Scotland where a rich oil baron wishes to drill in a remote and beautiful area of the Highlands, no doubt draws from this element of Scotland's modern history. As I write, recent political events in America, with the election of Donald Trump and his commercial interests in Scotland, resonate.

The early twentieth-century Scotland witnessed a new renaissance, echoing James V's sixteenth-century Renaissance Scotland, where Hugh MacDiarmid, like Gunn, wished to encourage Scottish expression through cultural pursuits. He created 'Lallans', or synthetic Scots, a Scots derived from numerous different codes of Scots, and wrote his famous work, *A Drunk Man Looks at a Thistle*. MacDiarmid was a founder of the National Party of Scotland, known today as the Scottish National Party. He believed that only Scots, albeit a synthetic Scots, could unite and express the distinctiveness and heart, or 'collective consciousness' of the Scottish people.

Throughout British history, the edges become blurred between there simply being a Scottish/English divide; complex conflicts of religion and wealth have acted as deciding factors for the fate of the rural or city poor in Scotland. Scotland's global perspective has endured, however. This was starkly emphasized in June 2016, following the British vote for Brexit, when the Scottish Member of the European Parliament, Alyn Smith, announced in the European Parliament that he was, 'proudly Scottish' but also, 'proudly European', not as one might imagine, 'proudly British'. He then stated that: 'I want my country to be internationalist… European' and ended with: 'Scotland did not let you down… do not let Scotland down now' (YouTube n.d.).

In June 2016, Nicola Sturgeon, Scotland's First Minister, suggested that a second Scottish referendum may be imminent, due to the UK vote for Brexit. This was largely fuelled by 62 per cent of Scots voting 'no' to exiting Europe. The 2014 Scottish referendum for independence was also revealing; only 53 per cent of Scots voted to stay in the UK. While I prepare this chapter, Sturgeon continues to work towards ensuring Scotland remains in some form within the EU. These recent political events again emphasize Scotland's modern sense of autonomy, identity and place beyond Britain and towards Europe.

Branding Scotland in literature

It is worth considering the branding that sits behind and helps to construct modern Scottish national identity and the impact such pervasive mnemonics have on Scottish educational policy and practice.

History plays an enduring role in the construction of Scottish identity. Highland 'nobles savages', wild and brutal figures yet with honourable morals, have languished in Scottish history to emerge later fully formed in Scotland's literature. MacPherson's *Ossian* (1762) and Scott's *Rob Roy* (1818) are just such examples. Scottish history and politics are also often depicted in film. Movies such as *Braveheart* (1995), *Highlander* (1986) and *Rob Roy* (1995) portray such 'noble savages' in glorious Technicolor. With *Local Hero* (1983), although the film offers a beguiling depiction of Highland life amid a robust political undercurrent, it unmistakably draws from the Kailyard tradition, again romanticizing rural Scottish life.

Scottish literature has proved to be a willing conduit to less positive productions of Scottish national identity, with some of its recreations of Scotland evidently being only loosely derived from Scottish history. Indeed, there endures a tension in Scottish literature between soporific and disingenuous 'Kailyardism' for example, and the often raw, honest and yet inescapably idealistic literature of the modern 'Scottish Renaissance'. This juxtaposition can also be found in film, where romantic depictions of Scotland, as above, are contrasted with realism, in the stark and violent representation of Scotland within productions such as *Trainspotting* (1996), *My Name is Joe* (1998) and *NEDS* (2010).

McCrone (1995) suggests that naïve but ubiquitous constructions of Scottish national identity were immortalized during the Romantic period. Influential texts such as MacPherson's *Ossian* (1762), Boswell and Johnson's *Journal of a Tour to the Hebrides* (1785) and Scott's many publications including *Waverley* (1814), *Rob Roy* (1818) and *Redgauntlet* (1824), helped to create a Scotland of: 'kilts, tartan, heather, bagpipes… romance, sadness, defeat' (McCrone 1992: 18). When George IV visited Edinburgh in 1822, Scott was at the forefront of reconstructing Scottish identity. His novel *Waverley* and his staged production of a 'tartanry' Scotland, harbouring Highland 'noble savages', had much to answer for in presenting to King and country a mythical version of a romantic Scotland (McCrone 1992: 18). Later Queen Victoria's procurement of Balmoral in 1848 helped to link 'tartanry' to royalty and eventually the military. As McCrone (1995: 52) states, this was 'a master-stroke by the British state in literally stealing its enemy's clothes'.

The Celtic Twilight and Kailyard movements in Scottish literature, Sharp's *Pharais: A Romance of the Isles* (1855–1905) and Barrie's *Auld Licht Idylls* (1888) for example, embedded the notion of a romanticized northern land, separate from newly industrialized Britain (Keay and Keay 1994). In part this was a reaction, embodied in Romanticism, to such swift change to workplace and landscape in the United Kingdom. Nevertheless Scotland is often depicted as possessing an 'aggressive spirit of independence and egalitarianism' (Wittig 1958: 95), autonomous to the developments of Britain at large. As such, it is not unanticipated that Scotland's literary tradition presents this forte for individualism.

Interestingly, the idea of Scotland claiming to own an egalitarian national character largely derives from the 'lad o' pairts' ideal, a mythical belief that can be traced back to McLaren's (1894) Kailyard text, *Beside the Bonnie Brier Bush* (McCrone 2008). The Kailyard, or 'cabbage patch', literary tradition presented Scotland as provincial and insular, yet interspersed with wise characters in high standing within small towns. 'Domsie' from *Brier Bush,* for example, was a schoolteacher who uncovered shrewd routes to send his talented boys of little means, his 'lad o' pairts', to university. No 'lass o' pairts' however, appeared to exist in this scenario (McCrone 2008).

The 'lad o' pairts', an inherently virtuous working-class boy of rural or small parish life, was robust and moral. He was a form of Scottish 'noble savage', empowered through education to escape his apparent 'barbarity'. Yet, that such a process occurred is somewhat lacking in credibility (McCrone 2008). Although this tale of egalitarianism is admirable in its aim for educational furtherance, it still implies the need to 'remedy' the uneducated poor and therefore became allied with notions of Anglicization and colonialism (McCrone 2008). However, such inequity arose from class structures rather than simply as a result of Anglicization. Anderson (2008) suggests that Scotland did not so much demonstrate a 'classless society' but instead a society where talent was valued above class, a 'meritocracy'. The egalitarian ideal of the 'lad o' pairts' endured; it was a valued part of Scottish identity, immortalized in *Brier Bush* and employed by Nationalists to help distinguish between Scottish and English national identities (Anderson 2008). Indeed, the Scottish education system largely appears to maintain 'a wider tradition of social egalitarianism' (McCrone 2008: 226), a remnant of the 'lad o' pairts'.

Emerging themes

The creation of Scottish national identity through history, literature and politics produces numerous emerging themes. These themes are useful when considering the educational policy surrounding Scottish studies in Scotland's Curriculum for Excellence:

1. Scotland largely and historically maintains a European perspective.
2. Tensions persist between British or Scottish Nationalist campaigns.
3. Religious divide, mostly between Protestant and Catholics, endures in Scotland. Commonly known as 'Scotland's shame', in 2005 *The Guardian* wrote about 'the dark side' of Scottish football when, as a result of a player's religion, death threats were made from opposition Scottish supporters, and the footballer was forced to seek refuge in a safe house.[1] The foundations of such political and religious conflicts, two of the six themes I discuss here, are no doubt linked to the Scotland's troubled past, as outlined above.
4. Scotland maintains its eighteenth-century reputation as a place of enterprise. However, ongoing tensions regarding the ownership of Scottish oil and the very much dwindling semi-conductor industry of 'silicon glen', the basin between Glasgow and Edinburgh, present a different picture.
5. The theme of Romanticism sustains in, for example, tourist towns such as Edinburgh, Stirling, Fort William, Aviemore and Inverness. It can be seen in the banal mnemonics of flags, tartan and shortbread, readily sold in such locations (Billig 2011).
6. Egalitarianism endures in the Scottish psyche, despite (as Scottish writer Hassan notes in his 2013 *Scotsman* article) the fact that, 'this is most definitely not who we are in reality: whether it be educational apartheid, health inequalities, or the 1:273 ratio between Scotland's wealthiest and poorest households in wealth'.[2]

Earlier I supported a more persuasive national identity for Scotland, founded on a contemporary 'Scottish Renaissance', where the 'collective conscious' reliably draws from tradition and memory and where contemporary culture is acknowledged and respected. As a nation and particularly in schools with young people, these persistent themes of Europeanism, 'Britishness' versus Nationalism, Sectarianism, Enterprise, Romanticism and Egalitarianism need to be challenged and problematized.

With these emerging themes and issues in mind, I return to Education Scotland's 'Studying Scotland', with reference to the SQA Scottish Studies Award document.

Here we discover that on initial analysis, at least some of these themes become apparent. With particular regard to the guidelines on Scots language within the former document, I would like to focus mainly on theme 2, with some mention of theme 6.

Scottish Studies in Scottish classrooms

When referring to Scottish Studies here, I allude to both the study of Scotland and its languages. The new 'Studying Scotland' school resource and Scottish Studies Award have gained a tenuous place in Scotland's schools (Lowing 2014). Education Scotland's 'Studying Scotland' resource places weight on developing a sense of nationhood in Scottish children: 'Scottish young people should have a clear understanding of the forces and events that have shaped our national identity' (Education Scotland n.d.). The Scottish government's creation and implementation of Scottish Qualification Authority's Award (SQA) in Scottish Studies is based on a belief that:

> understanding Scottish history, language and culture and connecting with Scotland as a place through our landscape and natural heritage are an important part of developing a sense of identity, confidence and wellbeing
>
> *(Scot Gov 1 n.d.)*

The suggestion in these two extracts is that understanding one's national identity, having a 'place' of 'our' belonging, by means of 'landscape' and 'natural heritage', creates assured and healthy young people. This statement follows the publication of such populist texts as Craig's (2011) *The Scots' Crisis of Confidence*, which highlights the 'pessimistic', Anglophobic Scot.

These references to national identity in the Scottish curriculum are in no small way related to the Scottish Nationalist Party's victory in 2015 and its influence on Scottish policy and practice thereafter. A resilient sense of national identity is also shared in Scotland's developing policy and practice for the arts and its heritage industry; patrons and consumers are encouraged to understand art and culture as, 'sit[ting] at the heart of who we are as a nation' (Scotland's 2016–17 Arts Strategy n.d.). An increasing sense of national place and identity, nationally and internationally, in the rhetoric of Scotland's municipal workings, appears to indicate the significance of national identity construction, its place and positioning, in an evolving post-2015 Scotland.

Nonetheless, it is worth considering in further depth 'Studying Scotland' and specifically its approach to Scots language. This is not to exclude Scots Gaelic, however, also a very important language of the Scottish classroom, but for the purposes of this chapter, I focus on Scots.

The application of language in educational policy can reveal much with regard to the governmentally endorsed and constructed national identity of a country (Hornberger 2008). When introducing Scots language, the document states:

Scots is the official name for all of the dialects of Scotland (eg Glaswegian, Doric, Ayrshire, Shetland, Lallands). Scots is recognised as a language in its own right by the Scottish and UK governments as well as the European Union.

(Education Scotland n.d.)

By referring to Scots as a 'dialect', the article infers that Scots is a dialect of an established language, i.e., English. Scots and Gaelic are Scotland's national languages, being recognized by the Council of Europe: European Charter for Regional or Minority Languages.

This initial passage of the text creates a tension between historically conflicting linguistic positioning in Scotland. The language required until recently in Scottish schools has generally been Standard English, the formally recognized language of much of Britain; the language employed beyond the confines of the classroom, however, has largely been Scots, the language of many Scottish people (Lowing 2014). This expectation of English being the lingua franca in Scottish schools has tended to remain despite changes to the contrary within the New Curriculum for Excellence (Lowing 2014). As language and identity are irrefutably linked (Joseph 2004), the contradictory positions offered within just this one piece of Scottish educational text project confusing messages for Scottish teachers and school children alike regarding the topic of national identity construction.

Active in overseeing the implementation of Scots, the Committee of Experts are a European Charter for Regional or Minority Languages group of independent specialists, required by the Council of Europe: European Charter for Regional or Minority Languages to be effective in 'the adoption of protective and promotional measures' (European Council 2000, 2007) for regional or minority languages. They ensure such languages are adopted and implemented by respective governmental bodies but in the case of Scots, experts noted in their 2007 report that 'the situation of the Scots language in Scotland however, remains unsatisfactory' (European Council 2007: 8). As McColl Millar (2006) notes, Scots is included in Part II of the European Charter for Regional or Minority Languages. This allows for government discretion in the application of Scots language provision, particularly in schools; McColl Millar states, 'the implementation of language policy on Scots at all levels of government... has been half-hearted, ill thought-out and buried in a swathe of other "cultural" issues' (2006: 63). One of these 'cultural issues' may very well involve language choice and the positioning of national identity between British and Nationalist locations in Scottish schools; this is despite the landslide victory of the Scottish National Party in 2015 and its impact on educational policy thereafter.

The 'Studying Scotland' article contradicts itself further, however, by refuting Scots as being 'slang'; it instead provides an etymology of the language, which imbues the tongue with significant standing. Yet thereafter the article suggests that during the seventeenth century, 'Scots began to decline. The Southern English language became the most popular written and spoken form. However, Scots was retained in the oral traditional tales and songs which provide a backdrop for the history of creativity in Scotland.' The article also states: 'In Curriculum for Excellence, Scots language is referred to both explicitly and implicitly' (Education Scotland n.d.).

This section is particularly damning of the Scots language and wholly inaccurate; that the article does not present further information regarding the standing of Scots beyond its decline as the language of officialdom is misleading; Scots has remained a spoken language to the present day (Lowing, 2014). As a language still employed freely throughout Scotland, academics such as McClure (2009), Macafee (2003) and McColl Millar (2006) remain active in the field of Scots. In addition, that it is referred to 'implicitly' throughout Scottish educational policy is somewhat ironic: Scots does indeed remain very much unspoken in many Scottish classrooms (Lowing 2014).

'Studying Scotland' also claims that the 2011 Scots census results are not yet available. The resource is outdated; the Scots census results are now accessible and they indicate that at least 30 per cent of Scottish people speak Scots in Scotland today. 'Studying Scotland' is undoubtedly questionable; the reader is left with the worrying realization that its representation of the Scots language is problematic and unsound but yet is currently being utilized in Scottish schools.

Acknowledging Scots as a minority language, the European Charter for Regional or Minority Languages pointedly highlights that language rights are a matter of social justice (see Madoc-Jones and Buchanan 2004). Maintaining equality and diversity in schools is not only a central component of social justice, but is also a sound model for developing positive citizenship in children. Unfortunately, however, the message to schools of 'Studying Scotland' with regard to the Scots language cannot draw on the Scottish egalitarian ideal. The document fails to fully support the collective voice and identity of Scotland that the Scots language is integral to. This is particularly concerning when Scots is often associated with working-class and/or rural areas in Scotland. It seems the Scottish speaking 'lad o' pairts' is not as welcome in Scottish schools as the Scottish egalitarian ideal might suggest.

Conclusion

The protagonist in *Trainspotting* (1996), Renton, is famous for his diatribe regarding a colonized Scotland. Unmistakably, Renton wishes to be 'ABE', 'anything but English' and solidly places himself in the Scottish Nationalist camp. Being 'ABE' is many steps beyond being anything but British and is a contentious and complicated area that requires not only a separate chapter but also a standalone text, in order to do this worrying subject justice. Renton in his controversial tirade, however, does pose a critical question: who are the Scottish nation? Renton here urges national meta-awareness and reflexivity in Scotland and it does seems that the national consensus is moving towards a more confident and self-aware national identity. *The Independent* on 25 September 2015 noted that:

While the national psyche of Scotland may have shifted, recent political polling has suggested that the way in which people describe themselves has stayed fairly stable. In an ICM poll in March, 62 per cent of Scots said they would describe themselves as Scottish rather than British, with 31 per cent stating the opposite – much the same as in previous years.[3]

A sense of 'Scottishness' before 'Britishness' generally remains in Scotland. However, repeated themes found in Scotland, clustering around place and national identity, require further consideration. So too do many of these recurring themes in Scottish educational policy. The accuracy of such documents and the nation's 'shifting psyche' and sense of nationhood therein necessitates change, change for the sake of a new Scotland where, through politics, there's a more positive and constructive outlet; where it's OK now to 'have a Saltire in your window' and where it's OK to celebrate a positive Scottish national identity, and a myriad of languages in the Scottish classroom, including Scots and Scots-speaking children.

Notes

1 *The Guardian* at www.theguardian.com/commentisfree/2011/mar/20/celtic-rangers-football-religion-sectarian.
2 *The Scotsman* at www.scotsman.com/news/opinion/gerry-hassan-equality-must-begin-before-it-goes-on-1-3248831.
3 *The Independent* at www.independent.co.uk/news/uk/politics/scottish-referendum-the-snp-and-identity-where-the-country-is-headed-as-the-dust-settles-from-a-10516590.html.

References

Anderson, B. (2006) *Imagined Communities*. London: Verso.
Anderson, R. (2008) The history of Scottish education, pre-1980. In T.G.K. Bryce and W.M. Humes (eds.) *Scottish Education: Beyond Devolution*. Edinburgh: Edinburgh University Press.
Benwell, B. and Stokoe, E. (2006) *Discourse and Identity*. Edinburgh: Edinburgh University Press.
Billig, M. (2011) *Banal Nationalism*. London: Sage.
Blommaert, J. (2006) Language policy and national identity. In T. Ricento (ed.) *An Introduction to Language Policy: Theory and Method*. Oxford: Blackwell Publishing.
Council of Europe (2000) European Charter for Regional or Minority Languages. Retrieved from www.coe.int/t/dg4/education/minlang/default_en.asp.
Council of Europe (2007) European Charter for Regional or Minority Languages – Application of the Charter in the United Kingdom, Report of the Committee of Experts. Retrieved from www.coe.int/t/dg4/education/minlang/report/default_EN.asp.
Craig, C. (2011) *The Scots' Crisis of Confidence*. Argyll: Argyll Publishing.
Education Scotland (n.d.) www.educationscotland.gov.uk/studyingscotland/about/why.asp.
hooks, b. (1992) Eating the other: desire and resistance. In *Black Looks: Race and Representation*. Boston: South End Press.
Hornberger, N. (2008) *Can Schools Save Indigenous Languages?* Hampshire: Palgrave Macmillan.
Joseph, J. (2004) *Language and Identity: National, Ethnic, Religious*. London: Palgrave.

Keay, J. and Keay, J. (eds.) (1994) *Collins Encyclopaedia of Scotland*. London: HarperCollins.

Kidd, W. (2002) *Culture and Identity*. Hampshire. Palgrave Macmillan.

Lowing, K. (2014) 'Ane Instructioun for Bairnis to be Learnit in Scottis': A Study of Scots Language in the Scottish Secondary Classroom. Retrieved from https://theses.ncl.ac.uk/dspace/bitstream/10443/2677/1/Lowing,%20K.A.%202014.pdf.

Lynch, M. (2011) *Scotland: A New History*. London: Pimlico.

Macafee, C. (2003) Studying Scots vocabulary. In J. Corbett, J.D. McClure and J. Stuart-Smith (eds.) *The Edinburgh Companion to Scots*. Edinburgh: Edinburgh University Press.

Madoc-Jones, I. and Buchanan, J. (2004) Indigenous people, language and criminal justice: the experience of first language Welsh speakers in Wales. *Criminal Justice Studies* 17(4): 353–67.

McColl Millar, R. (2006) 'Burying alive': unfocussed governmental language policy and scots. *Language Policy* 5, 63–86.

McCrone, D. (1992) *Understanding Scotland: The Sociology of a Stateless Nation*. London: Routledge.

McCrone, D. (1995) *Scotland the Brand: The Making of Scottish Heritage*. Edinburgh: Polygon.

McCrone, D. (2008) Culture, nationalism and Scottish education: homogeneity and diversity. In T. Bryce and W. Humes (eds.) *Scottish Education*. Edinburgh: Edinburgh University Press.

McClure, D. (2009) *Why Scots Matters*. Edinburgh: Saltire Society.

Scot Gov 1 (n.d.) www.gov.scot/Topics/Education/Schools/curriculum/ACE/Scottish Studies.

Scotland's 2016–17 Arts Strategy. (n.d.) www.creativescotland.com/resources/our-publications/plans-and-strategy-documents/arts-strategy-2016–17.

Scott, P. (1994) *Scotland: A Concise Cultural History*. Edinburgh: Mainstream Publishing Company.

Wittig, K. (1958) *The Scottish Tradition in Literature*. Edinburgh: Mercat Press.

YouTube (n.d.) www.youtube.com/watch?v=uZONWQ8VOOg.

11

'THANK THE LORD FOR THE INTERNET!'

Identity, social media and space online

Anna Llewellyn

Introduction

'Let me put it this way: planet earth has never been as tiny as it is now' (Karinthy 2007 [1929]: 21, cited in Seargeant and Tagg, 2014: 1). It may be tempting to assume that Karinthy's statement is current. In fact it was written in 1929, and was referring to the telegram and the ease with which people in the world were becoming connected.[1] Fast-forward 90 years and planet earth is even smaller. The virtual world and technologies have continued to change our relationship with time and space; they have made it possible to connect with people, places, information and events that are not in our immediate physical environment. Indeed, since the millennium, the web is no longer just somewhere to collect information and gain knowledge; instead Web 2.0 (O'Reilly 2012 [2005]) is a place to be an active contributor. It 'became a place where you participated; a dynamic space that was shaped (both intentionally and inadvertently) by your own actions and contributions' (Seargeant and Tagg 2014: 2). This digital revolution has brought opportunity, no more so than with the use of Facebook during the Arab Spring in 2011. Here, the ease, the immediacy and the accessibility of social media provided a perfect tool to facilitate rapid engagement from far and wide.

The opportunities that the internet provides through participation is the topic I examine further in this chapter. In particular, I want to explore how much the online world and social media – this 'third space' that blurs boundaries between reality and fiction – allow us to negotiate and play with our own identities. I am especially concerned with asking if this platform can break down discursive boundaries, norms and accepted ways of being. For young people and teachers, the subject of this chapter, identity, is particularly problematic. Teachers are exposed to a multitude of discourses that they negotiate in order to become the teacher they want to be. Young people are, of course, always already in the process of becoming; it is the age where people begin to search for a sense of self.

As such, I will take these discussions in two parts: first, exploring teachers and, second, examining young people and their relationship to the online world, with particular relation to social media. However, I begin with a more theoretical discussion of identity, and its relationship to discourses and space.

Negotiating identities in the online world

Following Foucault and educationalists such as Walkerdine (1997) and Walshaw (2007), I contest the idea of a fixed identity or a 'true' self, and instead suggest that our identities are multiple and always in flux. In simple terms, we are not always the same in every situation; for instance, a teacher may be different in the classroom, in the staffroom, in a meeting, at home, and so on – the student similarly so. Our identities are formed through a negotiation of discourses, which are 'practices that systematically form the objects of which they speak' (Foucault 2002 [1972]: 53–4). For instance, the 'outstanding' teacher, so commended by Ofsted and others, is a discursive construction; it is what we construct it to be. However, this is not passively done; structure does not remove agency. As Seargeant and Tagg state:

> People… actively and repeatedly co-construct and negotiate their identity (within the constraints afforded by a range of social and individual factors), and present themselves in different ways depending on the particular contextual circumstances in which they are operating.
>
> *(Seargeant and Tagg 2014: 5–6)*

Moreover, this is not a one-way relationship: the subject is produced through discourses, while simultaneously producing discourses (Walkerdine 1997); in this instance what it means to be a teacher or young person is the way it is enacted in the world.

Challenging the idea of a fixed individual can be controversial within educational discourses. Much of education is premised upon social cohesion and conformity, and as such normalization is always already in production (Walshaw 2007). This is intensified within the current climate of overt surveillance and performativity, where classrooms tend towards homogeneity. In addition, the child that is privileged in UK education is presupposed upon narratives of child development and the singular self (Henriques et al. 1998), historically through Piaget and Vygotsky and more recently via theories such as Bloom's or Dweck's Growth Mindsets. However, I suggest that this (or any) singular story can limit children and young people in their passage through school. How can it be that children and young people are cognitive beings that are devoid of cultural and social significance? How is it that they can be 'themselves' when the path of development is predetermined? Moreover, if we consider this singular developmental self to be true, then children and young people are never worthy as themselves but always in a process of becoming something else, and always inferior. If people are indeed discursive constructs then we may ask – is there space outside dominant discourses? Is there somewhere where we can become without restrictions and norms to follow? Furthermore, is it possible that this can be offered by an online space?

The key question here is – why is an online space different? Well… an online space is potentially accessible to anyone at any time (ignoring of course that some places and groups of people will have less access to the internet). Moreover, the second point to make is that the unreal online space allows very much for the play and creation of the self. We can more or less choose who we are, and present ourselves as such. Furthermore, modern technology not only allows us to connect with those around the world, and enables us to gain information from around the world, but much more than this, it gives us a space to 'play' – to play at who we are. As such:

> If identities are discursively (and semiotically) constructed and dialogically performed, then nowhere is this more evident than on social media, where people have relative freedom to choose how they wish to present themselves, have the opportunity to address new, diverse and potentially global audiences, and have at their disposal a novel set of resources for doing so.
>
> *(Seargeant and Tagg 2014: 9)*

This may be by engaging with role-playing games, blogs or vlogs[5], or social media. Online identities are often literally about 'writing oneself into being' (boyd 2001: 199). If identity concerns 'construct[ing] an image of who we are – for others and for ourselves – through the way we act, move and dress, the music we enjoy, the food we eat, the beliefs we hold, and the stories we tell' (Deumert (drawing on Ricoeur) 2014: 24), then the online world gives us the opportunity to do those things without normalcy and without restrictions on audience. Indeed the audience can play a role; much of today's online usage is about inviting the reader/viewer to participate, through, for instance, liking an Instagram photo, retweeting a Twitter tweet, or comments beneath a YouTube vlog, each of these adding validation (or not) to the identity of the online poster.

The final point I wish to consider is that the online space is outside dominant discourses, that it may be what Foucault termed a heterotopia – (an)other space, places that are outside the ordinary that do not follow the usual rules. Foucault himself cited prisons, rest homes, cemeteries and asylums among these (Johnson 2006). Of course this was long before the internet, but there are similarities to be drawn. Specifically, in heterotopias 'the displacement of time is matched by the disruption of space' (Johnson 2006: 72). While this may be easier to see with regards to a cemetery, the online world plays with both time and space; time can disappear, time can be preserved in its between-date-lines, time can have permanence as something is forever stored. It is not a physical space but allows for the creation of one. Furthermore, online space blurs a boundary between fiction and reality, another aspect of heterotopias (Foucault 1998); it is actual but created within the imagination and function of the online space.

Others have explored this idea through children and young people. McNamee (2000) suggests children find heterotopias and consequently deconstruct discursive adult boundaries within their leisure time, particularly through online video games. However, as mentioned, since she was writing in 2000 online spaces have shifted, and online activity now is exactly that, a place of participation; as such, I suggest there is more room for creativity and playing with identity. Regardless, a central argument that McNamee is making is with regards to control; she is suggesting that participation in online games allows children to 'play' outside the policing and surveillance of adult boundaries. The public world is, of course, an adult-designed and -experienced world. Children merely have designated spaces within it; for example, playgrounds and schools, which are under the control of adults.

This space outside adult supervision is even more important for young people, particularly as teenagers and young people often do not have space of their own; they do not belong in children's spaces, and they are not privy to many spaces frequented by adults, such as pubs or bars. For the teenager there is often nowhere they belong. Moreover, these barriers are 'bound up with assumptions about identity and attempts to construct socially acceptable identities' (Massey 1998: 127); young people are neither children nor adults but are caught somewhere in-between – a liminal stage of personhood. As such, many seek out disordered spaces, that are disused by adults, such as street corners or abandoned areas. Here they can be with their peers, and negotiate their own rules, without adult surveillance. Moreover, these seemingly disordered spaces of children are not to be defined or understood as mere disruption to the ordered striations of adult spaces. Instead, these spaces can be regarded as territories for becoming (Massumi 1992). This is crucial for young people, who are constantly becoming, who are in the process of figuring out who they are. This may be only possible where there is room for self-expression. 'Emergent identities require space of their own in which to assert themselves, and are also grounded in (if not tied to) the specificities of particular locations' (Hall et al. 1999: 505); the location in this instance being the vast world of online activity. The point is that there is some choice and agency over their identity, as adult dominant boundaries are displaced.

While a heterotopia may offer spaces of resistance, the idea of autonomy is, of course, contestable. Particularly within a neoliberal society, we are often governed into the decisions we make under the illusion that we are free to choose (Rose 1999). For young people, they may see certain online versions of their peers and be coerced into accepting this version of normalcy. The fictional presentation of the self may lead to unrealistic expectations of what young people should become, within the spaces to play. This could be furthered by the permanence of the mark left within the online world. Not only are digital worlds forever sealed, but also the data that is created constructs the version of the self that appears online. Carefully selected advertisements that appear within your social media sites and your browsing, of course, are not random and instead are chosen and marketed – they create your 'perfect' sense of place, and the 'perfect' self. Hence, the online world is heavily surveilled and nowhere and nothing is without permanence. Indeed there is a dark side to the space of the internet and the identity issues that may arise.

However, I would suggest here that agency is not lost, and online users are not passive. Indeed the market will respond to the users' needs; there are many examples of companies or platforms that trends have bypassed. Myspace, for example, the leading social media of the early 2000s, has largely disappeared from public use. A product is only viable if there is a market. This raises several points: that young people's interests very much adapt with fashions and fads; and, second, that the rate of change that occurs within Web 2.0 technologies is immense. Furthermore, it proposes the idea that young people may be savvy consumers, and not just manipulated by the market.

In summary, identities are shaped by discourses, which in turn shape them. The online world offers a vast space to play with this idea, particularly as it may operate as a hegemonic space – one that is outside dominant discourses. For the rest of this chapter, I want to explore how this works in practice with two examples. One concerns young people's use of social media platforms, but first I want to discuss teachers and their use of Twitter. In doing this I am asking how far the online world remains a heterotopia, or does it merely create its own hierarchies and dominant discourses?

Twitter and the celebrity teacher

Modern teachers are subject to extreme surveillance. Within school there are official managers, parents, governors, not to mention external pressures from government, official inspectors[2] and league tables. Their practice is no longer individual but instead is a product of and is judged by dominant discourses. The discourse of improvement abounds, and there are a multitude of ways to become 'outstanding'[3] – which must, apparently, be the pursuit of every teacher. Within this myriad of advice and official discourses it is questionable if there is space to 'become' a teacher in one's own variation.

One such place, potentially a disrupted space, is the social media site Twitter. Hence, in this section, I ask whether Twitter is a heterotopia – a third space that defies traditional hierarchies, for example, from educational research, government policy or school management, and allows for autonomy outside dominant discourses. Or is Twitter a place where hierarchies are created, and maintained through positioning, and where dominant discourses are merely reposited and made true by their literal writing into being?

Twitter and social media offer many things that a modern-day teacher, or young person, may seek. In the first instance it is speedy – which fits the modern world that seeks instant gratification; tweets of 140 characters are brief and can be constructed rapidly. However, more importantly, and as I have suggested, there is more space to play at self, and disrupt traditional hierarchical boundaries. For instance, there is space for the everyday teacher to become expert. 'Blogs, Twitter, and social media networks on the World Wide Web have opened up the conversation and levelled the playing field of the ordinary people to explore themselves without the usual gatekeepers' (Cross 2011: 1). A teacher, for example, does not have to have a promoted position to have their voice heard or to suggest areas of reform or pedagogical expertise. Furthermore, 'social media networks like Twitter seem to legitimize talking about yourself' (Cross 2011: 5): they can legitimize the identity you are creating, and you as a professional; particularly if your day-to-day teaching does not. For teachers this can be very rewarding. Teaching can be a lonely place; no longer are you limited to conversations in your department or school, but there is a world outside where you can have your own discussions, largely on your own terms. Social media has made the educational world a village full of possibilities.

If we look at the best-selling books on education, many of those are written by the twitterati; it is this domain that established their field in the first instance. Several of those are written by the self-styled 'most influential blog on education in the UK' (McGill 2016), with 140,000 followers – @teachertoolkit. McGill offers endless tips for teaching and general school practice. His blog is much more than himself, for there are frequently links to other educators; however, McGill is very clever in facilitating these ideas through clicking on his own pages. He is not writing from a distance: he is a deputy head teacher. This very much forms part of his practitioner identity and offers some legitimization. However in a truly neoliberal sense, he and his ideas have been validated by the market that perpetuated him, that read his blog, that buy his books, who favourite and retweet his tweets. Furthermore he proudly recognizes himself as a brand.

Another prominent tweeter is Tom Bennett, the founder of ResearchEd, a contributor for the *Times Educational Supplement* newspaper (TES), and an educational behaviour tsar for the current Conservative government – someone who became less involved in the classroom once more opportunities arose. ResearchEd professes to be 'the online home for anyone interested in educational research, what it means, and how it can – or can't – make a difference in the classroom' (ResearchEd 2016); as such it is a bridge between academia and the classroom, which more traditional educational research has been frequently criticized for not achieving. ResearchEd started by hosting conferences in the UK, but has since diversified to Scandinavia and Australia. The website is more recent. Its web-name is 'workingoutwhatworks' and the logo with a picture of a microscope clearly signals a move towards the scientific analysis of education, which follows recent trends in educational research. The work of both ResearchEd and the Conservative government tsar arguably would not have been possible without Bennett's success on Twitter.

These few examples could be seen as a neoliberal dream: people taking the opportunity to use their expertise, and to reach an audience they could never have fostered without Twitter and social media. However, once upon a time opinions about education were generally left to the 'experts' at universities. Hence, it is possible to suggest that hierarchies are being broken, and instead new ones (outside the university) are created in their place, ones that are less dependent on scholarship. For instance a recent group of self-styled 'education reformers' calling for action in education (Vaughan 2016) included not one single university academic. Instead, the list was made of several people who are prominent on Twitter, as well as some founders of academy chains, free schools and independent educational trusts. As such, it is worth asking if Twitter simply mirrors the privatization of education. Furthermore, the transfer of hierarchies would not be possible without the society in which we live, without the general moves towards privatization undertaken by the ConLib and Conservative governments, without the move away from state-defined education that was so dominant under the New Labour government. In addition, we may ask how much of this is identity negotiation and play, and how much of it is more akin to the corporatization of any product, and the establishment of dominant groups.

There are many other prominent users of Twitter who are not so brand-dominant; moreover, teaching-related hashtags are often trending as teachers actively discuss ideas and share experiences of practice. Here Twitter is the space where professional discourses are reborn; potentially there is space for a socialist collegiality. Indeed many of the twitterati often chat about meeting up at educational events. For many this permits the fiction to become reality, and potentially offers 'real' avenues for connections, friendship or collegiality. For those on the outside, it can of course exclude: it shows you what you are not a part of, the retweeting of conversations between the 'cool gang'. There is, clearly, a ranking system; there are favourites, retweets and followers – you can visibly see how popular you and your ideas are. There is the suggestion that popularity on Twitter is more akin to celebrity than professionalism, where image and popularity (which social media propagates) are central. For one of *The Guardian*'s Secret Teacher page, 'It felt like one big club I wasn't allowed to be a member of' (Secret Teacher 2016).

In summary, Twitter plays with traditional discursive boundaries; moreover, this challenges our ideas of authority and knowledge creation. Instead, the truths of Twitter are created by the users of the platform; it is this that makes it potentially more of a communal and equitable space. However, there is the possibility that within our neoliberal society, one traditional brand is replaced with another more polished one, and Twitter is instead a very modern marketplace. Overall, I suggest that there is room to play, and there is room for anarchy; however, these are some of the pitfalls of modern life – the celebrity teacher and the neoliberal brand.

Young people and the narcissistic self

In Hillary Clinton's recent US presidential campaign, the juxtaposition of two photographs demonstrates the change in the internet. A photograph from her campaign in 2008 shows young people grasping for her hand, or asking an autograph. The 2016 equivalent is young people turning their back, looking to take a selfie[4] with her. A once private interaction has become one that must be validated through sharing online; it is a blurring of our public and private lives. Many people condemned the recent photograph, and indeed all such narcissistic practices in the young.

When we consider how well adults can utilize the internet and social media, it is odd to think how heavily many people criticize young people and their reliance on social media and their phones for connectivity. As such, it is worth asking if we have different values for young people: are we judging them with moral conduct that adults are not expected to follow? An alternative is to suggest that our reasons for disliking social media trends for young people is more to do with online safety; however, this still presents the young person as less of an individual than the adult – someone without autonomy or agency.

It is important to see this criticism within the wider landscape of what is socially constructed for childhood and young people. Indeed many of these criticisms were similarly levelled in the 1980s at the box in the corner; it was said that the television would lead to the disappearance of childhood (see Postman 1982; Elkind 1981). As Meyrowitz (1985: 363) states, 'television removes barriers that once divided people of different ages and reading abilities into social situation'; if it is not automatically clear, he was saying this as a point of displeasure and concern. We can of course apply this sentiment to the internet and Web 2.0, but quadruple its implications. We can also flip Meyrowitz's meaning and suggest that the media disruption of classifications that are often socially imposed through age, place or position in society is a positive move – it blurs hierarchies.

What writers like Meyrowitz, Postman or Elkind are perhaps guilty of is taking childhood as a designated space with an essentialist meaning. In general, our perceptions of what a childhood should be are very much bound by idealized romantic notions. This rose-tinted positioning allows us to correct our own histories (Burman 2008), and present imagined pasts and hopeful futures, although I suggest that this romanticization does not acknowledge the here and now of children or young people's experiences. As such, interpreting childhood and youth through an adult lens is always that – one that is always already caught up in our own adult productions. As Moran elegantly summarizes, 'the category that is "the child" is not, in itself, anything but a cultural formation and an object of adult desire… we should not try to impose adult meanings on it' (2002: 157).

This is particularly problematic for young people who are neither adult nor child but occupy more of a liminal stage in-between; a place where becoming is always already in process, where rules and responsibility can become a burden that needs to be broken, where the search for identity is ongoing and in flux, where space is not easily found that is not defined by adult surveillance. Hence we may consider what the online world offers to young people; indeed, is there space to play with the self and to become in an 'authentic' manner that negotiates discursive constructs?

However, many, like Turkle, argue that online friendships are non-authentic:

> Their digitalized friendships – played out with emoticon emotions, so often predicated on rapid response rather than reflection – may prepare them, at times through nothing more than their superficiality, for relationships that could bring superficiality to a higher power, that is, for relationship with the inanimate. They come to accept lower expectations for connection and, finally, the idea that robot friendships could be sufficient unto the day.
>
> *(Turkle 2011: 17)*

While Turkle makes an important point about immediacy (and much of Web 2.0 is premised upon this), the implication is that offline friendships are somehow more valid, that they suffer none of the critique above; they are all genuine, trustworthy and 'real'. Indeed in previous years, young people's identities would primarily be formed through interaction with peers (Morris and Fuller 1999). For young people this is not always positive – the pitfalls online, such as cliques, bullying and isolation, are also found offline. One difference is that online there is more space to explore, more opportunity to meet someone you cannot find at your school or your peer group; the isolated child has more avenues to become who they want to be. Of course the unknown does bring very real risks, and there are important reasons to suggest that the virtual world can be unsafe for young people; it is often unregulated, and the dangers are very real. The desperately sad case of 14-year-old Breck Bednar, who was groomed and murdered by a 19-year-old through online gaming, is just one awful example.

However, we can acknowledge those angers, challenges and engage with them, as many young people inevitably will. Furthermore, the online world can offer a space to play positively with those challenges of growing up, and becoming. The online world can be 'playful, and even carnivalesque' (Danet 2001: 8); it offers a space for resistance, or for anarchy, which is often what young people are seeking. As suggested in the previous section, it can contest hierarchies and positioning, which is a gift for young people, particularly with regards to their own identity.

Indeed the clearest examples of playful versions of the self may come from role-playing games such as World of Warcraft. As such, a young person negotiating their identity may enjoy taking on an alternative one – in a 'safe' fictional world; as Bessière et al. (2007) note, they often take on idealized characteristics of the self, which can of course be positive or negative, but it does allow for play.

Another example of play and resistance would include blogs or vlogs, vlogging being a particularly fashionable activity among young people; its versatility being such that vlogs can be about lifestyle, make-up, friendships, travel, or they can be used to define an identity, for example 'coming out' as lesbian, gay, bisexual, transgender or queer (LGBTQ+) or about a young person battling with anxiety. The disestablishment of cultural and societal hierarchies can be shown through 'coming out', specifically as LGBTQ+ vlogs range from the celebrity to the unknown; 'coming out' vlogs include Tom Daley (celebrity and Olympian diver), YouTubers such as Ingrid Nilsen and Tyler Oakley, to the everyday person in projects such as 'It Gets Better' (www.itgetsbetter.org). As Tyler Oakley, an American YouTuber, states, '[There are] a lot of people grow up thinking, "Oh my Gosh, I'm in this small town. I don't have anybody around me who understands what I'm going through." Thank the Lord for the Internet! You do have people to relate to' (Oakley 2008).

Of course, vloggers, who are often YouTubers,[6] can become celebrities, Tyler Oakley being a case in point. He has recently developed the Tyler Oakley Show (an online show with Hollywood celebrity interviews) through collaboration with Ellen DeGeneres. Closer to home, one of the UK's most famous and influential young bloggers is Zoe Sugg, known as Zoella;[7] there is also her boyfriend Alfie

Deyes, and her brother Joe Sugg. All of these, and many others, have earned millions though their vlogs: it is, after all, their job. There is also add-on merchandise. For instance, Zoella has a make-up range, and a novel, which was the fastest selling debut novel since records began (Singh 2014) – it was also exposed as ghostwritten. Hence, again, we come back to the brand.

In contrast to this, vlogging can be used in a more 'authentic' sense; projects such as Youth Speak,[8] a mental health project for young people, or the 'It Gets Better Project'[9] aimed at LGBTQ+ inclusion; both of these involved sharing online 'confessional' videos. In a very old-fashioned way, there is something cathartic about sharing your pain with others. There is relief when you find others who feel the same, or who offer you comfort. Indeed, reaching out is something the online world very much permits. For communities that have been marginalized, such as LGBTQ+, this allows for a great deal of empathy, as Green et al. discovered in their analysis of online LGBT videos:

> The disclosure of experience allows contributors a degree of empathy with the viewer; as well as a means by which to seek empathy, they can identify and associate with each other. Furthermore, by allowing viewers to identify and relate to experiences, contributors are themselves acting prosocially.
>
> *(Green et al. 2012: 17)*

It is social, rather than anti-social; it is connecting with people, rather than isolating yourself. For every question young people have with regards to their identity, there is someone there to answer them. No longer does the young person have to grow up isolated because of who they are.

In summary, there are many negatives that are associated with the online world – from the very real dangers faced via anonymity and communication to the neoliberal branding that can ensue. However, a place that is outside adult boundaries, that allows for negotiation without hegemonic barriers, is important for young people who are actively negotiating their identities. They need these places to become; 'children have… been recognized as co-constituents of their own worlds – their own spaces – in ways which escape or even defy the ordered spatialities of adults' (Cloke and Jones 2005: 311). Nowhere is more open to opportunity than the spatialities that are offered online.

In conclusion

For teachers, an online space offers room for exploration, validation and professionalism; a place outside traditional hierarchies and space to explore their teacher identity. Teachers are no longer confined to their classrooms, their schools or their own ideas. For young people, the online world is dangerous, yet exciting. It is a vast place apparently away from the boundaries of adult-led society. This is vital for young people, who desperately search for a place of their own but who are bound by the adult-designed world in which they live. For both there is much space for exploration but also very real problems to negotiate, from the very dangerous to the neoliberal branded illusion of the 'real' self.

What we do experience is a blurring of boundaries between adulthood and childhood, personal and private, expert and amateur, consumer and product, and between reality and fiction. It is this fuzzy third space that, while risky, offers more hope of self-expression and identity formation than what is possible within the physical world, which itself cannot escape its roots and embedded hierarchal structures.

Notes

1 Discussed in more detail in Seargeant and Tagg (2014).
2 In England, inspections are carried out by Ofsted.
3 'Outstanding' is the top category for Ofsted, and what teachers, schools, universities, etc. should aspire to.
4 'Selfie' was the Oxford English Dictionaries word of the year in 2013; http://blog. oxforddictionaries.com/press-releases/oxford-dictionaries-word-of-the-year-2013.
5 'Blog' being a shortened version of weblog and 'vlog' of video blog.
6 Specific to the YouTube channel.
7 In 2015 she was listed on DeBretts 500 most influential people in Britain; www.tel-egraph.co.uk/news/celebritynews/11368331/Zoella-and-Alfie-feature-in-Debretts-500-most-influential-people-in-Britain.html.
8 www.youthspeakmh.com.
9 www.itgetsbetter.org.

References

Bessière, K., Seay, A.F. and Kiesler, S. (2007) The ideal elf: identity exploration in World of Warcraft. *Cyber Psychology & Behavior* 10(4), 530–5.

boyd, d.m. (2001) *Taken Out of Context: American Teen Sociality in Networked Publics* PhD thesis, University of California, Berkeley.

Buckingham, D. (2000) *After the Death of Childhood: Growing Up in the Age of Electronic Media.* Malden, MA: Polity Press.

Burman, E. (2008) *Deconstructing Developmental Psychology.* London: Routledge.

Cloke, P. and Jones, O. (2005) 'Unclaimed territory': childhood and disordered space(s). *Social & Cultural Geography* 6(3), 311–33.

Cross, M. (2011) *Bloggerati, Twitterati: How Blogs and Twitter are Transforming Popular Culture.* Santa Barbara, CA: Greenwood Publishing Group.

Danet, B. (2001) *Cyberpl@y. Communicating Online.* Oxford and New York: Berg.

Deumert, A. (2014) The performance of a ludic self on social network(ing)sites. In P. Seargeant and C. Tagg (eds.) *The Language of Social Media: Identity and Community on the Internet*, 23–45. Basingstoke and New York: Palgrave Macmillan.

Elkind, D. (1981) *The Hurried Child: Growing Up Too Fast Too Soon.* Reading, MA: Addison Wesley.

Foucault, M. (1998) Different spaces. In J. Faubion (ed.) *Aesthetics: the Essential Works*, 175–85. London: Allen Lane.

Foucault, M. (2002 [1972]). *The Archaeology of Knowledge.* London: Routledge.

Green, M., Bobrowicz, A. and Ang, C.S. (2015) The lesbian, gay, bisexual and transgender community online: discussions of bullying and self-disclosure in YouTube videos. *Behaviour & Information Technology* 34(7), 704–12.

Hall, T., Coffey, A. and Williamson, H. (1999) Self, space and place: youth identities and citizenship. *British Journal of Sociology of Education* 20(4), 501–13.

Henriques, J., Hollway, W., Urwin, C., Venn, C. and Walkerdine, V. (eds.) (1998) *Changing the Subject*. London and New York: Routledge.

Johnson, P. (2006) Unravelling Foucault's 'different spaces'. *History of the Human Sciences* 19(4), 75–90.

Karinthy, F. (2007 [1929]) Chain-links. Translated by A. Makkai. In M.E.J. Newman and D. Watts (eds.) *The Structure and Dynamics of Networks*. Princeton, NJ: Princeton University Press.

Massey, D. (1998) The spatial construction of youth cultures. In T. Skelton and G. Valentine (eds.) *Cool Places: Geographies of Youth Cultures*, 121–9. London and New York: Routledge.

Massumi, B. (1992) *A User's Guide to Capitalism and Schizophrenia: Deviations from Deleuze and Guattari*. Cambridge, MA: MIT Press.

McGill, R. (2016) Te@cher toolkit: The most influential blog on education in the UK. Retrieved from www.teachertoolkit.me.

McNamee, S. (2000) Foucault's heterotopia and children's everyday lives. *Childhood* 7(4), 479–92.

Meyrowitz, J. (1985) *No Sense of Place: The Impact of Electronic Media on Social Behavior*. Oxford: Oxford University Press.

Moran, J. (2002) Childhood and nostalgia in contemporary culture. *European Journal of Cultural Studies* 5(2), 155–73.

Morris, K. and Fuller, M. (1999). Heterosexual relationships of young women in a rural environment. *British Journal of Sociology of Education* 20(4), 531–43.

Oakley (2008) National Coming Out Day 2008. Retrieved from https://www.youtube.com/watch?v=HruqmAWjv3s.

O'Reilly, T. (2012 [2005]) What is Web2.0? Design patterns and business models for the next generation of software. In M Mandiberg (ed.) *The Social Media Reader*, 32–52. New York: New York University Press.

Postman, N. (1982). *The Disappearance of Childhood*. London: W.H. Allen.

ResearchEd (2016) Retrieved from www.workingoutwhatworks.com/en-GB/.

Rose, N. (1999) *Governing the Soul*, 2nd edn. London: Free Association Books.

Seargeant, P. and Tagg, C. (2014) Introduction: the language of social media. In P. Seargeant and C. Tagg (eds.) *The Language of Social Media: Identity and Community on the Internet*, 1–20. Basingstoke and New York: Palgrave Macmillan.

Secret Teacher (2016) Secret Teacher: I refuse to be a Kardashian with a PGCE. *The Guardian*. Retrieved from www.theguardian.com/teacher-network/2016/jan/30/secret-teacher-refuse-kardashian-with-a-pgce-social-media-toxic.

Singh, A. (2014) Zoella breaks record for first-week book sales. *The Daily Telegraph*. Retrieved from www.telegraph.co.uk/news/celebritynews/11268540/Zoella-breaks-record-for-first-week-book-sales.html.

Turkle, S. (2011) *Alone Together: Why We Expect More from Technology and Less from Each Other*. New York: Basic Books.

Vaughan, R. (2016) 'Education reformers' call for more tests and stronger discipline. *TES*. Retrieved from www.tes.com/news/school-news/breaking-news/education-reformers-call-more-tests-and-stronger-discipline.

Walkerdine,V. (1997) Redefining the subject in situated cognition theory. In D. Kirshner and J.A. Whitson (eds.) *Situated Cognition: Social, Semiotic, and Psychological Perspectives*, 57–70. Mahwah, NJ: Lawrence Erlbaum.

Walshaw, M. (2007). *Working with Foucault in Education*. Rotterdam: Sense Publishers.

Werbner, P. (1997) Introduction: The Dialectics of Cultural Hybridity. In P. Werbner and T. Modood (eds.) *Debating Cultural Hybridity*, 1–26. London: Zed Books.

12

A FABLE: *THE HAPPY TEACHER*

Deirdre Diffley-Pierce

Introduction

This chapter takes the form of an illustrated fable in which issues of teacher identity are explored. The importance of a teacher's creative life within and beyond the classroom walls is told in story-form, drawing first upon Blake's 'Songs of Innocence and of Experience'; second, upon two of Oscar Wilde's children's stories, 'The Happy Prince' and 'The Selfish Giant'. Barrs and Cork's research for *The Reader in the Writer* also underpins the story, informing the choice of fable and pictures as providing strong, narrative structures within which to explore the theme of innocence and experience within an educational context. Typically, the fable harks back to an idealized age of innocence in the mind of the teacher protagonist with idealized notions of education set against mechanized, assessment-driven approaches. It raises questions about the creative spaces open to beginning teachers and about what it might mean to be a teacher. Language, style and form are intentionally kept simple, enabling the fable to question, at a very personal level, the very ancient purpose of literature and the mystery that lies at the heart of both student and teacher response. The idea that prescriptive planning and formulaic delivery can strip lessons of a sense of mystery for both students and teachers lies at the heart of the story. So too does the idea that the creative spaces classrooms offer young teachers are powerfully and inextricably linked to their own sense of creativity and identity.

The fable

Once upon a time, there lived a young girl called Solas. She lived in a small, island kingdom that once, long ago, was famous for the might of its cities, the wealth of its kings and queens and for the learned scholars it produced.

FIGURE 12.1 Solas: Once upon a time…

Living in such a kingdom, once so confident in its long history of erudition, it was hardly surprising that when the time came to decide what she should do in life, Solas decided she could do worse than become a teacher. 'After all,' her mother remarked in the sometimes opaque way she had of speaking to her daughter, 'it's a good jumping-off point.' Solas chafed at her mother's words, wondering what indeed she meant by them. But, in the time-honoured way that daughters have of learning from their mothers, Solas trusted in her wisdom and squirrelled the thought away to ponder at her leisure.

What could be a better calling in such a privileged life, thought Solas, than to become a teacher? She had been raised to love God by parents who, while they didn't believe in *everything* to do with holy books, acquainted her with their stories, pictures and verses and thus impressed upon Solas' young heart a strong and active conscience.

So when the time finally came and she was called upon to make a choice, all things considered, Solas chose teaching as a way of life. And into that life came a youth; a wild boy who made her laugh and who had a fine, loud voice. In the mornings, he would sing almost as soon as he got up, while preparing his breakfast or shaving in front of the mirror. On Solas' darkest days, of which I'm afraid there were sometimes quite a few, his great capacity for cheer would fill her full of life no matter what cares or worries burdened her young heart.

Very soon, Solas and Gra became a pair and even sooner it seemed they had three wild, bonny and very distracting children to fill their days and nights. All this while, Solas worked as a teacher and was pleased to find that much of what she had surmised about her work and the life she had envisaged was true and had indeed come to pass. She had time in the spring holidays to paint the blue cornflowers and the green leaves of the wild garlic that grew in her garden and in the lane beyond. She had time in summer to use the tip of her finest, sable paint brush to pick out the detail in the eye of a richly coloured dragon she was busy painting – against the backdrop of a blue sky, against ochre mountains and the white ripples of the sea. When autumn came, she had time with her children to make 'fish bones' out of the brown horse chestnut leaves. In the crisp, dry air she crumpled the withered flesh from between the leaf veins, exposing the skeleton beneath for them to see. She had time in the early mornings, before school, to read the work of her favourite writers and poets and to carry their words into school with her, in her mind and in her heart, so that they were part of the ebb and flow of her teaching. All this and more, she took with her into the classroom to share with her students.

FIGURE 12.2 The dragon's eye

Teaching, she discovered to her surprise, was more than fun – it was her life blood. Solas poured her heart and soul, her love of life, family and learning and her own limited experience of death into the classroom. For why not? 'Here was life, all life!' she thought. And when Solas' beloved brother, John, died and her young heart quailed, she kept his memory alive in her classroom, talking openly of the sickness that killed him so that her students would understand that death too, as she now knew to her cost, was part of life.

At the end of the day, she would walk out across the playground (for schools still had them in those days), her head in the clouds remembering how beautifully Deepkamal had read – how when Desdemona died and Othello despaired at the treachery played upon his loving soul, you could have heard a pin drop in the classroom. In the shade of the oak trees, she would look up at the school buildings mapped against the sky and wonder, could there be a better life? For all of life was there to share with students, and to enjoy, and nothing in her own life was wasted, or not fed into her lessons, or went unrecognized by her as valuable.

And so the years went by and Solas matured as a teacher, a teacher who wanted time to probe the hearts of the students who came through her classroom. Year after year, the delicate layers of their young lives were shed and took new forms. Solas watched these fragile transformations. She saw how experience of the world slowly intruded on the quiet interior of their lives and it was language that helped her bridge the fissure that was sometimes left behind in them.

She remembered Vanessa who could sing unaccompanied – her strong voice filling the classroom as she entered with her bags and books thrown on the desk to begin the lesson. Further back, Lois, who was so bright that she had read books in her first year that were being taught to the cleverest students before they left for university. Ravneet, who wrote with the precision, control and humour of a Beckett. Chaandni, who carried herself with the grace and serenity of a young sage. Peter, who climbed into lessons through the window rather than use the door and ate the apples and cheese from the still life he was painting – a memory that stayed with Solas for all the days of her life and brought a smile to her lips each time she thought of it. Hans, who taught her about Ghana, drawing a makeshift map on the board in his haste to explain its complex history, and Rozlyn, from Ghana too, who taught her how high and far a young woman's dreams could take her.

Solas felt at home in her school on the west side of the great city. She loved her students, she understood their split loyalties to the lands their parents had come from and the land they found themselves in now. They talked about it often. They read stories and poems and plays together about the small dreams and hopes of ordinary people. They asked her question after question until it seemed that all the questions that came into their young and troubled minds might spill out into the classroom on any cold January or warm summer's day when the smell of cut grass stole in through the open windows. 'Is there a God?' they asked her one day after a line in Blake's *Tyger* had made them wonder about the creator as artisan, as blacksmith, shaper of all things, pounder of fierce metal in the burnished gold of fire and the orange glow of a tiger's eye – 'Is he my God, or yours?' they had asked one another.

And Solas let the questions ripple, and sometimes rage, around the classroom until they would ignite in the raw fire of their minds to burn to the end of their days, she hoped. Fervently. For what is a lesson, Solas believed, but a space in which to share the rich, dark heart of a verse, a line or an image? Towards no discernible end, she saw sometimes, but simply because their questions were what mattered.

★ ★ ★

And then one night, while Solas slept at Gra's side, a great change came. Creeping slowly through the darkness, it came to break her life in two. It came to sever, to separate the living from the dead, to make clear the triumph of death over life. On a raw winter's morning in early January, far away across the sea, Solas' mother Bridie, suddenly and without warning, sank down on the still floor and died. When the news reached Solas across the sea, she beat her breast in anguish. She tore at her skin and bent double in her seat but the pain was here to stay. And stay it did.

Every day, in the numb weeks and months that followed, Solas went off to work, to teach her students in the same way. But nothing was the same. Everything had changed in her mind and in her heart and Solas was no longer the happy teacher she once had been. This time her loss swept into the classroom behind her like a cold wind, trailing its icy draft. Beset with grief, she saw her students through hollow eyes now, for she no longer cared about the future they would one day inherit. Every word she spoke to them and every word she wrote in response to them reminded her of Bridie and of her free spirit, her laughter, her strength and truth. Her mother, the bedrock of Solas' young life, was gone and a terrible sadness took root deep within her soul.

With a heavy heart, she reflected anew on the advice of her mother who had told her so long ago that teaching 'was a good jumping-off point'. What did the words mean? Jump off into what? And why was teaching not a good enough pursuit – in and of itself? What had her mother really wanted her to do in life if this was not it?

Solas brooded. She grew unhappy with her lot and looked out beyond the classroom walls, no longer content to stay within them. Restless and unhappy but not sure what else she could do, she at last found a job teaching young people who wanted to be teachers, like her – in the very centre of the great city and in a noble university where the erudite scholars of the land published greatly esteemed papers. Solas trod the hallowed passages quietly, sometimes looking in through the half-open doors of the learned doctors and professors. To begin with, Solas' heart was so heavy that she barely noticed what was said in the dark lecture theatres where young teachers came to learn. She was drawn though to the young people who had chosen teaching as their work in life, as she had done once. So, as the years went by and her sense of loss burrowed its way so deep that, some days, she no longer knew it was still there, Solas' spirits rallied and she threw herself into her new life. She tramped the pavements all over the great city, visiting school after school, classroom after classroom and watching lesson after lesson of the young teachers in her care.

★ ★ ★

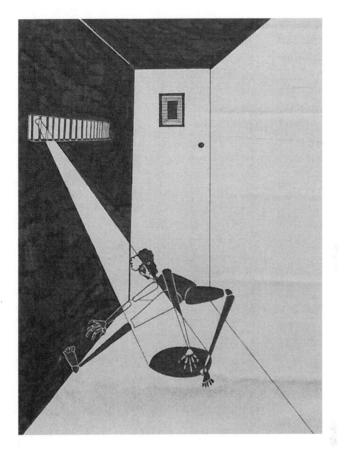

FIGURE 12.3 Enclosure

And the years went by again and Solas found herself, quite suddenly, in the middle years of her life with her three children grown up and with time to look around her. She saw how the world of teaching had changed since the early days, so long ago now, when she had begun. And she wondered at it all. 'Where have all the teachers gone?' she asked Gra suddenly one evening as they looked out through the three long windows that framed the orange sunset beyond.

It seemed a strange thing for Solas to say but, she told Gra, the type of teacher she had once been seemed no longer to exist. In classroom after classroom, she saw teachers beginning lesson after lesson in the same way. And in subject after subject, she wondered at what she saw. For teachers now, it seemed to Solas, were encouraged to act as if they weren't in the classroom at all. They should fade into the background of a lesson and hand over quickly something called 'learning' to the students. This puzzled Solas greatly. What was learning? All the young teachers seemed very confident that it existed. They talked knowledgeably about its existence, telling Solas eagerly about the checks and balances they had set up to prove it was there. They employed elaborate tricks to catch the students 'learning' and to help them all catch each other learning. A good lesson, they told Solas was one where they did little and the students did a lot.

All this Solas pondered in her heart.

And more. For Solas noticed other things had changed too. Students could tell her as she moved around the breezy aisles of the spacious, new classrooms and the cramped spaces of the older ones, exactly what they could do and what they could not do. Many described themselves not in words but as numbers or 'levels' and everyone knew where the lesson was going, how it would begin and how it would end up. Solas, sometimes sitting silently, sometimes talking to the children around her, marvelled at it all and at the confident predictions of progress made by the young teachers she encountered.

She observed how lessons no longer flowed one into another, as she remembered long ago. They were tidy, carefully divided into sections and neatly wrapped up at the end. Solas looked on as her young teachers asked their students to identify their 'learning' at the close of lessons. Silently, she recalled the classroom discussions of long ago that had carried on after the sudden ringing of the school bell had interrupted them, when students hung around after the lessons to talk more or simply to chat to her as she packed her things away. Solas said nothing but she considered afresh – would her students of yesteryear have been able to tell her exactly what they had learnt from their lessons? Would they have cared? Solas wondered to herself. Would some of the value of her memories have seeped away over the years if that's all she had wanted from them?

But most of all, she marvelled at the 'activities'. At the time spent in front of screens planning complicated lessons. Lessons with beginnings, middles and ends. Lessons with activity after activity elaborately designed, Solas could see, to bring about the 'learning' everyone was talking about, and everyone but everyone wanted at the heart of their lessons. Her head would spin as 'activities' followed thick and fast, one upon the other in lesson after lesson.

Plans handed to her at the beginning of the lessons would leave her blinking in bewilderment at their density. 'How long does it take to write these plans?' she found herself wondering aloud to Gra who, tired of the fiendish complexity of his own job, shook his head wearily, having no answers for her. 'And at what cost? They don't have time to really read the poem anymore, to get to know it, to think about why they chose it or what they feel about it,' she worried. But Gra didn't answer. Feelings were given short shrift in his world. He still sang in the mornings but less so than before for he had his own troubles navigating the shifting tides of greedy commerce in the great city. He looked at Solas, his soulmate of many years now, and gazed out with her as the sun quietly dropped below the horizon.

In almost every lesson she watched, there were complex instructions to follow, complex and involved activities, and complex arrangements to meet the needs of children judged to be lagging behind. Solas herself floundered at the pace and speed of it all. She found herself sympathizing with the many students she saw who shut themselves off from the legion demands made upon them to *learn,*

learn, learn – and to divide their 'learning' up so that it could be measured all the more accurately. Solas wondered at the lack of privacy; at the loss of the myriad interior worlds students had seemed, in her mind's eye, to inhabit long ago when teachers were not privy to the mysterious and oblique ways in which students chose to learn.

And all the time, she walked to and fro among the hundreds of schools in the great city. Day by day, the schools seemed to change around her and day by day she would wonder at what it all meant for the students at the heart of it all. Solas arrived in schools across the city to be greeted by television screens in foyers that no one ever watched and wondered who had put them there and why. The lessons she watched, it seemed to her, were repeated again and again, retrieved countless times from computers and yet teachers planned more and more of them as if there could never be enough. Oh God, that there should be any unaccounted for space left in a lesson to pause, to linger, to feel. Solas despaired. Time. What to *do* with it? How to fill the space, quickly oh so quickly, with *learning*!

Poems, books or plays she observed, were rarely taught whole, as they had been written, but chopped up into bits of paper so that 'learning' could take place. What then, if not learning, Solas puzzled, *was* taking place in children's minds when they first heard the rhythms of Blake's *Tyger*? In its entirety, as he intended it to be experienced? Everywhere Solas looked, there were fragments and scraps of 'learning' as though the young teachers she came across had been told that students might choke on the 'whole' of anything they were exposed to. In vain, Solas quietly lamented the loss of shared experience with students. She lamented the loss of sharing a poem for the first time, in the way it had been written, like a jewel on the page, in the ear, mind and heart and shared as one together. Silently, she fought the urge to swat aside the Steri-strips of mangled verses that littered the tables of the classrooms she visited and left behind her.

Like 'learning', Solas noticed 'discovery' was greatly prized by the teachers she spoke to and took place, she was told, with complete conviction, always in groups and pairs, very rarely alone and never in silence. All learning was social, she was told, and rarely took place in solitude or through listening to a teacher talk. Student talk, Solas learnt, was desirable but teacher talk most definitely was not, and was frowned upon with the greatest severity of all, by *everyone*.

Solas kept her own counsel but remembered in her heart how happy she had been talking to her classes about the books, poems and plays she had loved. With eyes wide, she looked on as in school after school, fledgling teachers who had wanted to soar soon lost all confidence in the relevance of their personal vision of a poem, book or play and fell quickly to lower, safer and more prosaic ground. Love and knowledge of the spoken and written word were no longer to be shared with children at the expense of 'learning'. Solas' young teachers were told in no uncertain terms that 'learning' was in the grasp of all students, whose powers merely needed to be tapped like water in a bottomless well. Or better still, Solas learnt, to be facilitated through managing 'activities' – held in the greatest esteem by all for their ability to unlock the 'learning' within children.

And in every lesson, there was talk of 'learning' and after lessons there was talk of learning and often there was talk of students' responsibility for learning and of teachers' responsibility for planning evermore complex levels of learning. Solas gazed at the colourful slides on the great white-screens, at the bubbles, bullet points and boxes. She watched the children filling in grids, charts and worksheets reducing and reducing until they had a gobbet sized concept here or the skeleton, pith or bare bones of an idea there. Until all the frail, tantalizing and ragged flesh of thought had been trussed up – well and truly bound. And she contemplated the fear she saw at the heart of it all. She saw how the plans, grids and boxes made her young teachers feel better. For with them they could fill the black holes of incomprehension, bag up the spiral of unanswered questions for later and fill the vortex with any meaning rather than none. This was distraction on a grand scale, it seemed to Solas, and beneath it all a terrible paucity of faith, she despaired, that students would ever be clever enough, or interested enough to be trusted with a text, idea or experience unreconstructed, without filtering.

Solas looked on in wonder, all the while remembering a very different time. And a great sadness grew in her for the students of whom so much was now demanded, for how quickly they had to grow up! How carelessly tossed-aside their childish worlds in the hungry quest to improve on the raw material of self. And for the young teachers who might as well have gone into another job for the little that was demanded of *them*, in contrast, as teachers.

Years went by and Solas still worked at the university, teaching teachers in the heart of the city. She had grown older and her hair was grey now but she continued to tramp the streets of the great city, visiting schools in one capacity or another. Tirelessly she walked, keeping her memories close and her thoughts quiet. At home, she still spoke to Gra about the teachers and students which meant so much to her and about the changes she had seen in the great city.

Early one morning, tired out by a restless night and by now in her old age, Solas sat in her chair by an open window and looked out on the blue cornflowers and wild garlic in her garden. On the walls of her room hung the pictures she had drawn during the holidays in her years as a teacher. Two were of her nieces and she remembered the slow process of deciding on composition, colour and design. Quietly, at the kitchen table and in full sight of the white daisies on the lawn outside, she had brought the pictures into being for her own pleasure and in the happiest moments of her life. No thoughts of progress had troubled her. She had needed no one in the moment with her. All around her were the rooms she had lived in, had raised a family in and seen life and grief.

Solas quietly mourned the part in lessons she had once played. She mourned the type of teacher she had been, lost now forever, whose life experience had been so much a part of the students she taught. She thought of the joyless lessons she had seen in which the teacher's experience of life, knowledge and love of subject was no longer of any great consequence to anyone. She thought of the exhausted young teachers she knew now planning endless, whirly-gig activities, and pitied them for what they had never really experienced – the joy of a lesson that could go

FIGURE 12.4 Eléonore with wild garlic

anywhere. She pitied the loss of exposition that had robbed the soul from the role of teacher and rejoiced in the mutual sharing of knowledge she had once enjoyed – gone, she knew now, forever.

Solas' eye rested for a moment on the slain dragon in her picture – on its writhing serpent's body and ferocious eye as it lashed the air with tongue and tail. She wanted to know if there was a way back to innocence. Back to her classroom before the reptile slithered under door and desk to claw the tiled floor between the students' feet. There was once, she knew, a time when its hot breath had not befouled the air of classrooms across the city and she recognized the serpent for what it was – a thing grown frenzied and desperate on the neurosis of process, of failure and on a crisis of belief in anything worth teaching. Deep in her soul, Solas suffered no such crisis – for her own teaching had been born not out of process but out of response to her subject and to her students; these things first, she nodded at the dragon, above all else, first.

And what of Solas' heart and the blows dealt it? The loss of her brother, John, and her mother, Bridie, now long gone and so deeply mourned? What of these and other blows life dealt her? Happily through time, she learnt how to understand

FIGURE 12.5 Héloïse with green leaves

her loss, though Time was not her only friend in this. Through it all, Solas leaned heavily on the power of words to heal her. As a little girl long ago, growing up in the great kingdom with all her life ahead of her, Bridie used to brush Solas' hair in the mornings before school with long, confident brushstrokes. Her mother's lips had moved in time then with the rhythm of the brush, reciting the words of poems she loved and which found a place in Solas' heart too and sustained her. She could not say why or how she had learned them and was glad of it – for the feeling of the words and the sound of her mother's voice were what Solas had first cherished, without knowing their meaning at all and that voice was with her still.

On this morning early in May, with her eye drawn slowly from her picture to the blue Iris in the garden and the forget-me-nots at the pond's edge, Solas thought of Shelley's elegy to Keats and the words she had clung to when her mother died:

> Stay yet awhile! Speak to me once again;
> Kiss me, so long but as a kiss may live;
> And in my heartless breast and burning brain
> That word, that kiss, shall all thoughts else survive.

FIGURE 12.6 The serpent's body and ferocious eye

'What words,' thought Solas, 'and how they have stayed with me!' She thought of all the lessons she had seen in all the classrooms of the great city. She remembered the many poems dissected, butchered and splayed out on tables for the cursory gaze and hostile interrogation of students bent on 'learning' what was to be 'got' from them. For what? Solas thought. For an exam, was it? For a level, was it? For certain, it was not to sustain life, or love or to help explain loss, thought Solas.

She thought too about how in her darkest moments in life, she had sometimes felt as though her heart might turn to stone inside her. Looking back, Solas thought that she understood in some small, infinitesimal way a little of how experience of life, or death, could calcify the human heart – slowly, secretly and with unforeseen consequences. At times, Solas recalled, she had been beyond the reach of any help, save that offered up to her in words. She thought now of the shut-off children she had watched in lessons in the busy heart of the city and looked at the great, hard oaks standing tall in the garden. It seemed to Solas that such mighty living things had once been the slenderest, most delicate of saplings and had been let grow with feeling towards the light and air, uninterrupted and with grace.

FIGURE 12.7 Sorcha, waves, light and sky: 'That word, that kiss, shall all thoughts else survive,' Percy Bysshe Shelley

Solas thought of her mother and of how in her mind over the years she had grieved for her loss and pleaded, like Shelley, for her to 'Stay yet awhile!' for one last conversation. She wanted to tell Bridie of the deep gladness she had felt as a teacher and how such gladness had somehow begun long ago with her. She wanted to talk with her as with her students long ago in her classroom on the edges of the great city – of a world that may or may not be godless but where there were words to heal, to enlighten and to help make whole again.

Gra stirred upstairs in his sleep. He slept peacefully these days and some of his old optimism had returned now he no longer travelled into the city every day. Solas shifted in her chair, distracted anew by the beauty of the morning light on grass, trees, flowers and water. She decided that hers had been a life well-lived at a time when teaching was still magical. And she did not regret it. She remembered the mystery at the heart of her lessons, the aching, dizzying, defying space – long ago when learning took you anywhere, without you knowing. Oh, without you knowing. When innocence and experience mattered more, so much more than anything else – when simply knowing that alone had made her happy to be a teacher. For much of life, in those days, had been so simple to share.

Reference

Figures 12.1, 12.2, 12.6 and 12.7 adapted from *Icon with St. George Slaying the Dragon*, Russian (Novgorod), early sixteenth century in Cormack, R. (2007) *Icons*, London: British Museum Press, 92.

INDEX

alienation 5
Arabic 30–7, 102–3
Arab Spring 135
Arendt, Hannah 109

bilingualism 31
Blake, William 148
Blood Hunt (Neil M. Gunn) 124
Blunkett, David 29
book clubs 116–20
Bourdieu, Pierre 68
'Brexit' 56, 83, 94, 127
Britton, James 42
Buell, Lawrence 4
Buryatia (Russian Federation) 67, 70,
     72–9
Byatt, A. S. 43

cheder 29
Cliff Hodges, Gabrielle xv
Clinton, Hillary 141
Collective Unconscious 124
Conservationism (in
     New Zealand) 6
cosmopolitanism 68, 71, 96
Council of Europe 123, 131
creative writing 42–4, 46, 60
creativity xiv, 28, 44, 65–6, 148
critical literacy 11
cross-curricular education 3
Cruel Century 67, 77–9
Curriculum for Excellence (Scotland) 123,
     129, 131, 132

democracy 79
dialect 131
diaspora 31, 38, 39, 124
Durham Cathedral 57, 60

ecocritical literacy 10–11
ecocriticism xiv, 4, 10, 62
ecology 1
emergent identities 138
endangered species 3–4
English (language) xiv, 36, 65
English (subject) 4, 14–16, 23–5,
     42–3, 62–3
English classroom 23, 25
English literature 43, 47–8
English pedagogy 56
English subject knowledge 16
environmental identities 4–8, 11
environmental knowledge 7–8

fables 148
Facebook 135
faith-based complementary schooling 29
fiction series 115
film (in education) 14–26
Foucault, Michel 65, 136, 137
France xiii, 94–109
Free Voluntary Reading 113–14
Freire, Paulo xi

General Certificate of Secondary Education
     (GCSE) 46
Genghis Khan 77–9

Georgian House (Bristol) 47–9, 51–2
global citizenship 94
global eco-being (New Zealand context) 6
global imaginaries xiii, 95–9, 104, 108–9
globalization 95, 109
Goodwyn, Andrew 113
'governing myths' 68–9

Habitus 68
haiku 8–9
Harry Potter series 115, 119
Harste, Jerry 115
heterotopia 137–9
Hughes, Ted 86

identity xi, 124
imagination 95–6
immigrant-background children's
        identities 94–109
inclusivity 18
Initial Teacher Education 15–16, 44–6,
        55–7, 60
interethnic speech 103
International Literacy Association 113
internet 38
Islam 30, 35–6
Islamophobia 29–30, 33
It Gets Better project 144

kaitiakitanga 5, 6
Kalashnikov, Isay 67
kennings 2–3
Key, John (New Zealand Prime
        Minister) 11
King Lear 67–9, 72–6
Kiwi 3

language arts xii, xiii, 1, 68
language change 60
language heritage 29
Lear of the Steppes, A 73–6
LGBTQ+ issues 143
literacy 5, 10, 11, 16, 24, 29, 42, 44, 50, 91,
        112, 115–17, 119–20
literature 28, 31, 37, 47, 61, 67, 73, 75, 79,
        113, 115, 118, 120, 124, 127–8, 148
Local Hero (film) 126, 127

McCarthy, Michael 3
Macbeth 70
MacDiarmid, Hugh 126–7
McEwan, Ian 84
Maori experience 5–7, 9
maps 86, 99–107
Marxism 71

Massey, Doreen 25, 83, 85, 91
May, Theresa 29
Meek, Margaret 50
Midsummer Night's Dream, A 70, 72
Mohammed 35
monolingualism 32, 36
Motion, Andrew 1, 3
multilingualism 28
multiple identities 136
Muslim youth identities 28
Myspace 139

narrative imagination 96
nasheed 33, 35
National Curriculum (England) 15, 42–4,
        69, 86, 116
national identities xiv
nationalism 68, 71, 124–5
National Writing Project (UK)
        45, 49–50
National Writing Project (USA) 45
neoliberalism 138
New Zealand xii, 1–12, 15
normalisation 136

online identities 137
online space 137
origine 98–9
Otherness 97–100, 102–6, 109

Pakeha 5, 7, 9
patriotism 83
performativity 14, 15, 17
personal growth and English 4
place 1, 4–5, 8–11, 14, 16–25, 47, 49, 50,
        55–7, 61–6, 82–92, 94–6, 103, 127,
        130, 133, 135, 142
place-based education 16, 63–4
place-related literature and media 82
poetry xiii, 30–4, 58–9, 85–92
poetry and song 30–1
'Poetry by Heart' 32, 39
Post-Graduate Certificate In Education
        (PGCE) xiii, 16, 44, 46, 49, 55,
        57–8, 60–4
Punjabi 31–2

Qur'an 33–4

Reader Response theories xiii
ResearchEd 140
Ricoeur, Paul 94, 99, 108
risk aversion (in teaching) 26
Roma 103
Romantic(ism) xi, xv, 85, 128, 129

Rosenblatt, Louise xiii, 118
rural deprivation (UK) 83–4
rural poetry 85–6

Scots language xiv, 123, 130–2
Scottish heritage industry 124
Scottish history 125–7
Scottish Literature 127–9
Scottish Nationalist Party 123, 130
Scottish Qualifications Authority
    (SQA) 123
Scottish Renaissance 124
Scottish Studies 123, 130
Secret Teacher 141
Shakespeare, William xiii, 67, 69, 70–3
Siberia xiii
' *Silent Spring* (Carson 1962) 2
social class 38
social media xiv, 137
Sparrow (poem) 1–2
spatial turn 82
Sturgeon, Nicola 127
Sunday Schools 29

teacher identity xii, 144, 148
Teachers as Writers (Bristol) 45–50
Teachers' Standards 46
'third space' 135, 145
Tracey Beaker series xiii, 117, 120
Trainspotting (film) 132
Trans-Siberian Railway 75
Trump, Donald 83
Turgenev, Ivan 67, 73
Twitter 139–41

United Kingdom Independence Party
    (UKIP) 83
Urdu 31–2, 35–7
utopian function 99

Wilde, Oscar 148
Williams, Raymond xv, 84
Wilson, Jacqueline xiii, 112–15, 117–20
Wordsworth, William 47, 59, 85
World of Warcraft 143

Youth Speak 144